# CHRIST AND THE MODERN CONSCIENCE

# CHRIST AND THE MODERN CONSCIENCE

*by*

JACQUES LECLERCQ

*Translated by*
RONALD MATTHEWS

SHEED & WARD—NEW YORK

*Nihil obstat* Daniel Duivesteijn, S.T.D.
*Censor deputatus*
*Imprimatur* E. Morrogh Bernard, Vic. Gen.
*Westmonasterii, die* 17a Maii, 1962

This book was first published under the title *Saisir la vie à pleines mains*, by Editions Casterman, in 1961

*Library of Congress Catalog Card Number : 63-7790*

*Made and Printed in Great Britain*

# CONTENTS

Chapter Six

*Moral Values* . . . . 218

# Chapter One

## *How the Moral Question Arises*

### I. THE ORIGIN OF MORALITY

The fact of morality precedes moral reflection.

The fact of morality is that men consider there is a rule of conduct. It is a social fact, characteristic of community life. Everywhere, men consider that they ought to behave in a certain way, and that certain actions are particularly praiseworthy or blameworthy. Those who practise morality perfectly are the good or the wise. They are greatly venerated. And this is so among every people, from the most primitive up.

Furthermore, virtue is regarded everywhere as a sign of intellectual eminence, and the good man as a man worth consulting, that is to say a man whom one can trust over one's behaviour in life. Even from the strictly intellectual view, on the plane of pure knowledge, he is believed to hold the solution to every problem.

If, however, a rule of conduct is to be found everywhere, problems are to be found everywhere too, that is to say that the rule of conduct does not in itself solve every practical problem. And when uncertainty arises, the wise men are consulted. Among primitive peoples, they produce solutions which are guaranteed by their authority, an authority which must be called *moral*, since it commands respect on account of the veneration felt for the man who is speaking. The wise man is little concerned to justify his judgment. He sees things in such a way and he is believed because he is wise. But this leads also to reflection on morality, and this in its turn results in what we today call moral philosophy.

A man is drawn to study morality if he considers that life sets problems. These arise from observation of the lack of coherence in the customary pronouncements. Now incoher-

1

ence means lack of unity. A lack of unity or of homogeneity is observed in men's attitudes and in the pronouncements which dictate them. But what is wanted is to direct life or conduct, and to direct is to unify. To unify is to reduce heterogeneity or multiplicity to unity. Ethics is thus essentially an answer to the problem of man's management of his own life or conduct. In this it is opposed to other sciences, such as medicine or biology, which also claim to direct life in a certain sense. In ethics it is a matter of regulating action with a view to the general orientation of life.

Reflection on morality also originates from the fact that man has the impression of being free. He may find himself in a world which forces itself on him, but he can still move on his own and direct his actions to some degree. Moral philosophy thus results from a sense of autonomy and this sense of autonomy results from the fact that man is conscious of something in himself which will later be called intelligence, and which endows his personality with an inner independence which other beings do not possess. That is what we mean today when we say that man is a person.

In so far as a man acquires this sense of inner independence, it seems to him the most precious and the noblest thing in the world. If I am a person, the preservation of this characteristic, that is to say this autonomy, transcends everything and demands that everything should be sacrificed to it, because to be a person implies a greatness in me that surpasses every other.

The moralist is thus essentially a nonconformist. His conduct is inspired by the dictates of his conscience and not by that of his environment as expressed in customs and general opinions. The phrase, dictates of conscience, means an inner vision. The moralist is thus profoundly different from most men who are at the mercy of instincts or customs. He generally wins the admiration of some and the distrust of others. Admiration comes to him from those who realize his greatness and see that they can expect truthful teaching from him, whereas others are only out for their own advantage and success, both on a strictly social and material plane. Distrust comes from those who realize that it is impossible to be certain what attitude he will take up towards the circumstances of

2

life, because this attitude will depend on his own inner vision and not on the habitual judgments of the environment. That is why wise men are almost always surrounded by fervent disciples, at the same time as they are cold-shouldered by the powerful. The crowds listen to them gladly and admire them without following them. The same thing is as true of Confucius as it is of Socrates and of Christ and his great disciples. Sometimes, as in the cases of Socrates and Jesus, the wise man's life ends with a catastrophe which appears later as the supreme manifestation of his wisdom.

\*　\*　\*

Another starting point for moral philosophy is to be found in a more intellectual aspiration. The moralist asks himself what is the meaning of life, and in this he is at one with all philosophy.

The ordinary man never asks himself this question. He lives according to instinct disciplined by social usages. Good is what is regarded as such in his environment. There are things which 'are done' and others which 'are not done'. Since he is constantly spurred on by immediate ends, he does not think about things as a whole or seek to discover an end by which everything is co-ordinated.

Now to think about the meaning of life implies that life has a meaning, or that a man thinks it has one and is inquiring into it. What is more, to talk of *a* meaning presupposes that life is regarded as a unity, and since its natural appearance is that of a multiplicity, that a unity is being sought to which this multiplicity can be reduced. The operation falls into two parts. First this unity has to be discovered, which is purely a problem of knowledge. Then it must be decided in what way actions are related to it, which is another problem of knowledge. Finally life must be organized accordingly, which is a problem of action. But all this presupposes first and foremost that a man is conscious of being a personality: is conscious, that is, that his behaviour depends above all on himself, on his inner vision and his autonomy.

\*　\*　\*

We have just described the moralist in his original state.

But the picture changes later. Once moral philosophy has come into existence and certain men have put forward formulas of unity, it no longer exists only in the form of a social phenomenon expressed by mass opinions and attitudes, but also in the form of systems of thought. And thinkers appear who consider these systems in order to criticize or to modify them.

From then on, ethics appears as an abstract phenomenon. Ethical thinkers are not concerned with their own lives. They are not wise men. They are philosophers, and they treat morality simply as subject matter for speculation, one object of knowledge among others. They have not necessarily got any taste for it; they do not reflect on life in order to do good; they reflect simply in order to know.

It is possible for example to reflect on morality in order to deny it. It is obvious that this happens because morality exists. Those who deny morality would not think of considering the conduct of life had others not considered it before them and proposed solutions.

The reaction against morality is all the more vigorous since ethical thinkers are tiresome people. They claim to lay down rules for the whole of life and to impose the primacy of their own point of view. Now alongside the moral philosopher, who is concerned first and foremost with the purity of actions, in the sense of the relationship of the act to the dictates of conscience, there are other types of men. There are the political thinkers, who are concerned with public action, with varying motives. There are aesthetic philosophers, who are concerned with the beautiful, which also assumes many forms. There are the speculative thinkers, who are concerned with knowledge for its own sake, and the scientists, a modern term for those who seek knowledge of the material world, not to speak of the mass of men who are concerned first and foremost with satisfying their own appetites and vanity. The moral philosophers embarrass them all, for they claim to subject action to a rule foreign to the interests which have just been enumerated. We therefore find a permanent revolt against ethics, which with most people takes a purely practical form : they let the moral philosophers talk and pay no attention to what they say, and there is every kind of variation and nuance of this attitude. With other, more intellectual minds, the revolt takes a form which is itself speculative. In every age there have been thinkers who have constructed a theory to destroy all ethical theories; a formula which means that in their eyes ethical rules are laid down by the environment, or by a certain number of men of whose attitude they disapprove, and that they react against this. Take André Gide's novel, *The Immoralist*. No writer of our times has been more haunted by the moral problem, that is to say, by the problem of the conduct of life; it might be said that there is no other theme in all Gide's work. But his moral ideas develop almost exclusively as a reaction against what he saw as *morality,* that is to say, an existing reality, taking the form of a series of rules generally accepted by a body of men who were the representatives of morality, and of a collection of principles which appeared to him false.

The same was the case with the Sophists of antiquity, and the equivalent is to be found in China and India, in short in all the great civilizations.

\* \* \*

This reaction against ethics grows stronger as it ceases to be the free reflection of a conscience concerned with the problems of life or of wisdom, and a body of professional moral thinkers comes into being.

For one thing, morality grows set. In social life, that is to say, precepts are handed down in abstract form, as established rules to which men must submit, whatever their personal desires: 'thou shalt not kill; thou shalt not steal; thou shalt not commit adultery.' These imperatives are taught as absolutes and no attempt is made to provide proof of them. A child is told: 'You mustn't lie; you mustn't be greedy,' although it seems to him that in a given case, it is in his interest to lie or to be greedy. And the word 'interest' here means that the child feels that he will gain from the forbidden act an advantage which will provide him with a means of satisfying his deep-lying propensities or of developing his personality. For example, a lie that gets him off a punishment is a means

5

of preserving his personality, since it does not detract from this and is what the lover of abstractions would describe as 'a means of self assertion'. Thus he does not feel that this lie is evil—this particular lie, for him, at that moment and in those circumstances, not the lie in itself, the abstract lie.

That is a first explanation of the revolt against ethical thinking. Again, ethics has become a subject of teaching and study, and that is a characteristic of modern times.

The curricula of philosophical and theological studies include courses in ethics. A man is appointed professor of moral philosophy, not because he is a wise man concerned with the orientation of life for himself and for others, but because a professor of moral philosophy is required, and when the chair becomes vacant the candidate who has displayed his intellectual attainments and who is free at the moment is nominated to it. A professor of moral philosophy teaches moral philosophy because he has been given the chair. Most of them would never have taught moral philosophy otherwise. If they had been appointed professors of metaphysics, psychology or logic, they would have taught metaphysics, psychology or logic. If they are responsible for teaching philosophy as a whole, ethics merely represents a certain number of lectures. Moral philosophy for them is thus not a problem they set themselves, but a problem others set them, which they study and whose data they teach.

Moral philosophy thus becomes an 'object', a collection of ideas which are to be found in authors and their circles, of ideas which are talked of and discussed. But the man, the ethical being, is not committed to it.

The point of view which was the origin of moral reflection, the problem of living as it concerns personal life, therefore falls into the background. The moralist by vocation is replaced by the moralist by profession.

\*　　\*　　\*

The systematization of ethics and the activities of professional moral philosophers leads to the distinction between speculative and practical ethics.

The origin of moral reflection is practical: the wise man

6

asks himself what should be done. He starts off from a conception of life which he teaches. The great moralists who are known as such in history are of this type, whether they are concerned with what is known as philosophical or as religious morality. It is the approach of Confucius, of Buddha, of Socrates, of Jesus and of Epictetus.

But with the organization of teaching, the outlook changes. Other branches of study come out with views on man, and a great number of thinkers draw conclusions about human conduct from neighbouring disciplines, from metaphysics, for example, or from psychology. They are, it should be added, hardly concerned with conduct; their interest is in knowledge and explanation. Their speculations or their observations lead them to certain conclusions on the meaning of life; they draw these conclusions, but they stop short at general formulae. For what interests them is not the way in which men behave —themselves or other men—but the harmony of their system of ideas. Ethics thus becomes the part of philosophy which deals with the guidance of life, a practical philosophy or a philosophy of practice. But knowledge is still the goal; the aim is no longer to influence action. This 'practical' philosophy remains theoretical or speculative.

In other words, this philosophical ethics is not concerned with coming to conclusions bearing on a particular act and leading to action. Its conclusions deal only with the act in general and stop short there.

Once ethics takes its place in the array of philosophical studies, there will be moral philosophers who are exclusively concerned with introducing order into it, determining its exact field, for example, and linking it up with general philosophy.

In moral philosophy, studies and discussions will be concentrated on the definition and the essence of good, of obligation, of wrong and of remorse. The aim will be to reduce the moral code to order by precise formulae. And there will be little concern over the origin of morality; it is a datum.

These discussions are useful; they permit the clarification of many ideas. But a moral philosopher who stops there never gets to what is the real object of ethics and is in danger of straying into fields which have little interest for moral philosophy, or which even contribute nothing towards achieving its real object.

Thus the place which ethics occupies in the hierarchy of philosophical sciences or the determination of the real object of morality and of the essential character of the moral fact are useful ideas for the moral philosopher on condition that he goes on to use them for a study of the conduct of life. But when he stops short there, he never reaches what gives ethics its peculiar character and is even in danger of arriving at an inaccurate conception of it, because the essential feature of the moral act only becomes evident in connection with action. It is action, concern over actions and over the conduct of life, that characterizes ethics, and that is quite a different thing from a speculative inquiry directed towards knowledge for its own sake.

Those who study moral philosophy from a speculative point of view therefore end up by distorting it. It is the same when we apply ourselves to defining virtues and vices, classifying them and clarifying our ideas of them without applying ourselves to the question of what we should do. There may be important elements in an action which are refractory to intellectual analysis. The man who is concerned with having a clear mind and not with life disregards these elements, which annoy him. He thus formulates an ineffectual moral system. Now efficacy is the aim that moral philosophy should pursue.

All this is worsened by the fact that the different aspects of moral philosophy are considered by different men. Those who study practical ethics are not the same as those who study what is called theoretical ethics—what is called by that name, for in reality it is only a part of ethics, and theoretical ethics is a false moral theory if it does not issue in action. There is little contact between the two factions. The students of practical ethics have the impression that the work of the theoreticians is useless; they content themselves with opinions inspired by concrete situations which they do not relate to principles. The theoreticians have the impression that the practical men are the bone-setters of moral philosophy and that their opinions are without value. The true philosopher should unite the two points of view, but the approach which produces results in action is the practical one.

Now when we talk of moral philosophy we are usually talking only of morality studied from a speculative angle.
Attempts have even been made to translate it into a formula.
The German philosophers of the school of Kant used the term
*ethics* for the part of moral science designed for the elucida-
tion of the fundamental principles, and the word is tending
to become universal. But the term ethics is merely the Greek
word which designates moral philosophy in the most general
sense. Aristotle's *Ethics* is a free reflection on the problems of
life. Cicero is credited with having invented the term *Moralia,*
derived from *mores,* and it has the same meaning. In our times
the British and the Americans use the word ethics, with the
same meaning again. In France the terminology has not been
fixed. Taking things together, the position is a confused one.
And since everyone uses the term he prefers without pointing
out that it is not universally accepted, the reader has considerable difficulty in finding his bearings.

\* \* \*

Professors of moral philosophy thus form a community
which claims to be the official world of ethics and is generally
accepted as such. Alongside them, however, there remain the
practitioners of ethics, most of whom do not write. In
the Catholic Church especially, these practitioners also form a
community, that of the confessors and directors of conscience,
and their teaching often diverges considerably from that of
the professors. But the problem set by Christianity and
particularly by the Catholic Church is a special problem
which must be studied separately. For it is important as well
as special and we shall be unable to understand the way in
which ethics presents itself in the modern world, and particularly in the Western world, if we disregard it.

Again, ethical thinkers of the type of the old-time wise men
are still to be found outside the Christian world. Keyserling
was an example of this in the present century and his case is
not unrepresentative, for he enjoyed considerable authority
among the non-specialist public, but little credit in the professors' world. His thinking was concentrated on the conduct
of life, and people concerned with this found him enlighten-

9

ing. The world of specialists, however, reproached him with having little system in his ideas, with using terms he did not define and in short with not putting his thinking into shape as he should.

This will show the services which the moral philosophy of the professors renders and the dangers it harbours. It clarifies a certain number of given ideas, but it may easily distract the mind from the genuine aim of ethics. That explains the resounding indictment of moral philosophy launched by Lévy Bruhl at the very beginning of the century, in his *La Morale et la science des moeurs*. 'Ethics is useless,' he said in substance, 'for while moral philosophers may argue about principles they are agreed on practice. When you read the history of ethical philosophy, you are impressed with its chaos—there are as many systems as there are men. But they all come to the same conclusions.'

Lévy Bruhl could utter that criticism because he was acquainted only with the moral philosophy of the professors. In reality, he did not know very well what ethics is. His criticism is not true of the moral ideas of the wise men. There is a great difference between the Confucian, the Buddhist and the Christian, and between the Stoic, the Neo-Platonist and the Epicurean. The Christian wise man who is called a saint is very different from the Stoic sage. Every school has its type of wise man, but what differentiates them is certainly not the Ten Commandments. Lévy Bruhl, like many others, believed that people were agreed on practical ethics once they were agreed that it was wrong to kill, to steal and so on. But is that the aim of ethics? That is what we shall have to ask ourselves later.

Moral philosophy has in short been a victim of organized teaching, though it has benefited from the clarification this has brought to some of its ideas. The ideal development of ethics would call for the theoretical lectures to be a mere introduction, the essential teaching being given in the form of a school of wisdom where a master would live with his disciples, trying at the same time to elucidate the problems of life and to live in conformity with the principles he established. For the moral rule should constantly be verified in moral experience, just as moral experience should constantly

10

be reduced to the rule. A morality without principles is like a body without a skeleton; a morality without life is like a skeleton without flesh.

Since the teaching of moral philosophy has evolved as it has, we are involved today in a jungle where it is extremely difficult to find our way. The aim of this book is to try and map one out.

## II. THE MORAL PROBLEM IN THE TWENTIETH CENTURY

At first sight, the twentieth century seems an ideal time for ethics, for a preoccupation with action and the value of action might be said to dominate thinking in general.

To understand this evolution, we must go back to the preceding period, for the ideas of an age always develop in reaction against those of its predecessor.

The starting point is the rationalism of the school which is today called Classical and which is generally traced back to Descartes.

The philosophers of the seventeenth century believed they had found a new orientation for philosophy, which rectified the flaws they held against the Scholastic philosophy of the preceding age. So well did they succeed in relegating this to oblivion that even today most people treat philosophy as if Scholastic thinking had contributed nothing to the intellectual heritage of humanity, and as if the Classical authors had caught up the torch of ideas from those of antiquity without any intermediaries. Now Descartes was completely imbued with the Scholastic philosophy in which he was brought up, and this Scholastic influence is still to be found in Kant, a century and a half later.

Classical philosophy is essentially rationalist. It set out to establish a purely deductive philosophy, starting from a small number of principles, and if possible a single one, which should be obvious to the mind, and from which a complete explanation of the world could be deduced by reasoning. The Classical philosophers attempted to eliminate everything that was not reasoning: they distrusted sentiment, which is not a source of intellectual knowledge. Their ideal was an interplay

11

of purely abstract concepts, axiomatic to the mind, and on which the mind got to work with no recourse to the affective element. Knowledge for them should be reduced as far as possible to a body of purely cerebral ideas; the ideal of philosophy lay in geometry. What was not reasoning was sentiment, and sentiment was worthless.

Rationalism led to the idealism of which Kant is generally regarded as the father, and of which the most important form is represented by transcendental idealism. Of this Hegel is looked on as the master: he may not be the most distinguished member of this school, but his historical influence seems to have been the strongest.

As a result of this evolution, man *qua* person is watered down. There is nothing left but thought. But the very exaggerations of the system led to a reaction, and two currents of ideas took form in the nineteenth century.

On one hand criticism extended further and further, introducing ever new subtleties into idealism to the point of dissolving any sort of reality and of being unable to conceive of anything but a thought knowing itself. On the other, positivism or sociological reflection accepted the premise that nothing can be known intellectually of the outside world, concluded that it was unnecessary in practice to take philosophical knowledge into account and that philosophy in the traditional sense of the word must be discarded, and limited knowledge to what we learn from the senses, with a view to founding a science in which man and human society should be the crowning data. The philosophers would be left free to dispute in the clouds, and a science of man and of society would be founded, a positive science in which the problem of knowledge would no longer be raised.

Positivism and sociological reflection might thus be called the adulterine children of idealism. They presuppose it; they are inconceivable without it; but they set out in a diametrically opposite direction.

Since reason is incapable of knowing the outside world, they maintain, this can only be known through the senses, and since there is no means of proving the validity of this knowledge, rational proof need not be taken into account; the only thing to do is to trust to practical experience. The

12

scientific development which coincided with these trends of thought supported them both by reducing physical knowledge to more and more abstract mathematical formulae. On the one hand it was founded on sense-experience whose validity it did not attempt to question; on the other it reduced matter to formulas and abstractions till no one could say just what reality it corresponded to.

Thus the inability of reason to reach reality served as a justification to those who said we must be content with what sensible knowledge teaches us. Now this indicates society as the supreme reality. Again, intellectual knowledge grew so complicated and subtle that it became lost in formulae, which were themselves so abstract that the link between knowledge and reality was lost.

\* \* \*

It is against all this that twentieth century thinking is reacting, principally by way of the phenomenological and Existentialist schools.

It is true that the sociological-positivist and idealist currents still persist and exercise their influence on the new schools, but a new point of view appears.

This is a very complicated and often confused trend of ideas. I shall try and bring out one or two elements in it which seem to me to be fundamental.

### 1. *The return to realism*

This is an attempt to get beyond idealism : reality is the object of an immediate apprehension of the mind, and there is no need to question the validity of this : it is the prime phenomenon of knowledge. In this way idealism and the whole problem of knowledge are transcended.

This trend of thinking asserted itself in France as early as the end of the nineteenth century, with Blondel's philosophy of action and the intuitionism of Bergson. We cannot separate the knowledge of ourselves and of thinking from knowledge of the outside world. We know the outside world in the act of knowing ourselves, and we cannot know ourselves or become conscious of ourselves without knowing the outside

13

world and assigning ourselves a place in relation to it. This conception becomes the fundamental idea of Existentialism.

Existentialism presents us with various formulae a number of which have been produced by philosophers trained in university discussions, devoted to abstraction and expressing the simplest ideas in the most abstract terms. (I have spoken earlier of scientists' liking for technical jargon.) For example, they make subtle distinctions over the words 'to exist' and 'existence'. At the basis of the whole trend of thinking, however, there seems to lie a simple human phenomenon which is not talked of in the universities.

The idea of a direct apprehension by the mind of the world, and the idea that all knowledge derives from this, and that consequently if this apprehension of reality is eliminated, the phenomenon which is being analyzed is eliminated too is doubtless quite a commonplace one. That is how men have always philosophized; they started from there, and no other starting point is possible. The ancients did not question the existence of the outside world. But in our days, after interminable discussions on knowledge, the question is dealt with in a complicated vocabulary and amid subtleties which obscure the simple elements. These elements were at the start of everything, however, and they still are. It is desirable to refer back to them constantly, but scholars do not like this attitude, which puts them on the same level as the man in the street. In any case, the Existentialist school is a reaction against idealism and against the inclination of scholars to attach no importance to anything but essences and intellectual definitions.

One of the Existentialists' fundamental ideas is that it is more important to know that an object exists than to know what it is. The philosophy of the ancients distinguished between the question *an est*? and the question *quid est*? The Classical philosophers had a tendency, which as we have seen comes naturally to scientific thinking, to consider that we are not sure of the existence of a being—*an est*?—till we are able to define it—*quid est*? Existentialism is a healthy reaction against this cerebralism.

Its starting point is the 'existential shock'. This results from the simple phenomenon that, for man, what exists has a com-

14

pletely different value from something that merely corresponds to an idea, and that to come into contact with an existing object is quite different from encountering an idea. This is simple and it is fundamental. Innumerable examples of all kinds can be given.

Men have been reading the *Iliad* for more than two thousand years, and the question of the existence of Troy was long discussed. Why? Whether Troy existed or not makes no difference to the value of the epic and in any case, if Troy did exist, it was only an unimportant little town.

One day, archaeologists digging in Asia Minor discovered the foundations of Troy. This created a sensation throughout the world. There was not a paper that did not inform its readers of this vital news. The fact that Troy did exist turned the *Iliad* into quite a different thing. That was the existential shock.

Again, everyone is familiar with the controversies which crop up from time to time about the identity of 'Shakespeare'. Here once more we are concerned with literary works that stand on their own, no matter who was their author. But men feel it is important to know if the person called Shakespeare existed, and if he really was the author of the plays. Serious scholars throw themselves into the question, exchange arguments, undertake arduous researches. Why? Because, if Shakespeare did exist, something important has changed, and also if we know he existed we possess an important datum: the existential shock again. Some pure intellectuals, whom the cast of their mind inclines towards idealism, will say that this has no more importance than the existence of Troy; but they will give the impression of flaunting paradoxes.

Examples can be taken from everyday life as well. It is often said that a driver only becomes careful when he has had an accident. All the same, before it happened he knew the trouble the accident would bring him and what was likely to cause an accident. But he only knew this in the realm of ideas. When the accident happened, it gave him the existential shock.

The existential shock corresponds to what in everyday language is called experience. People often say that a man who has never been hungry does not know what hunger is. He can

15

perfectly easily understand it intellectually, however. The idealist does not realize this difference, and Existentialism arises from a reaction which is based on the start that is man's response to the first-hand experience.

The Existentialist philosophers do not, of course, employ examples as concrete and as commonplace as this. Their vocabulary is as abstract as that of the idealists.

For example, Existentialism takes to pieces the word *exist*. It traces its derivation back to *ex sistere*, to place outside oneself. Consciousness of existence consists in being conscious that an object is real outside of our consciousness, and that there is thus something other than the idea. There is nothing particularly new about that. Existence has always borne this meaning. The new formula and the insistence on recalling that consciousness of existence consists in positing a reality independent of knowledge results simply from the reaction against idealism.

The origins of Existentialism date some way into the past, for it has been traced back to Maine de Biran, who died in 1824, and its development in the course of the nineteenth century can be followed in thinkers as different as Kierkegaard and Nietzsche. It should, moreover, be noted that these thinkers were unknown to each other and that Maine de Biran in particular was plainly a forerunner, and that his great reputation is due to his *Private Diary* which was published a hundred years after his death. It should also be noted that none of these thinkers was a professional philosopher except Nietzsche, who taught for a time but was a failure. They were independent thinkers, as are most forerunners.

## 2. *The philosophy of action*

The role of action in knowledge is characteristic of twentieth century thinking, even though all Existentialists cannot be described as philosophers of action.

Already at the end of the nineteenth century Blondel was formulating a philosophy of action, whose fundamental postulate was the exact contrary to that of Descartes. He replaced 'I think, therefore I am' by 'I act, therefore I am'. And Existentialist phenomenology is profoundly imbued with the role of action.

Once more this can be explained by the reaction against idealism, because the consciousness of existence is stronger in action than in thinking. The independence of the object is more obvious when we bump into it than when we think about it.

This rôle of action in philosophy disposes the mind to ethical considerations, since ethics is the rules of action. Most philosophers, however, are men of thought, not of action, and among them the concern with action is chiefly directed towards the discovery of a source of knowledge which is certain. Their interest generally lies in orientating thought, not life, though certain of them, such as Kierkegaard, were chiefly prompted by anxiety to orientate life. But Kierkegaard was more of a religious thinker than a philosopher.

It has just been said that the consciousness of existence is stronger in action than in thinking. We must go even further and say that in action, the question of the existence of the object does not arise. That is so in all action, as much in scientific observation as in action on the outside world, and moral action is included in action in general. Ethics confines itself to looking at action from a special point of view, that of the entry on the scene of the free agent.

On the plane of action, it is quite immaterial that the agent and the object do in fact exist. That is why men of action never tackle this question. From the point of view of action or of the aim in view, it does not matter whether it is an ideal I that is driving an ideal nail with an ideal hammer into an ideal wall, or whether a real I is driving a real nail with a real hammer into a real wall. The problem of knowledge which consists in discovering whether and how we know the object, or of discovering whether the object exists is thus an academic problem which only interests the speculative.

Existentialism is in revolt against a philosophy divorced from life. Discussions on the problem of knowledge, and idealism in general, are excellent representatives of a purely cerebral philosophy. A philosophy of action finds its guarantee of truth in the success of the action; it is action that provides me with the guarantee that I was not mistaken in believing in the existence of the nail, the wall and the hammer. That is the only problem the man of action sets himself, and the moral

17

philosopher is one of the men of action, or at least of the men concerned with action. That is why we never encounter in moral philosophy the problem of knowledge, or the problem of discovering whether the outside world exists and whether we exist.

## 3. *Anthropocentrism*

Twentieth century philosophy is definitely anthropocentric, in contrast to certain scientific currents, which stress the limited and even fugitive place that man occupies in the universe. The problem of philosophy today is no longer, as it was for the ancients, the problem of the cosmos, but the problem of man. It is from him that philosophers start and with him that they end. Thinking is dominated by the problem of destiny, and under the influence of the concern for social affairs, this tends towards concern for the collective destiny of men, who are regarded as forming a whole. This is clearly the same as the problem of civilization so arduously studied and so fiercely discussed in our age. When men today ask the question : 'Where is man going?' they are asking about the fate of the human race. 'Where is man going?' no longer means : where is each man considered as a unit going? It means : where is mankind going?

The ancients did not ask this question. For them humanity as such was going nowhere. There were men, individuals working out their own life, and there were discussions as to whether this led to another world; but that other life, like life on this earth, was proper to each person. Mankind was thus an eternal beginning over again. Each generation and each individual accomplished his destiny; then others started all over again. Today we think of the human race as a whole, as an entity advancing along a road, and we ask ourselves : 'Where does this road lead?' People believe that it must lead somewhere, that everyone has his part to play in the collective task, and that the meaning of life can even be identified with this part. This attitude is common to thinkers of every school; it is to be found even among Catholic theologians, who see the task of the human race in the form of the building up of Christ in this world.

For this world is the centre of the picture. Should there

18

be another world, our world is a preparation for and a pre-figuration of it. For a great many contemporary theologians, the point of the present world is no longer simply to garner the elect, but to achieve on earth a collective task which will be attained by common labour, associating men in a single whole down through the generations.

This problem of destiny was already apparent in Maine de Biran; it haunted Kierkegaard; with Nietzsche, the problem of the future of civilization came to the forefront, and the trend continues, the emphasis being sometimes on man as such, sometimes on humanity.

Gabriel Marcel founds his philosophy on two fundamental ideas. First comes the awareness of concrete existence—I am I—a knowledge that is primary and empirical, a fundamental reality. Secondly, this first fact has neither meaning nor value unless it is taken up by thought and included in a system of relations situated in the I that thinks.

It will be seen that this conception derives from both idealism and realism, and endeavours to overleap the opposition between the two by what might be called personalism. In any case, the only problem is that of man. The only interesting problems are the problems of man, for nothing can interest me except in so far as it concerns me. But to concern me is to concern the man I am. There you have anthropocentrism.

## 4. *Anti-rationalism*

We have seen what the Classical rationalist conception amounted to. When Bergson launched his offensive against that attitude at the beginning of the twentieth century, at first nobody understood him. Now contemporary philosophers are diverging more and more from the old point of view.

To begin with, they admit that there are things which cannot be explained. They readily talk of 'the ineffable'. A certain number have even put forward with a provocative air a philosophy of the 'absurd'. Against the idea that the world forms an ordered and coherent whole whose explanation must be sought, and that the explanation is to be found in a unifying principle, they set the idea that the world is a chaos, with no unity apparent and none to be discovered, that we are travelling in a fog and that everything is absurd, that is to say irrational. Then they catch at the instinct to live in order nonetheless to find a meaning in life.

For the absurdity of the philosophy of the absurd is that nothing can be inferred from the absurd, and that its exponents want despite everything to end with something. But to end with something means ending by finding a meaning in this life, which they began by declaring to be without meaning, and to find a meaning signifies finding a unifying principle, when they began by saying that none was to be discovered. All this verbiage can only be explained if we know what it is reacting against.

Thus we come to a presentation of philosophy whose manner is very different from the Classical one. The philosopher imparts his impression on a certain number of things. He says: 'This is how I see the world'; he imparts a vision and is little concerned with justifying or reasoning. He and his fellows do not believe in reasoning. They talk a lot about feeling; they say 'I have a feeling that'; and in their minds feeling has a meaning different from that which it has in the Classical tradition. Feeling for them is a total impression resulting from a body of mental images which impart a conviction and a certain vision of reality. They worry very little about furnishing it with a rational foundation, that is to say one based on an argument or on a series of well arranged arguments.

But this is fraught with consequences for moral philosophy. Earlier writers had built up moral philosophy on the same lines as metaphysics, starting with a few fundamental principles and deducing by successive stages till they reached immediately practicable rules. Present day thinkers are in violent reaction. For them a moral theory must be discovered from experience of living. It is not ready made, it is always in course of making itself; it evolves, it undergoes transformations; the mind must defer to the fact. In any case, there are many ways of attaining certainty; the mind must close in on reality by all the means of approach at its disposal. Hence the role of fiction in present-day philosophy. Many philosophers write novels or plays which occupy as important a place in their thinking as their systematic volumes and theoretical writings; for ideas can equally well be set forth in connection with a slice of life. They bear witness, and philosophy is more witness than theory.

Since anthropocentrism concentrates thought on man, it directs it towards the problems of life, for man is more interested in his destiny than in his nature. It is more important to know where I am going than to know what I am, for this last piece of knowledge is only important in so far as it sheds light on the first. But that leads up to ethics.

Characteristic of our age are the 'tormented' philosophers or ethical thinkers, those who themselves describe their philosophy as a philosophy of anguish. They are uneasy philosophers, for they are seeking the solution of the problems of destiny with no cosmic synthesis to lead them to it. The ancients were untroubled, because for them destiny followed from their view of the world. But the new men have not got a view of the world; in their eyes it is nothing but a chaos. How is man to find his way in it without a light to guide his steps?

For the thinkers of today, doubt is no longer a 'downy pillow', it is a torture. Their thinking is tragic; before anything else in action and in reality what they see is the evil. Sartre's *Nausea* is typical. The sense of what exists merely fills him with disgust, whereas a man might with just as much reason take the opposite point of view and find in what exists a source of exaltation.

These pessimistic thinkers who start off by affirming the absurdity, nothingness and chaos, and who then attempt despite everything to build it all up again are generally amateurs, as has already been remarked.[1] The professionals are generally cheerful, because they adhere to a tradition. Generally speaking, all those who accept a system of metaphysics are cheerful.

5. *The return to intellectual spontaneity.*

This follows from everything that has gone before, but should be emphasized. The cult of spontaneity is moreover a

---

[1]An exception must be made here for Germany. Almost all the thinkers responsible for the progress of German thinking have been professional philosophers, from Kant to Hegel and right down to our contemporaries Scheler, Husserl and Heidegger. This not so in any other country.

particular characteristic of our age, and is one more result of the reaction against the artificial aspect of technological civilization. Jazz in music, camping and nudism in a quite different field, the craze for hiking at a time when it is no longer necessary to walk to get about, all the forms of poetry and painting in which the artist concentrates his attention on the spontaneous expression of his inner vision, without worrying whether he is understood, all this is related to the trend of philosophy.

When Husserl describes the starting point of philosophy as a 'naive attitude in face of the object', he is taking the same line as the protagonists of jazz. What is more, the trend is accentuated by an inverse development. The natural sciences are becoming more and more technical and less and less accessible to the man in the street. Logic, transformed into logistics, is perfecting reasoning to the point where it becomes a technique so subtle that only a few initiates can understand it. Under these circumstances, those who look for a certitude which will enable them and everyone to direct their lives adopt a course which consists in surrendering themselves to spontaneity and abandoning the scientifically mapped-out route. They are like the hiker who seeks out stony by-paths just when the countryside is being criss-crossed with scientifically planned and mathematically levelled concrete highways.

There is something a little paradoxical about this spontaneity, for it is the spontaneity of ultra-civilized men, impregnated with artificiality. These thinkers remind one of people who go in for camping and the return to nature with complicated equipment carefully chosen in the appropriate shops. As the vogue for camping grows, the shops that sell camping kits increase in number, and the goods they sell consist of methodically designed equipment manufactured with all the resources of modern technique.

It is difficult not to see a humourous side to Husserl's phrase recommending a naive attitude in face of the object when it is realized that he wrote it at the age of fifty or sixty after a life devoted to studying the subtlest thinkers and the most abstract problems. Does not the naivety consist in believing that under those circumstances a man can still be naive?

But an attitude of this kind is frequently found among philosophers. It springs from the state of mind which I mentioned earlier: concentration on ideas without reflecting on one's own personal position or taking into account the influence of one's environment. Many philosophers give the impression of thinking of their mind as an object they can dispose of as they please, a magic lantern they can place as they will. They talk of training their thoughts in this or that direction, of envisaging reality in this or that way, as if they believed they could do what they wanted. Indeed they do believe it; but surely that is where they are naive.

## 6. *The question of the next world.*

Finally we must revert to metaphysics, for there is the watershed which separates the two slopes.

The trends of which I have been speaking are common to many philosophers, and it can even be said that all are more or less affected by them, but these trends are adaptable to the most diverse systems.

The division arises over God. Some philosophers stop short at man and lapse into anguish, for life ends in death, and after death we cease to exist. But if we cease to exist after death, life is dominated by anguish, says Heidegger, for a man who knows he is going to die and thus to return to nothingness is already carrying nothingness within him. What is the use of being, if being leads only to nothingness?

Other philosophers such as Marcel, Le Senne and generally speaking all the thinkers who have remained more or less faithful to Christianity discover God in value. They usually avoid the mention of the word God. For Le Senne, man finds within himself the sense of value, and what he calls value is what is traditionally called an absolute. Value is unlimited. When a man resigns himself to the idea of ending, of being finite, he becomes materialistic and loses the sense of value.

This is very like Neo-Platonism, and recalls the importance attached by the Christian tradition to meditation on death.

Such, it seems to me, are the trends of twentieth century thinking which lead up to ethics. They consider it from a point of view which often appears novel, thought it is sometimes more novel in its terms than in its essence. After this opening survey we are now able to tackle the problem with some hope of avoiding ambiguities.

## III. CHRISTIANITY AND MORAL THINKING

The trend of contemporary thinking, whose main lines I have just sketched, has had a considerable repercussion on Christian thinking and on the trend of Christian ethical thought; and this, on the other hand, holds a central place in Western moral thinking. The influences are reciprocal. But if we are to understand the evolution of ideas, we must try to clarify the form these influences take.

Most members of the public regard Christian thought, especially in the Catholic Church, as an unalterable monument completed centuries ago, and many do not believe that it is possible to change the least thing in it. Many Catholics believe that the one thing to which they should apply themselves is to uphold and reiterate it. A historical view of Catholic thinking, however, shows that it has been on the move the whole time. The Scholastics' thinking was not the same as the Fathers'; that of the seventeenth and eighteenth century theologians was not that of the mediaeval Scholastics. Christian thinking may have reacted strongly against certain trends of thinking of our own day, but that is no reason for assuming that it will be any less capable of changing than it has been in the past. The moral philosophers of the Classical age felt the influence of the thought of their own day, and those of today are surely equally likely to come under a similar contemporary influence? But in order to understand the problems, we must come to know the peculiar character of the way ethical reflection and teaching in earlier periods were presented.

\* \* \*

We have discussed the Classical rationalism against which present-day thought reacts. Now Christian thinking from the Middle Ages on has continuously developed in an increasingly rationalistic direction. All doctrinal teaching must conform with the rules of logic and the principle of clear ideas. Every exposition must be made in the proper form, that is to say the syllogistic form.

St Thomas was imbued with this intellectual exactitude. The method of exposition he adopted in his books, as was the custom in his times, was based on the rule of demonstration. For example, he demonstrated by means of reasoning (*Summa Theologica* p. III, q. xlvi, art. 10) that Christ suffered in the place where he was meant to, and advanced three arguments (*ibid*, 2nd rep.) to prove that he died outside the walls of Jerusalem. St Thomas was however very prudent from the point of view of the time in which he lived. When he argued, he often used restrictive formulae, such as *oportet* or *quodammodo*, which showed he was under no illusion as to the decisive character of the reasoning. But in the environment in which he lived, it was not possible for him to declare himself incapable of explaining. Once or twice he did say that there could be no certitude on certain points, for example as to whether the origin of the world went back to all eternity or occurred in time. Today these passages are often quoted, and St Thomas is praised for his reserve. But he could not have written like this often in his own time.

All doctrinal teaching was thus subjected to the law of reasoning as it was then understood. Logic, the science of syllogistic reasoning, and training in the syllogism dominated theological education. In the schools men engaged in dialectical tourneys, in which they had to fight according to the rules. Nothing except what could be demonstrated was of interest. What was not an object of reasoning was 'vague', and this term was a condemnation. There was no need to take vague ideas into consideration.

The starting point for philosophy was logic. It was by classes in logic that pupils approached the study of philosophy. Indeed, in the mediaeval schools, at the beginning of the Scholastic Renaissance, the teaching of philosophy boiled down to logic. First a man learned to reason; then he reasoned. What could be more 'reasonable'?

The Schoolmen thus proved by syllogisms the existence of God, of the soul, of freewill, of the nature of good and of evil.

St Thomas proved the existence of God by five arguments, around which an enormous literature has accumulated. The question of the number of proofs was regarded as important, as was their statement in the proper form. What could not be reduced to a syllogism was worthless.

This tendency has been even more accentuated in modern times, for the whole of philosophy has shared in it. Descartes, Spinoza and all the thinkers of their time, as we have seen, wanted to establish a philosophy on the pattern of mathematics. It could be used to defend religion as well as to attack it. Descartes, it is known, was prompted by considerations of apologetics and later theologians tried to adapt Kantianism to the defence of the faith.

It is true there were parallel currents of thinking, especially in mystical circles, but they were generally regarded with suspicion and pushed into the background.

The same attitude was to be found in moral philosophy. Men proved by syllogisms the nature of good and of obligation, the existence and nature of freewill and the divisions of ethics. The syllogism supported with its authority the statement that there are three theological virtues and four cardinal virtues. There had to be that number, neither more nor less, and they had to be those virtues and no others. For each virtue and each vice, there is a demonstration why it is so described, why it must be such as it is, defined in such a manner, integrated in such a way into the system and occupying such a place in the hierarchy of virtues and vices. Everything was rationally necessary; nothing was a matter of convention. Nothing was merely the result of a historical development which might have worked out another way. The ideal was to achieve a system which started off with a definition of good and culminated in labelling every act in a completely clear fashion. As regards sin, it was necessary to determine just what each sin consisted in. It was not enough to know that an act was evil; it was necessary to know exactly what sin it constituted. The label on it must be an accurate label, and it must be known whether the act constituted one sin or two, as well as the particular commandment of which it was a transgression.

I have known professional philosophers who demonstrated

everything in this way: everything, from the first principles to the most concrete applications. They shed an absolute light; there was no chiaroscuro, not a single shadow. And they did it proudly, certain of possessing the truth and possessing the whole of it. Their light was a pitiless one, so dazzling that it caused a certain uneasiness. The listener asked himself: but if everything is so clear, how is it people are still arguing the matter? That did not worry the professionals and they went ahead, with never a doubt to cross their minds.

All this, of course, has some point in quiet periods, like army regulations in peacetime. When no serious problem is being raised, when the doctrine is accepted and all that is necessary is to clarify it, the syllogistic method allows men to define terms, to link up ideas and to produce corrections of detail. It makes the mind supple: it is a form of gymnastics.

But it reveals its inadequacy when it comes to dealing with fundamental trends, because these spring from and can only spring from a global vision. As we have seen, it results then in a denial of all value, indeed of all reality, to what is not clear and distinct. To describe an idea as vague becomes a condemnation without appeal.

\*     \*     \*

Men had thus spent a thousand years constructing piece by piece a monument that was to last for ever. Its thick slabs, meticulously quarried, seemed solid enough to stand up to any test, and every generation added the finish of a hand-wrought detail. Was there anything that could still shake it? Everything had been a hundred times verified, put in place and perfected. The majestic lines of the edifice dominated the world, life and thought.

But then, about the second quarter of the twentieth century, a corrosive flood suddenly cataracted down on it. Not that anyone was attacking the monument with the idea of breaking through its walls; it was strong enough to repel any attack. But abruptly it seemed that everything was dissolving. The indestructible slabs that had defied the centuries seemed to be turning to gelatine; the ancient edifice was shivering and quaking.

You are cutting up reality into clear and distinct concepts, the assailants had said; but these concepts are false in so far as they are clear, for reality is obscure and the greater part of fundamental experience cannot be reduced to clear concepts. Even less can it be reduced to distinct concepts, for reality is a whole, and once you start to split it up, it is no longer reality. Besides, reason is incapable of accounting for anything. For man with his knowledge—his knowledge is part of him—forms a whole together with the world. You can only know anything by knowing the whole. There is no starting point; the starting point is a global knowledge which becomes progressively clearer by concentric circles, and the syllogism proves nothing.

It was an appalling hurricane. What could be done to save the great thousand-year-old work?

It is true that a certain number of schools took a long time to become aware of the crisis, but almost everywhere people were worried; students were asking questions. They were reading contemporary authors and they saw no relation between what these men were writing and what they were themselves being taught. In the system that was officially imparted to them they found no answer to the problems of the age. The teaching seemed out of date. Most of them felt this vaguely; very few dared to say so.

The long and the short of it is that contemporary thought does away with the very idea of demonstration. For it has substituted that of explication. Certain truths are apprehended in a global and more or less obscure manner, and critical reflection is necessary to determine what this knowledge comprises and implies. Thus the certitude of the existence of God is perceived in the very nature of things, forces itself on the mind in a series of converging approaches and is consequently found to be much harder to express and to formulate than was believed in the old days. To many people however, a formulation of this kind seems the only satisfying one. In short, demonstration is superseded by analysis, and this replaces immediate, simple and confused knowledge by a clear, not distinct but global knowledge. The ancients sought for the first principles to which everything could be attached; the thinkers of today believe that the starting point is the whole perceived globally, without any distinction of its elements.

28

In 1870, at the end of the classical age, the Church was reacting against rationalistic agnosticism, which denied God on the pretext that his existence is incapable of proof, and the Vatican Council laid down that God *can* be shown to exist. But with a lucidity which may be called prophetic, the Council refrained from laying down that there was any form of demonstration that forced itself on the mind, and theologians have continued to discuss the formulation of the proofs. Today the position has been transformed. The contemporary attitude is much nearer St Paul than the linear method of the classics, for in the eyes of St Paul, everything shows that God exists.

In moral philosophy, the activities of contemporary thinking have restored its prestige to the 'prudential judgment' which we find in St Thomas, and to which Maritain has drawn attention. This is a global judgment, resulting from a comprehensive view of the act, and is certain in so far as the man who pronounces it is endowed with the virtue of prudence, a mental balance which is the fruit of moral life as a whole. Thus moral judgment is linked with life at the same time as it is with the mind. We shall come across this conception again. It contradicts the conception of the Classical ethical thinkers, for whom moral judgment was a purely rational activity which reached its conclusions thanks to a mere manipulation of ideas, alien to life.

This trend of thinking leads to a contempt for reason that is often disturbing. Under the influence of non-Christian teaching, a certain number of Catholics have little but sarcasm for traditional moral philosophy. Since they have nothing to put in its place, they become engulfed in a sort of anarchy which glorifies spontaneous judgments, as often as not alien to the virtue of prudence. The ecclesiastical authorities then become alarmed and demand that they should abide by tradition, for it is no part of the duties of these authorities to examine new problems. They approve or they condemn, but it is for the specialists to suggest. Catholic thinkers are called on to do a big job of rethinking.

\* \* \*

Another point where the evolution of ideas in the twentieth century has had profound repercussions on Christian teaching is the separation of philosophy from theology.

This has come about progressively in the course of the centuries. It was unknown to the ancients. In the Church of the Fathers, Christian wisdom was opposed to pagan wisdom, as if 'wisdom' had the same meaning in both cases. The credit for asserting the distinction is generally attributed to St Albert the Great and St Thomas.

St Thomas asserted it, but rarely applied it. He was above all a theologian, and was constantly interlarding philosophical with theological arguments. But from the sixteenth century onwards, the distinction became more usual, following the division of Christendom caused by the Reformation, and the secularization of thought.

With the development of anti-clericalism, it became part of the arsenal of polemics. Catholics were taxed with being incapable of studying philosophy because their faith debarred them from freedom of thought, and they defended themselves by arguing that the domain of philosophy was different from that of theology. Both sides supported their theses *a priori* for reasons which had little to do with the question itself. Since the end of the nineteenth century, the Neo-Scholastic movement has devoted considerable efforts to demonstrating that there is a Catholic philosophy completely independent of theology, claiming to recognize it in the Middle Ages, and propagating it today. The men responsible for the Scholastic Renaissance show themselves very touchy on this point, and in Catholic courses pains are taken to put forward nothing that depends on Revelation.

The evolution of contemporary thinking has turned the positions topsy-turvy by transforming the vistas of thought. If we are to understand the scope of the development, we must examine more closely the consequences of the separation of the two disciplines.

\*     \*     \*

The general ideas of the Christian on the subject of the world and man are obviously dominated by Revelation.

It could hardly be otherwise. Hence the saying 'philosophy is the handmaid of theology', which was in current use in the Middle Ages. Today their critics bring it down on the Neo-Scholastics like a club, and that generally annoys them.

Now this saying can be understood in two senses:

(a) Philosophy is subject to theology, in the sense that it must abandon its positions if there is a contradiction between the two.

That presents no difficulties, for the Christian is convinced that theology cannot result in an error, at least where revealed doctrine is concerned. If a chain of philosophical reasoning ended up in an apparent disagreement with theology, the Christian philosopher would suspend judgment.

(b) But there is another way in which the saying can be interpreted, and this is more dangerous.

Philosophy can be the handmaid of theology in the sense that its object is to serve it. If that were so, the only important questions in philosophy would be those that were going to be dealt with in theology, and they would be studied with a view to allowing theology to solve its own problems. There would thus be no autonomous philosophical thinking. And that is just how the teaching of philosophy was organized in many Catholic schools that were theological schools. The aim of the philosophy courses was not to teach the students to think in an unbiased manner, but to prepare them for their theological studies. A whole series of questions was tackled which no-one has ever thought of outside theological circles: for example, the ideas of personality and nature, in order to explain later on the mystery of the Incarnation; the possibility of separating substance and accidents, in order later to explain the mystery of the Eucharist; or, again, the division of natural law into primary and secondary, in order to justify certain precepts of the Jewish law.

Thus on the one hand the separation of the two disciplines was being proclaimed and on the other theological considerations were constantly coming up in philosophy.

But there is another and more serious difficulty.

The truths of Christianity are taught in the following way. First the fundamental natural truths, which are the domain of philosophy, are expounded. Then comes the authenticity

31

of Revelation: Christ's teaching is indeed the teaching of God. After that, the study of Revelation, which is the word of God, is tackled. From now on, the student is in the domain of faith, of trust in the God who has spoken. On this plane, there is nothing more to be discussed. Since God has spoken we must trust in everything he said; the only question is to know exactly what he has said.

Consequently the essential argument of theology is the argument from authority. All the same, theology has made a lot of use of the syllogism; it is used to demonstrate the inferences to be drawn from Revelation, starting from an inspired major premise. The rationalism of the time gets in from this angle.

\*    \*    \*

The methodology of teaching has extremely serious consequences in ethics.

Christian ethics is a unity. The Christian must follow all the precepts of natural ethics transformed by Revelation, for divine teaching takes over and reinforces the essential principles of natural ethics as seen in the Ten Commandments. Moreover the Church is the trustee, not only of directly revealed teaching, but of the natural ethics that Revelation presupposes. The result is that the whole of ethics is taught officially, as a Revelation of the divine will, and that teachers have hardly worried to distinguish between what is properly speaking natural and what Revelation adds. Take certain fundamental commandments, such as that of charity or of worship and prayer. Little effort has been made to distinguish the difference between human mutual aid, as it can be pictured on the natural plane, and Christian charity. And no more has been done to discover what contemplation of God can be on the natural plane—as among the Neo-Platonists or in Moslem mysticism—by comparison with Christian contemplation.

The concern of Christian ethical thinkers is to decide what the Christian must do. Indeed that is their mission. Now Christian ethics as a whole depends on Revelation; it is therefore taught as part of revealed truth.

In the early period, we know, the distinction between

philosophy and theology was not clear. Christian wisdom was taught, and nobody worried much about distinguishing its two planes. But later on, when teaching was systematized, a distinction was made between natural and revealed ethics.

Nevertheless, ethics is one. Man has only one life, and he can have only one rule of life. To separate natural from revealed ethics, to distinguish in actions what is dependent on Revelation and what would be forced on the mind even if there were no Revelation—though indeed the second element is taken over by Revelation—all this was so complicated that it seemed almost impossible to realize. The decision finally adopted was to accept the only solution that seemed practicable: to make the teaching of applied ethics the responsibility of theology. The study of moral philosophy was thus limited to a few general principles or a few psychological analyses, which would provide moral theology something to work with. For example, the notion of conscience was elucidated: it was asked in what moral consciousness consisted, and in what circumstances man must be for his acts to have a moral value. Or again, the idea of law was examined, the various kinds of laws and the special character of moral law. These are abstract rules: when analyzing the conscience, it was asked in what the prompting of conscience consisted, but no attempt was made to discover its object. When the notion of law was analyzed, it was not asked what the moral law demands. These rules can be used to formulate any system at all. When we have analyzed conscience and decided what it means to follow our conscience, we still know nothing about what it lays down.

What it lays down is the content of ethics. The rules fixed by moral philosophy are only a container, a recipient into which ethics can be poured once it has been decided what must be put there. But this last question is tackled only in theology, that is to say after it has been established that the Christian doctrine is divine truth.

Christian ethics is thus prescribed to the Christian by the authority of God; it is not for him to discuss it, but simply to accept it. The question that dominates moral theology is to know what God commands. The whole moral code is taught like this: why cannot I kill? Because God forbids it. Why must I be chaste? Because God commands it. And so on.

Once it has been stated in this way, Christian ethics cannot be set alongside other ethics or discussed like one of them.

It cannot be represented as one variety among the different kinds of human wisdom, for it is not a human system of wisdom, it is the word of God. There is no question of showing that it is the loftiest form of human wisdom, for to do that comparisons would have to be made, and there is nothing to compare it with. The divine command is an absolute. We accept it because it comes from God, and we accept it without discussion. The word of God cannot be assimilated to human pronouncements.

But since Christian ethics is taught like any other ethics, many Christians have the impression that ethics, without any more qualification, is Christian ethics, and that there is thus no ethics outside Christianity. That results in more than one kind of trouble. There are people who believe that if they were to lose their faith, they would have no ethical rules. There are others who are disturbed in their faith if they meet non-Christians who are concerned about ethics, or who suffer the same disturbance if they study philosophy or history and learn that there are authentic moral values outside Christianity.

This leads to a very tangled situation. For example, a lecturer on moral philosophy will talk of the Stoics' ethics and of their ideal of mortification. Mortification will not however be discussed in a Catholic course on moral philosophy, because mortification falls in the domain of religion and therefore of theology. But theology teaches what God commands without justifying it and without comparing it with anything else. We should be lacking in the respect we owe to God if we undertook to justify what he teaches, as if God had any need to justify himself before us. Thus students will never have the opportunity of comparing Christian asceticism with Stoic asceticism.

Again, altruism occupies a considerable place in the moral philosophies of today; it is not referred to in the Catholic teaching of moral philosophy. When it is discussed in theology, it is discussed as if it were founded solely on Revelation.

Thus there is no opportunity of comparing Christian charity with other forms of love of one's neighbour.

But if Catholics do not draw such comparisons, others do, since for non-Christians the distinction between philosophy and theology does not exist in moral philosophy. For them there is no other ethics than philosophical ethics; Christian ethics seems to them one form of wisdom among others, and they discuss it freely. They criticize it or they praise it; they undertake to clarify it. No attempt is made to answer them in official Catholic teaching, and there is no sector of Catholic education where a corner is reserved for such considerations.

The histories of philosophy that are being written today emphasize the influence on thought of religion, Christianity among others. There are Catholics who tackle the question too, but they do so in written or oral commentaries outside the official teaching. And the young people who take Catholic courses in moral philosophy find nothing in these which permits them to assess what they read elsewhere.

This is accentuated by the fact that a certain number of Protestant philosophers, who have no part in the divisions peculiar to Catholic teaching, put forward a philosophy imbued with Christian values. In short, everyone is talking of Christianity in philosophy, some attacking it and others being inspired by it—everyone except the Catholics.

\*      \*      \*

All the same, Christian ethics is human, preached by one man, transmitted by other men. To those who do not accept the divinity of Christ and the mission of the Church, Christ's teaching appears to be one form of human wisdom among others and must be discussed on this plane. Those of us who are Christians are certain that Christ's wisdom is the most perfect there is, because he is the son of God. But it has value in itself; it is thus still the loftiest form of wisdom, even if we rule out the fact that he was the son of God. What is more, one of the reasons why Christ attracts people and why they divine that he is unique among men lies in the wisdom of his teaching. This is probably, indeed, the chief reason why he attracts people. 'No-one has talked as this man does' said those who

35

listened to him. Now this element falls into the background in the demonstration of the divinity of Christ as it has been systematized, because his divinity is demonstrated before his teaching is approached.

It is therefore extremely important to explain the value of Christianity as a system of human wisdom; only then does the question of who Jesus was arise. That indeed was how he proceeded himself. He came forward as a man among his fellow-men. He started to preach. He drew crowds by his teaching, and only little by little did he reveal who he was, as the disciples were gradually convinced by what he said. In modern apologetics, Christ's miracles have been made a decisive element of proof, separated from the rest of his activities, because the method of exposition demanded it. In the Gospels, however, the miracles are an integral part of the teaching and the wisdom of living displayed by Christ's attitudes as a whole.

Now this position is what present-day philosophy comes down to. It is perfectly conceivable that a mind steeped in the ideas of this school may discover God in Christ, though from a philosophical point of view the proofs of the existence of God do not satisfy him. The wisdom of Christ will lead him to the transcendence of Christ, and this will lead him to God; he will accept God because God reveals himself in Christ. All this is in line with what happens in the Gospels. But it is in direct opposition to the linear rationalism of modern times, which insisted that the existence of God should be demonstrated first, then the divinity of Christ, and that only then should Christ's teaching be tackled.

What is more, conversions confirm this, for they do not follow anything like the course that apologetics claims to map out.

\*　　\*　　\*

If we are to get a comprehensive view of the question, we must restore Christianity to its setting among other religions and all religions to their setting in the general current of human thought. In the Western world, we too often talk of 'religion' as if there were no religion but Christianity, and as

36

if the religious problem was simply one of whether to accept the Christian faith. In this respect, the contact we have today with the systems of thought of the Far East may have a salutary effect.

Now Christianity is one religion among others, but it is a very unusual religion on account of the personality of its founder and of the role he himself plays in the Church he founded.

Most religions have no founder. They are traditional religions, founded that is to say on an immemorial tradition; they lack organized religious authorities and thus possess no touchstone to sound doctrine. Their tenets are generally vague, and they consist principally in ritual practices.

Most thinkers, outside the Christian world, speculate in harmony with the religious ideas accepted in their environment, but since the doctrines are vague they admit of any sort of gloss that may appeal to the thinkers. This was the position of the ancient Greeks, the Chinese and the Hindus. There is no difference between their position and that of the modern philosopher, whether he be a Cartesian or a Kantian, or a disciple of Durkheim, Bergson or Husserl.

Moreover, there is no such thing as a man thinking by spontaneous generation. The philosopher speculates on the basis of the influences he has undergone. The *tabula rasa* of Descartes is a myth, and if we try and make it the actual starting point of reflection, we end up with illusions.

In the classical epoch from which we are emerging, religion was regarded as demanding assent to a body of truths whose intrinsic value its followers had not personally verified, while the philosophic approach on the contrary implied personal verification of everything that was asserted. Today we realize that this opposition is purely mythological. Most philosophers work out their system before they are thirty; they have obviously not considered personally everything it implies. The philosopher's attitude is based on a vision of reality; so is the attitude of the religious believer. A man may accept a religion because he believes it to be true as a result of personal reflection, and many people accept a philosophy solely because they come under the influence of a master, because chance has made them the disciples of this or that

37

teacher. The opposition between religion and philosophy thus becomes blurred.

Man thinks on the basis of a body of convictions which are already fixed at the moment when he starts to think. He has acquired these convictions under the influence of his environment. When he begins to think, he sets to work considering them, and it matters little whether he has acquired them under the influence of Christ, of the Church, of Karl Marx or of Durkheim. Whatever the case, these convictions and this turn of mind form the starting point of his thinking.

Now Existentialist phenomenology, which takes into account all the elements of knowledge and makes its starting point the spontaneous vision of the universe, assumes that allowance will be made for all these *de facto* convictions, whatever their origin.

Furthermore, the ethical thinkers of our day are agreed on the considerable influence of the social environment on moral convictions. But, to look at it scientifically, religions form part of these social influences. The *tabula rasa* is finished with, as is the 'naive attitude in face of the object'.

If we want to get a comprehensive view of ethical thinking and moral feelings, we must take into account all the elements which come into play, and religions have in fact exercised a much bigger influence than philosophies. The trend of contemporary philosophy thus obliges us to state the moral problem in quite a different way from that which has hitherto been habitual.

# Chapter Two

## *Wisdom Morality and Code Morality*

AFTER THE general views which have just been stated, we must define the object of ethics and to do that we must start at its starting point. We shall then see how moral philosophy has evolved and be able to reach a clearer idea of its present condition.

### I. THE STARTING POINT OF ETHICS

We saw in the last chapter how ethical reflection arises. It is founded on an existing morality. It is essential to realize that morality exists before ethical reflection does, that it exists wherever there are men, and that is useless to hunt for its chronological origin. Like all fundamental phenomena, it constitutes a datum. But we can try to find its psychological origin by attempting to pin down the phenomena which gave birth to the concern with morality.

The ancients were not worried by it: morality existed. They examined its bases and constructed a system by which they linked their metaphysical principles with the practical conclusions accepted in their society, though they might modify some of these with a view to co-ordinating the system. The problem is a little more complicated for the thinkers of the present age.

It seems to me that we can distinguish three interesting trends in the moral thinking of our time.

### 1. *The monist trend*

The word monist is used here in a somewhat special sense. Generally it is used in the metaphysical sense of a system which reduces all reality to a single element. Here it designates ethical monism, that is to say a conception which reduces all ethics to a single element; this element is a subject to which everything is referred. The subject may be absolute thought, as in Hegel, or the superman, as in Nietzsche, or any man at all, as in Guyau. In any case the subject has nothing to take into consideration but himself. He thus enjoys absolute freedom.

The freedom referred to is not, of course, the fact of free will but the *right* to do what the subject wishes. It is moral freedom as against psychological freedom, which consists in the *objective power* to do what one wants; moral freedom consists in the *right* to do what one wants.

In these systems, this ethical subject has therefore nothing to worry about except what he wants. He is subject to nothing; he is supreme. Moreover, these authors want to be done with the word good, because in their minds it is bound up with traditional ethics, which sees in good a rule imposed on man from the outside. Hence they try to avoid the word, though the idea remains the same. Nietzsche wrote a book called *Beyond Good and Evil*.

This primary subject need not necessarily be man. For Hegel, it is absolute thought and, from a practical point of view, society or the State, the supreme expression of the thought. Individuals are completely subordinated to it; for the individual, the only moral rule is subjection to the thought. This idea reappears in a great many contemporary ethical systems, particularly in Communist ethics, where the individual is completely subordinated to the community and has no other moral rule than this subordination. In reality, the individual under this system is no longer a person, in the sense that the Christian tradition attaches to this word.

For Nietzsche, no rule holds sway over the superman. He seeks only his self-realization; he is his own final aim. But men are not all supermen. The others are herd-men, and for them there is a slave morality which subordinates them completely to the superman.

In Guyau's eyes, there is no ethics in the traditional sense of the word. He puts forward an 'ethics . . . without obligations

40

or sanctions'. This consists simply in sifting out the various human requirements, that is to say the conditions of man's development, his needs, desires and inclinations. These then become the equivalents of the old ideas of good and duty. This is mere psychological analysis.

If we consider these systems—there are others, but a complete enumeration of them would do nothing to serve our purpose—we shall find in all of them the idea that the ethical subject has no other law than that of his own nature. The authors indeed avoid the word nature, because they are in reaction against tradition. They also avoid the word good, and yet talk of nothing else. The whole question is to know who or what the supreme subject or being is.

Everyone would agree with the abstract principle that the subordinate being should submit himself to the supreme being, because the object of his existence is not contained within himself. This is the principle that Christian ethics applies to God. The main thing is to know who is the supreme being and who is subordinated to whom.

## 2. *The sociological trend*

This combines Hegelian monism with positivism. Man is a product of society. Everything that he thinks and feels, and everything that inspires his action comes from society. The sole object of a science whose aim is to regulate human conduct is to analyse the way in which society is evolving, imposing this or that way of looking at things. There is no going beyond this analysis of social facts, and ethics is thus eliminated.

All the positivist sociologists from Comte to Durkheim have put forward this formula, but very few have been able to hold to it. The case of Durkheim particularly is highly symptomatic. He is obsessively concerned to propose a system of ethics to the people, and constantly shows himself unfaithful to the system which he advocates theoretically. But the system exists.

## 3. *The phenomenological trend*

This reduces ethics to the awareness of personal destiny and of the value of man. From the Positivists, phenomenolog-

41

ists inherit the scientific attitude which accepts morality as a fact, but they consider it more from the psychological than from the sociological point of view. They thus inquire how the moral sense is awakened in the conscience.

Most of them think that the moral sense does not come to life spontaneously through the sole consideration of the end or aim, but believe that it must receive a shock. This is Kierkegaard's and Heidegger's anguish (*angst*); or Le Senne's *obstacle*.

In short, their idea is that man is drowsy and torpid as long as everything is going without any difficulties, but that he wakes up when he runs into an obstacle. The obstacle, Le Senne says, produces a 'split'.

With variations, the same attitude is to be found in all the Existentialists. Sartre and Camus, for example, start with a radical assertion of human autonomy, a little in the Nietzschean manner, while stressing their conception of nothingness and of absurdity. After this they fall back on an ethics of action in order that man become aware of himself.

\* \* \*

The interesting thing about the analytical method of the phenomenologists is its analysis of the moral phenomenon. It is true that conscience is awakened by comparison. That is true of all knowledge and is not peculiar to the moral phenomenon. But that is the only truth there is in the theory of the *obstacle*.

This notion comes down simply to the law of the manifold which is one of the elements that give rise to knowledge. Man exists in a multiplicity; the world is a datum for him, and he himself is a datum. He does not come first; he wakes up in a datum, or to be more precise, surrounded by a body of data. And it is because of the multiplicity that he becomes conscious of unity. He would not know colour, he would have no idea of colour, if there were only one colour; he would have no idea of sound if there were only one sound.

The awakening of moral consciousness follows the same pattern. Conscience is brought into being by comparison. But comparison is a more general idea than those of obstacle or anguish. The obstacle is only one occasion among others for making a comparison, and anguish is only one of the feelings which can arise from comparison in certain conditions.

We have already remarked that the moral philosophy of our time is pretty generally pessimistic. It is a moral philosophy that starts with a bad conscience. Its analysis of moral consciousness starts with the phenomenon of remorse, which gives the impression that man only becomes conscious of the fact of morality or of moral values when he comes up against evil. Ethics is the science of evil rather than of good.

The origins of this go back some way. Modern Catholic casuistry has focussed moral philosophy on the problem of sin. The object of moral theology was to decide what was sin. It seemed that the essence of the moral problem was to avoid sin. It seemed that to avoid sin was to do good, and that the latter raised no further problem. The concentration of ethics on duty, which was Kant's conception, thus formed part of a trend in which Catholic theology as well as Protestant Puritanism and pietism participated. This explains why the ethics of duty which Kant had put forward met so little resistance, in Catholic circles as in others. Even today most people, in the most varied circles, are convinced that what characterizes moral consciousness is the sense of sin. Catholic novelists such as Mauriac, Bernanos and Graham Greene write as if there were no other problem. It was Mauriac, I think, who defined the Christian as the man who is aware of sin—not aware of God, not aware of the divine love, not aware of redemption, but aware of sin. The same outlook is to be found in Bernanos's *Under the Sun of Satan* or *The Diary of a Country Priest* and in Graham Greene's *The Power and the Glory* or *The Heart of the Matter*. Chesterton is probably the only Catholic writer of our time who has set against this a more cheerful conception of Christian morality.

All this seems to be based on a profound misapprehension of the moral phenomenon, a misapprehension which is due to social conditions, particularly to the code morality of which I shall be speaking later. We are faced with a far-reaching historical development, which extends over centuries, but for all its persistence and its influence, it has profoundly perverted the moral sense.

The kernel of truth in it is that the moral phenomenon or a concern with ethics derives from comparison : comparison between actions. But there can be other comparisons than that between good and evil. Comparison can arise from the profusion of good, or the presence of a number of good alternatives. Indeed, as things happen, good is manifold, and comparison is born of this multiplicity.

If I have some money, I can think of a lot of uses for it. I have a choice not only between a good and a bad use of it, but between a series of good uses. I can give it to the poor, buy a work of art, endow a university or make a journey. And I can ask myself : Which is the best thing to do? Concern with ethics can arise from the attraction of good and the desire for perfection, as well as from opposition to evil.

The moral sense can be awakened by concern for my own fate, this last term being used, however, in a sense that has nothing catastrophic about it. And moral experience seems to indicate that the men most representative of the moral sense suffer very little from anxiety.

For the sinner is not the most authentic witness to the moral sense. On the contrary, the sinner is a man whose moral sense has become atrophied, and whose conscience usually only awakens by fits and starts. The man who is the best representative of the moral sense is the man whose moral sense dominates his entire life : the saint and the wise man.

It is true that some saints are converted sinners, and in their case the attraction of perfection is supported by personal experience of sin. But most saints, like most wise men, display from their youth a consistent pattern of conduct, and are the most untroubled of men. The ethics of remorse and of anguish is corrupt in the etymological sense of the word.

To regard remorse or a bad conscience as the typical phenomenon of moral life is as if indigestion were regarded as the typical phenomenon in the study of organic life. So far as I know, it is digestion and not indigestion that doctors study. It is only after they have mastered the workings of digestion that they inquire how indigestion can be avoided. Now remorse is to moral life what indigestion is to organic life.

It is true that the man who has got a good digestion does not think about it, and that concern about digestion arises from the fact that it becomes difficult, that is to say from the obstacle. This is a simple practical phenomenon. But to conclude from it that indigestion is the typical phenomenon of organic life, and must therefore be the starting point for any study of the latter, is quite a different matter.

We shall return to this analysis of the moral sense when the question of obligation arises. But even at this stage it can be pointed out that if we want to study it in itself, the representative figures who should occupy our attention are those in whom the moral sense exists in the purest state. They are not those with whom other thoughts come first, and who look on morality as an external constraint against which they react in one way or another. Those in whose eyes morality is an obstacle difficult to clear are just those who fall into the second category.

\*     \*     \*

Moral philosophy is thus in the same position as any other branch of knowledge: it originates with comparison and comparison presupposes multiplicity. To a certain degree it is true that moral consciousness is awakened by the comparison of good with evil, and that it is thus linked with the sense of duty. But it also involves other elements.

Take a well brought up child, who has grown up in a respectable family where he has never seen anyone tell a lie. It will not occur to this child to lie; he will not think of a moral rule, because he has never chosen between telling the truth and lying, any more than a healthy man chooses between dishes which are easy or difficult to digest.

When this child goes to school, he will meet schoolmates who do tell lies. He can react in two ways. He may be bewildered, fail to understand and tell his parents that some of his schoolmates are mad. Since respect for truth is for him an obvious good, there will in this case be no awakening to the sense of the moral rule, for this implies choice and therefore implies that the subject is faced with two courses of action and considers the possibility of choosing between them. On

45

the other hand, the child may be indignant, and this indignation will indicate that he is conscious of the moral rule, that is to say that he is aware that it is possible to act otherwise but knows this should not be done.

The child's indignation thus shows that he knew the rule, and yet previously he had not been aware of it. He had never thought of it, since he had never dreamed of lying. He knew it all the same, otherwise he would not have become indignant. So good men often find it quite natural to be good, cannot imagine that anyone could be otherwise, are astonished that people should admire their goodness, are puzzled by bad men. Does this mean that their goodness is not a moral value? On the contrary, it is such men who give an example of the purest moral consciousness. This indicates that there are several layers in moral consciousness.

It is true that awareness of the moral sense is often dependent on awareness of evil. Much has been written on this subject in connection with the story of original sin in Genesis. This is one of the applications of the law of multiplicity; but it is not the only one.

The example that has just been given shows that we should not confound knowledge with awareness. A man can know unconsciously.

Sometimes happy people who are going through a trial will say: 'We didn't know how happy we were.' Here the word 'know' is synonomous with 'be aware'. Let us not quarrel about words. They enjoyed their happiness, and the fact that they enjoyed it shows that they were aware of it. There are however two forms of awareness: spontaneous consciousness and reflective consciousness. The latter is awakened by comparison. We can thus talk of sleeping consciousness and awakened consciousness.

As for the sociological conception of morality, it should be noted that moral consciousness is essentially non-conformist. The social environment may prescribe certain attitudes, but moral consciousness asserts itself as an attitude of autonomy. The moral man, as we have already seen, follows the dictates of his conscience. This attitude corresponds more or less with Bergson's celebrated distinction between open and closed morality. The moral sense is concerned with good, so we follow the attraction of good. This is quite a different thing from the dictates of the social environment. Moral consciousness passes judgment on the social code; it may follow it or oppose it, but it obeys only its own promptings. If we want to understand the starting point of ethics, we must do our best to grasp this primitive and spontaneous phenomenon.

*     *     *

At the starting point of ethics, then, we shall find in experience what we may call the 'moral shock'. It does not result from coming up against an obstacle or from a split, but from meeting with an object which appears desirable, beautiful or good.

In order to make the question quite clear, it will be well to give a characteristic example.

Many readers know Kipling's poem *If*. To reproduce it in full will be a good way of showing what the moral phenomenon is.

If you can keep your head while all about you
Are losing theirs and blaming it on you;
If you can trust yourself when all men doubt you,
But make allowance for their doubting too;
If you can wait and not be tired by waiting,
Or being lied about, don't deal in lies,
Or being hated, don't give way to hating,
And yet don't look too good nor talk too wise:

If you can dream—and not make dreams your master;
If you can think—and not make thought your aim,
If you can meet with Triumph and Disaster
And treat those two impostors just the same;
If you can bear to hear the truth you've spoken
Twisted by knaves to make a trap for fools,
Or watch the things you gave your life to broken,
And stoop and build 'em up with worn-out tools:

If you can make one heap of all your winnings
And risk it on one turn of pitch-and-toss,
And lose, and start again at your beginnings
And never breathe a word about your loss;
If you can force your nerve and heart and sinew
To serve your turn long after they are gone,

And so hold on when there is nothing in you
Except the will which says to them : 'Hold on!'

If you can talk with crowds and keep your virtue,
Or walk with Kings—nor lose the common touch,
If neither foes nor loving friends can hurt you,
If all men count with you, but none too much;
If you can fill the unforgiving minute
With sixty seconds' worth of distance run,
Yours is the earth and everything that's in it,
And—which is more—you'll be a Man, my son!

This poem is undoubtedly the most famous that Kipling wrote. It has not only been translated into every language; it has been reproduced in the form of a broadsheet, and many people have framed it and hung it up on their walls. That means that thousands of readers have found it an extremely eloquent expression of their moral aspirations. Now it will be noticed that it speaks of nothing but suffering, endurance, failure, hard times and disappointments, and that it promises no recompense, in the human sense of the world. The supreme recompense, the climax of the whole thing is simply : *You'll be a man, my son!*

There is no philosophical doctrine in it either. There is no question of a future life, or of the soul. There is nothing but the moral shock in all its starkness. Yet no reader can read the poem without feeling himself nobler for having shared its ideas.

No doubt most of its readers are incapable of realizing these ideas in their own lives. They do not even dream of it. But the admiration they feel for the poem shows that it corresponds with something to which they aspire.

There is not a single echo in it, either, of anguish, bad conscience, remorse or the split. The poem puts forward an ideal, something noble, pure and strong. And the mind accepts it. That is the moral shock in all its purity.


## II. WISDOM MORALITY

We have seen that the first ethical teachers were wise men. It has always been so outside Christian civilization. That is why it is worth while studying the moral phenomenon from

48

this point of view, for Christianity has obscured the problem a little by linking ethics with religion. The perfect Christian is the saint; but sanctity is a religious value. An essential element of Christ's preaching is that man cannot practise virtue without the help of God, which is a religious force, and that on the other hand he cannot please God except by virtue. In this way ethics is linked up with religion and religion with ethics. This manner of presenting ethics has had an influence on the whole civilization which has come under the sway of Christianity, including even the Western philosophers who would appear at first sight the most alien to the Christian faith. That is why, if we want to scrutinize the moral phenomenon in its pure state, it will be useful to start by looking at it outside the Christian world.

The wise man's idea of things is different from the saint's, then. The saint's contains both religious and ethical ideas. On the other hand, the wise man's idea includes an intellectual idea which is not to be met with in the saint's.

The wise man is in the first place the man *who knows*. In Greek antiquity, the Stoics added to this picture the idea of the man who *does* or who achieves. This conjunction of action and thought had already been taught implicitly by Socrates and Plato, since for them the principal cause of depravity was ignorance. That is incidentally a conception which occurs spontaneously to the good man. Even in Christianity, where other elements come into play, saints feel a spontaneous pity for sinners and exclaim: 'Unhappy men! If they only knew.' And a favourite theme of Christian preaching is to try and convince the sinner that sin will not bring him the happiness he expects from it.

Nevertheless, Christianity itself turned this conception upside down with the notion of original sin. St Paul wrote: 'It is not the good my will prefers, but the evil my will disapproves, that I find myself doing.' It is true that we can find parallel texts among the pagans. Ovid wrote: *Video meliora proboque, deteriora sequor (Metamorphoses,* VII, 19). Plato thought that wisdom dwells in the mind, but that the mind can only reach it by fighting against the wild beasts that are the lower instincts. The fact of human unbalance is thus a patently obvious one; but the doctrine of original sin which

49

explains it has given it a completely new prominence in Christianity. Christian thinking is impregnated with it, and the idea of the Fall has come to the forefront of every conception of life since the rise of Christianity and as a result of Christianity. Today those who are reacting against the idea of the Fall react against Christianity too, and those who are reacting against Christianity usually react against the idea of the Fall.

Let us return to the wise man. He appears everywhere as soon as reflection develops. The man who reflects is a thinker when his reflection is chiefly about the world, and a wise man when it is chiefly about the meaning of life. We have already seen that it is the same in every civilization, no less in China and India than in Greece, among the ancient Persians, the Jews and all the civilizations we know. The patriarchs and prophets of the Old Testament are types of wise men, as well as teachers.

The moral teacher is thus first and foremost a man who wants perfection and who has made it the essential object of his life and his reflection, and his teaching is based first of all on his experience of life. It is not an intellectual system, alien to life in general and his own particular life. His teaching corresponds to the *contubernium* which Seneca advocated. In this the master and his disciples would live together and the latter would model themselves on their master's example as much as on his teaching, since the doctrine would be lived before it was set down in books.

Moreover the great thinkers of the non-Christian civilizations generally pursued their systems to the point of their appropriate applications in life. That is just as true of Plato and Aristotle as it is of Lao Tse, the most metaphysical of the Chinese wise men. This unanimity of the greatest minds all over the world and right down the centuries is extremely symptomatic. It never entered their heads that reflection should stop short when it had reached a satisfactory speculative solution of the problems of the world.

In this respect, Christianity has transformed the outlook by linking ethics with religion, which is itself revealed. The result is to give the impression that ethics is given and that there is no need to reflect about it.

But the terms which we have just used are again ambiguous. When we say that, for the Christian, ethics is given, what is meant is the moral *rule*. The moral *fact* is itself double. There is the fact of a moral rule accepted in the community, and the fact of the more or less conscientious practice of this moral rule, this practice being traditionally called morals. Alongside this moral fact with its two meanings is the reflection on the moral rule which is characteristic of the wise man. In Christian society, the impression is widespread that since the moral rule is given and is not discussed, because it is accepted on religious grounds, the problem of moral reflection is merely a problem of exposition. The meaning being that reflection should be concentrated on the best way to explain and to teach ethics, but without modifying its content, any attempt to modify it being indeed ruled out.

This, however, is more apparent than real. In Christian society, and in the Catholic church in particular, there are thinkers who reflect on morality just as the ancient wise men did. But these thinkers are not professional teachers, nor are they philosophers, in the sense in which the philosopher is a man who studies the foundations of thought. They are therefore not referred to in the histories of philosophy, nor even in those of theology. They are, for example, the founders of religious orders, St Benedict, St Francis of Assisi, St Ignatius Loyola, who put forward an extremely personal vision of Christian perfection. But this only shows the confusion reigning in education. A course in the history of philosophy may deal with Epictetus and Marcus Aurelius. But the students go away with the impression that they have no equivalents in the Christian world, because the men who form their counterparts are unknown to philosophers.

In our day, as we have seen, concern with moral philosophy has come back into prominence, as a result of the concentration of thinking on the problem of fate. But what these philosophers are interested in is not wisdom; it is to discover in the question of fate a starting point for knowledge, which will permit them to resolve the fundamental problems of philosophy. Hence the 'tormented philosophers', who founder in pessimism and anguish because they do not like the good. There is no anguish in Kipling's *If*, but Kipling is not classed among the philosophers. All the same, the whole of his work is imbued with a conception of life, that is to say with an ethical idea; but the ethics is not at the service of a system of thought. It is easy to see how fraught with ambiguities all this is.

\*     \*     \*

The wise man is thus concerned with the good life. The wise men of whom history speaks are in addition concerned with teaching others to live well. That is, indeed, why history does speak of them. It would be a mistake to believe that these are the only wise men there were, but the others are not spoken of; we know little of them.

This 'good life' consisted in the realization of an ideal of perfection. The ideal assumed widely varying forms. It was contemplative in Lao Tse or Plotinus. It could be active through an equilibrium between inner life and life in society. It was more individualistic with the Stoics, more social in Socrates, Plato, Aristotle and Confucius. In all of them, however, perfection lay in the truth translated into rules for action. Perfection consisted in living according to the truth. The link between truth and good was always very close. All the wise men noted that ignorance is extremely wide-spread and regarded it as the principal cause of depravity and unhappiness.

Generally speaking, the wise men's optimism is a little disconcerting. They contemplated life very calmly, and did not seem to find virtue difficult. Christianity, as we have seen, spoke differently. Yet when we put the wise men back in the pagan environment as we know it through history, we see that its ways were brutal and cruel. The wise men did not seem to notice it.

Those who are known to us in history were generally masters of wisdom. Epicurus, Epictetus, Plotinus and Confucius lived surrounded by disciples, who had come to be trained at their feet. They were more like the novice master in a monastery than the professor of moral philosophy in a modern university.

Some of them were concerned with social affairs. They noted the communal character of life, and quite often we find them believing at the outset of their careers that could they succeed in converting the rulers, the latter would convert their subjects, first by making good laws, then by giving good example. They all of them failed, for the rulers were not converted.

The best story in this respect is that of Confucius. He lived at a period of the monarchy when China was a feudal State, with a number of practically independent kings. Nevertheless, the idea of Chinese unity and of the Emperor, the Son of Heaven, dominated men's thinking, as that of the Holy Roman Empire dominated medieval Christendom.

Confucius was convinced that if the sovereign practised virtue, it would spread among his great court officials by force of example, and would thence by successive stages penetrate the entire nation. He spent nearly fifteen years travelling through China in search of a king who would apply his doctrine: the kings showed the greatest admiration for him but did not change their behaviour. His story resembles that of Plato with Dionysius of Syracuse and that of the eighteenth century encyclopaedists with Catherine the Great of Russia, but is more striking since Confucius went from ruler to ruler. Finally he returned disillusioned to the kingdom of Lu, which was his native country, and opened a school of wisdom which met with considerable success. All China looked up to him, and he is said to have had as many as three thousand disciples. But these were young people who came for some years to be trained in wisdom, then returned to the world and generally became pretty much like other men, once they came into contact with life.

Seneca too, in his old age, complained of the ingratitude of the disciples who absorbed their master's doctrine when they were young and forgot him afterwards. The phenomeron is universal.

Chinese thinking is concerned in the highest degree with the ethical and the social. By this last characteristic, it comes near echoing the interests of our own day. Furthermore, Chinese ethical thinking is without a doubt the purest and the most continuous that has ever existed outside the Christian world. The case of Confucius, in particular, is unique in history.

Confucius did not claim to be putting forward an original system. As he saw it, he was doing no more than continuing the Chinese tradition. He can be compared with St Thomas Aquinas, who also laid no claim to be putting forward a system of his own. But the two men alike carried out their modest work with such genius that they became heads of schools to whose authority a whole succession of thinkers has continued to appeal. Confucius thus became the uncontested master of Chinese thought, and for more than two thousand years China quoted his tradition, which became the official teaching, as an authority.

The interests of Confucius were purely ethical. From the doctrinal point of view, he accepted the Chinese tradition, which amounted to a more or less naturalistic and somewhat vague deism. But at the root of his system lies the idea of the dependance of moral value on knowledge. 'When a man has examined the nature of things,' he wrote, 'knowledge attains its highest degree. When knowledge has attained its highest degree, the will becomes perfect. When the will has become perfect, the impulses of the heart are controlled. When the impulses of the heart are controlled, man is free from failings. After a man has reformed himself, he establishes order in his family. If order reigns in the family, the country is well-governed. When the country is well-governed, the Empire also enjoys peace.'

Plato and Aristotle would have objected to none of that. Everything starts from the Emperor who is at the summit of the hierarchy: 'He who governs the country by setting it good examples is like the pole star, which remains motionless while the other stars circle around it.'

The practical advice which Confucius gives to the man who wants to put wisdom into practice much resembles that given by the Stoics. We get the impression that the moral rule commands recognition so unequivocally that wise men discover the same principles in every latitude.

### III. CODE MORALITY

In our times, code morality is to be found principally in

the Catholic Church. We also find it among certain Protestants and among Orthodox Jews, but in the world as a whole it is on the wane, and it can even be said that the contemporary world is in reaction against it. Since, however, it has played and still plays an extremely important part, we shall never understand the moral problem unless we get a clear idea of what code morality comprises, of the causes which led to its appearance and of the conditions which it presupposes. All this must be founded first of all on an analysis of certain historical aspects of the development and the teaching of Christian ethics.

## 1. *The ethics of the Old Testament*

Christian ethics derives in part from the Jews. Jesus was a reformer of the Jewish faith; he forms part of the continuous tradition. Christian ethical teachers are brought up on the Bible, and not only on the New Testament, but the Old Testament. The latter has exerted a profound influence on Christian consciousness. Even today, the greater part of the passages in the breviary, which forms the basic food of the Catholic clergy's spiritual life, is drawn from the Old Testament.

Now when we open the Old Testament after reading the Chinese, Greek and Indian moralists, we are struck by the violence of the religious sentiment and the harshness of the moral sense.

I have noted elsewhere the difference between the religious and the moral sense. The religious sense arises from the conviction that there exist one or more divine beings who must be reckoned with; the moral sense arises from the apprehension of the value of the person. The wise men possess the moral sense in the highest degree; Confucius is one of the most representative examples of this, partly because of the weakness of his religious sense. The religious question does not worry him; all his life is centred on the moral problem.

Now the greatness and the beauty of the Old Testament lie in the vigour with which it asserts divine transcendence at the same time as the personal and active character of God. And the 'active character' of God refers to his action among men.

Now among other peoples, the sense of divine transcendence rules out any action by God in the world. The acute sense of divine transcendence to be found in Aristotle, the Neo-Platonists and Hindu wisdom leads them to isolate God in ignorance of the world. In the popular religions, of course, gods are to be found mingling with men, but divine transcendence disappears. The special character of the Bible lies in the energy with which it simultaneously asserts divine transcendence and divine intervention in the world.

Its moral teaching on the other hand, is rather matter-of-fact. In this respect as in others, of course, the Old Testament forms a composite whole. When the Bible is described as a book, this term is ambiguous. In reality, the Bible is a collection of extremely disparate books, and the spiritual tone of the prophetic books, to take an example, is very different from that of the historical or the wisdom books.

The prophetic books, however, are above all religious : the prophets' chief concern is to warn the Jewish people of God's plans with regard to them. The best place to find the ethical ideas of Judaism is first in the Mosaic law and then in the wisdom books, the latter being principally or exclusively ethical. The wisdom books which date from the Hellenistic period represent the culmination of the Jews' ethical thinking. And their exhortation to virtue always ends with the promise of an earthly recompense.

Let us take a few examples at random, so that the reader may get the existential shock from them :

> Nor let anxious thoughts fret thy heart away; a merry heart is the true life of man, is an unfailing source of holiness; length of years is measured by rejoicing. Thy own self befriend, doing God's will with endurance, and giving all thy heart to the holiness he enjoins, and banish thy sad thoughts; sadness has been the death of many, and no good ever came of it. Jealousy and peevishness shorten a man's days; cares bring old age untimely.
> (*Ecclesiasticus* XXX, 22-26)

> Blessed is the man who lives, for all his wealth, unreproved, who has no greed for gold and puts no trust in his store of riches! Shew us such a man, and we will be loud in his praise; here is a life to wonder at. A man so tested and found perfect wins eternal honour; he kept clear of sin, when sinful ways were easy, did no wrong, when wrong lay in his power. His

treasure is safely preserved in the Lord's keeping, and wherever faithful men are met, his alms-deeds will be remembered.

(Ibid., XXXI, 8-11)

There is quibbling talk that will earn thee enemies, and an empty belly.

Blessings the wise man reaps from all around, to see him is to praise him.

Among our people the wise man wins an inheritance of honour, a deathless renown.

(Ibid., XXXVII, 23, 27, 29)

These texts have been selected at random; the wisdom books are all in the same spirit. If they are compared with the Kipling poem quoted earlier, the contrast is striking. The moral teaching of the wisdom books is one of moderation and of respectability, of measure, not of heroism. It teaches dignity, an orderly pursuit of earthly possessions, not detachment.

*　*　*

When we then inquire how Jewish ethics came into being, we find a phenomenon of a very unusual and purely religious character. It is the Pentateuch that tells this story: the Jews were at that time a rough and worldly people, passionately attached to all the good things of this world. Jahweh imposed his law on them by a decision which is depicted as arbitrary. After that, he kept them faithful to him by force: as soon as Israel showed signs of turning away from him, Jahweh recalled them to obedience by overwhelming them with misfortunes, and the recompenses he promised them if they remained faithful were all earthly ones. There is a violent contrast between this moral crudity and the purity of the idea of God lodged in this worldly people like a foreign body.

The Jewish moral law is thus not the fruit of reflection. It is imposed by God; it is a law that comes from outside, from a master. Or to be more precise, the moral law is part of the law, for the Jewish law also comprises ritual and political

57

precepts and rules of civil law and even hygiene. The word 'code' comes to one's mind unprompted. Jahweh said to Moses: 'These laws thou shalt promulgate to them . . .'

What we have before us, then, is a law dictated to a people, an entirely different thing from a wisdom in living proposed for the acceptance of those who are willing to comply with it. This law is composed of a collection of positive prescriptions which enjoin precise acts; there is no question of any reflection directed towards action and based on a general conception of life. If there is a general conception in the Jewish law, it is God who has it. The Jews confine themselves to receiving concrete commandments applicable to definite situations.

Thus the only general rule is obedience to Jahweh. He commands and there is nothing to do but obey. The sanction for these precepts is a social one, human happiness: 'I thy God, the Lord Almighty, am jealous in my love; be my enemy, and thy children, to the third and fourth generation, for thy guilt shall make amends . . .'

This is quite another thing from a school of wisdom. We are a long way from Epictetus and Confucius. What we have here is a law applying to an entire population demanding recognition. It is not *proposed*, it is *imposed*. The Jewish people as a whole showed no sort of desire for moral purity, quite the reverse. They were sensual and eager for every sort of material enjoyment, but Jahweh imposed his law by threats.

From this starting point the Jewish law developed. It was not a reflection on wisdom, not an ideal of wisdom; it was a law. And on the basis of this law, a tradition of casuistry took shape. Confronted with the law, men wanted to know exactly what it constrained them to. The 'cases' that might come up were studied, and it was asked how they could be resolved, taking into account the precept or precepts that applied to each case. At the end of antiquity, a corporation of interpreters of the law had been formed. It was the corporation of the Pharisees, and their task consisted in specifying the application of the precepts as far as was possible, so that everyone should know exactly what he ought to do.

The point of view is clear: men had a master whom they

must try not to displease, and for that they must know exactly what were the acts they were bound to do. Certain of these acts were moral acts in the sense that the wise men gave to the word, but others were simply marks of respect for the master; a gesture, for example, or a detail of clothing. Casuistry thus originated with the rule imposed from outside, with a rule which men had not chosen, with which they did not comply because they loved it, but which was imposed by the authority of one who was stronger than they. I do not think the same thing can be found in such an emphatic form among any other people. We can find elements that resemble it, but they are only a shadow of it. In ancient times, at any rate, the Jews were regarded by all the peoples who met them as beings apart.

## 2. *The ethical attitude of Jesus*
The personality of Christ presents many aspects, primarily religious. He is first and foremost the Saviour, and the revelation of salvation is linked with the revelation of his divine sonship. The ethical attitude of the Christian forms part of his religious outlook.

All the same, it is possible to place Christ's attitude in relation to the moral problem as it manifests itself in the history of mankind, and from this point of view, Jesus appears as a wise man. He calls on his disciples to translate into fact an ideal of purity put forward as a value in itself. 'You have heard that it hath been said: An eye for an eye and a tooth for a tooth. But I tell you that you should not offer resistance to injury; but if a man strikes thee on the left cheek, turn the other also towards him.' Here we are on the plane we found in Kipling: a summons to a value attractive in itself.

Christ, however, was also a Jew. He lived in Palestine and it was among the Jews that he preached. All his preaching referred back to the Old Testament. Its starting point was the Jewish tradition: we have just seen that in the text quoted above. But he reacted against a great number of the elements in this tradition.

He reacted particularly against code morality and against casuistry. For him the moral attitude is essentially a matter of impulse, of an orientation of life, of purity of heart and readiness to be used by God to serve. The disciple of Christ abandons himself to God, lets himself be possessed and borne up by him. And the love of God leads to the love of his neighbour, which at the same time expresses his love of God.

The rational aspect of Christianity is to be found in the purity of heart which results in that readiness to serve, and that aspect is common to Christianity and most ethical teachings. But this readiness is completely directed towards the divine surrender, and Christ's message is dominated by the revelation of the divine love. In one way, his entire message comes down to proclaiming that God loves us and to revealing the way in which this love was made manifest. Christ himself is the manifestation of this love. All this is put forward as the fulfilment of the Jewish law, but is opposed to it at the same time.

The rational aspect is therefore to be found in the ethical ideas of purity of heart or of readiness to serve. The Christian is detached in regard to every sort of worldly goods. Now the Jew, as we have seen, was not, and Jahweh never asked it of him. On the contrary the Jew was drawn to virtue by the lure of worldly recompense. The ethical notion of purity of heart is thus in violent contrast with Jewish ethics. To a great extent it is in contrast with Greek ethics also and that is why it struck the Western world as so new. All the same, it is the least original part of Christ's message, and being the only point many people have seen in Christian moral teaching, it has provided an argument to those who later considered this teaching to lack originality. This ethics of renunciation is principally expressed in the Sermon on the Mount, which is often represented as the essential passage in the moral teaching of the Gospels, and even as the essence of Christianity. Now the originality of the Sermon on the Mount lies in the general atmosphere of thinking it expresses, and not in this or that isolated passage. When we take isolated passages, as people often do, we find parallels in the works of most of the great moral teachers, especially in the Far East.

This atmosphere appears very clearly from the first verses on :

Blessed are the poor in spirit; the kingdom of heaven is theirs. Blessed are the patient; they shall inherit the land. Blessed are those who mourn; they shall be comforted. Blessed are those who hunger and thirst for holiness; they shall have their fill. Blessed are the merciful; they shall obtain mercy. Blessed are the clean of heart; they shall see God. Blessed are the peace-makers; they shall be counted the children of God. Blessed are those who suffer persecution in the cause of right; the kingdom of heaven is theirs. Blessed are you, when men revile you, and persecute you, and speak all manner of evil against you falsely, because of me. Be glad and light-hearted, for a rich reward awaits you in heaven; so it was they persecuted the prophets who went before you. (*Matt.* V, 3-12)

The first striking thing about this passage is the calm assurance of its opposition to accepted opinion, and the peace which contrasts with the toughness of the Kipling poem quoted earlier. What next strikes us is its religious character. God and the Kingdom of Heaven constantly recur and values such as 'to see God' are presented as the supreme values. All is bathed in an atmosphere of sweetness and joy, in striking contrast to painful experiences spoken of, experiences which are transformed by it. Suffering is given a halo of peace, and it leads to God. Whereas Kipling ends up: 'You'll be a Man, my son!' Jesus ends up: 'They shall see God' or 'the Kingdom of heaven is theirs'.

\*       \*       \*

Christ's attitude towards code morality is purely and simply one of reaction. Christ comes forward as a wise man as well as the Saviour. He summons men to love and 'he that hath ears to hear, let him hear'. He shows infinite pity for every weakness. He grows angry only with those who claim to limit man's duty, who set themselves up as just men and refuse to love. When he is asked casuistical questions, he refuses to answer, and though he often talks of sin and presents a picture of a world dominated by sin, he does not go into the practical consideration of what is allowed or forbidden. What he wants to do is to awaken men to love, to persuade them to give themselves, and he is constantly coming up against the Pharisees, whose attitude is the exact opposite. The Pharisees were the prisoners of a rigorously logical system; they understood nothing of the attitude of Christ, and they did not attempt to put themselves in his shoes. There was a head-on collision, and Jesus replied to them with invective. The Pharisees were the only people he grew angry with, and it was they who finally sent him to his death. In short, for Christ, the worst offence is pride, which is an attitude of life and which there is therefore no way of treating casuistically.

### 3. The twofold aspect of the teaching of Christian ethics

Later on, in the course of the centuries, moral teaching in what is known as historical Christianity developed on two lines which seemed at certain moments to be divergent, though they were really in agreement.

First of all, a wisdom morality like that preached by Christ was taught. This teaching, however, was concentrated in the religious orders and linked with religious vocations. It was imparted in spiritual, ascetic and mystical literature by the schools of wisdom represented by the religious orders. It was closely associated with the religious life, in the strict sense of the phrase, and prayer and direct and intimate relations with God occupied a predominant place in it, which differentiated it from the non-Christian schools of wisdom.

On the other hand, since the life of the religious orders is organized on the fringe of the world, this spirituality was not put forward as applicable to all Christians. It was an ethics for an elite, optional, not imposed but proposed for acceptance, like the wisdom morality found among non-Christians. I remarked earlier that if we want to find in the Christian Church a parallel phenomenon to the non-Christian wise men and their schools of wisdom, we shall have to go to the founders of religious orders and not to professors of moral philosophy.

This ethics for an elite was thus proposed for the acceptance of those attracted by it. Since it is applicable to religious, it only considers the aspects of life which concern them; hence its partial character. The mass of Christians were taught a code morality.

These two kinds of ethics do not contradict each other; indeed they would better be described as two ways of teaching ethics, or two aspects of it, rather than as two kinds of ethics. The elite which aspires to live up to wisdom morality starts by submitting to the code morality. The latter might be described as constituting the foundation of moral life.

Christian moral teaching, particularly as it developed in the Catholic Church, undoubtedly showed originality in the systematic way in which it combined solicitude for a moral training for the elite and for one for the masses. It was original to have tried to put forward simultaneously an ethics of perfection, a wisdom morality, and a popular ethics, a code morality. And it was an innovation to have combined the pursuit of complete purity with a concern for the people of God who were subject to a law, itself linked with the faith in a law-giving God, a God who cares for men and guides them.

Undoubtedly, too, prefigurations of this attitude will be found elsewhere. For example, there were the Essenes, who at the end of antiquity set up in Jewry communities of ascetics more or less resembling what the Christian religious orders were later to be. In the same way, the Buddhists have two moral rules, which apply respectively to monks and to ordinary believers. But nowhere else has this conception been taken so far as in the Catholic Church.

Code morality evolved in the Catholic Church under the influence of certain characteristics peculiar to the teaching of Christ.

To begin with, the Christians, like the Jewish people, form the people of God. The difference is that a man is Jewish because he is born so. In principle, a man is not a Jew as a result of personal choice, and the Jewish people itself is not the people of God by free choice. The whole initiative came from Jahweh. On the contrary, all men are summoned to become Christians and they become so by a personal choice. They enter the Church through baptism, and this in principle is voluntary. The practice of infant baptism came in because parents were regarded as qualified to speak for their children. The people of God is the whole body of Christians.

The Church thus forms a people, a human society, as does the Jewish people, though its members are recruited differently. It is a visible and organized society, and membership of the Church is subject to certain outward conditions.

The Church is a visible society, yet membership of it is linked with the supernatural life which is invisible. The Church continues the work of salvation that Christ came to carry out. It continues it first of all by introducing men into an order of life, the supernatural order, and by so guiding them that they retain and develop this supernatural life. The supernatural life is itself linked with objective conditions.

Now the supernatural life is the condition of salvation. It is thus the most important thing there can be for man. The state of grace, which is the state of supernatural life, is entirely different from the state of sin. A man who has lost supernatural life through sin has lost the essential element of good and of happiness. Hence nothing is more important than the possession of grace.

Theologians of earlier times somewhat over-simplified this. Though they came progressively to realize the possibility of a man being mistaken, they did not take this into account in practical application and treated as sinners all those without the faith. Nowadays, their attitude is less hard and fast. Since Christ has founded a supernatural order of life, all those who succeed in learning of it are obliged to become part of it, and the Church's mission is to bring this order to the knowledge of all mankind: 'Go out and preach the Gospel to the whole of creation.' When a man is ignorant of this order of life, however, we cannot automatically draw the conclusion that he is damned. A man who does know of the order and refuses to join it is guilty. If he does not know of it, he stands before God, who is above everything and treats everyone according to what is in his heart. That does not alter the exigencies of the Christian order, and emphasizes the duty of the Church, that is to say of the Christians who form part of the order founded by Christ and represented by the Church, to make Christ's message known to the world. But this conception makes us more wary of drawing absolute conclusions about the eternal fate of those who do not know of the Christian order.

It is thus understandable that Catholic theologians should be particularly concerned with the conditions of the state of grace. Grace is lost by sin, but it was soon realized that not every sin results in the loss of grace. Men are all sinners; never to commit a sin would be to be perfect, and no one is. Unless we are to lapse into a rigorism which would exclude all humanity from grace and be contrary to the spirit of Christ, we must distinguish between grave sins, which do deprive a man of grace, and minor, accidental and inevitable sins, which even men of good will commit. Hence the distinction between mortal and venial, which was destined to play a key role in the elaboration of Christian ethics.

With this notion of the state of grace is also linked the distinction between precepts and counsels, and between duty and perfection, sin and imperfection. The conditions of the state of grace must first be laid down; these conditions follow from the definition of grave sin. But grace can develop in a greater or less degree. To be in a state of grace is a minimum; to develop grace is another matter. A distinction is thus made between the things that are obligatory and the development of grace, which is optional. Thus the double line of teaching takes shape: that of the ethical minimum, which is obligatory, and that of wisdom morality, which is an ethics of free choice.

This distinction is further followed up since it is linked with the doctrine of the sacraments, which is more precisely defined in the Catholic Church than in other Christian communities. Certain sacraments are designed to open the way to the supernatural life by erasing sins; others presuppose that a man is in a state of grace. There are thus practical disciplinary reasons, linked with the daily life of the Christian, for defining accurately the distinction between mortal and venial sin on one hand and between sin and imperfection on the other.

All this intellectual labour is rational speculation. Christ's revelation on its own sheds no light on these questions. But men have had the impression that all this is theology because the problems involved are linked with the order of grace, which derives from revelation, and because their interest derives from this order. And it is thus that a casuistic ethics came into being in the Church, though Christ refused to consider this point of view.

Under the influence of these factors, the teaching of moral theory in the Church acquired ever more casuistic precision. The focal point in the teaching of morality is the sacrament of penance, whose object is the forgiveness of sins. To know what the faithful must confess and in what conditions the priest must give absolution, it is essential to know exactly what is a sin and what the dispositions of the penitent must be. Theologians investigated these questions tirelessly: in the Middle Ages, casuistry was less precise than it is today. I have analysed elsewhere, in *L'Enseignement de la morale chrétienne,* this trend of ideas. What interests us here is to appreciate the human character of this evolution.

Since this casuistic ethics is the only form to be taught systematically, it is regarded as *the* Christian ethics: those whose concern it is are moral teachers. The term 'moral teacher' thus assumes a different meaning from that it had in the ancient civilizations. Spirituality is seen as a sort of annexe of ethics. The result is that the teaching of ethics strikes a note rather different from the Gospel teaching of ethics. Not that Jesus condemned the search for a positive solution to these problems. But he reacted against the attitude which sought to minimize man's duties in order to reconcile his pursuit of and attachment to worldly possessions with the anxiety to satisfy God considered as a master.

All the same, Christian casuistry is very different from that of the Pharisees. To begin with, Christian casuistry is the work of men imbued with spirituality or wisdom morality in their private lives. Most of them are religious who have devoted their personal existence to the pursuit of perfection. They study code morality for others, in a spirit of compassion, so as to discover the minimum that must be demanded of the weak. It is true that since code morality deals with other forms of action from wisdom morality the same men sometimes practise code morality over certain points, justice for instance, and wisdom morality where humility or prayer are concerned. In certain fields there is no other teaching than that of code morality. Justice is a case in point. The question of honesty in money matters has not been studied from the point of view of wisdom morality.

Then again, the whole of Christian moral teaching is steeped in the doctrine of grace, since the whole aim of code morality is to determine the conditions of the state of grace. Now grace is the same thing as love. And though abstract words sometimes obscure this reality, concern for love can never completely disappear. The specialists may sometimes lose sight of it, but they feel its influence all the same. Christianity forms a whole, and we must take the whole into account if we are to judge the parts.

All this does not prevent people from thinking that Christian ethics is moral theology, that is to say the ethics of duty or the ethics of sin. This results in ambiguities, and in an uneasiness which broods over the whole evolution of ethics and affects moral teachers who are unacquainted with theology. When Kant made duty the focal point of ethics, he was unconsciously under the influence of the trend of ideas of which Catholic casuists were the principal authors, though he only came into contact with this trend through the pietism of the German Protestants. And we end up with attitudes like that taken in our days by Le Senne, who would confine philosophy to the study of duty, and puts above it what he calls 'morals', a tendency to good and a concern with the general direction of life which corresponds exactly to what we have here been calling wisdom morality.

It is easy to see the ambiguities which arise from this situation, for Le Senne uses the term 'morals' in a sense different from the usual one. Morals is generally used to designate the common or social practice of morality. We say that the morals of a people or a class of people are high or low according as the moral rule is well or badly observed. Le Senne's 'morals' is quite a different thing, and the uninitiated reader who thinks that the term employed by Le Senne is an accepted term will understand nothing. This is the more so since Le Senne, following the practice on which I remarked earlier, fails to say that he has changed the usual meaning of the word.

\*   \*   \*

To understand the teaching of Christian ethics we must therefore put it in its context in the main stream of ethical thinking. But at the same time it is impossible to understand the evolution of Western ethical thinking if we do not take into account the teaching of Christian ethics, though this is put forward first and foremost as a religious ethics and is always referring back, implicitly at least, to revelation. All these questions have become tangled over the centuries; the ambiguities and confusions are innumerable, and there is a big job of clarification to be done today if we want accurately to define the ideas involved.

Those of code morality and wisdom morality are fundamental; they are keys. We shall be coming across them constantly in the course of our inquiry. For the moment, it will be enough to remember that code morality is a popular ethics applying to a people and depending on the voice of a master who lays down the rule, and that it is thus obligatory on those believers who do not aspire to an ideal which is itself ethical. It corresponds, in short, to a parting of the ways between the moral rule which a man must respect in order to satisfy the master, and thus obtain the recompense he desires, and immediate personal satisfaction, which lies on another path. Wisdom morality, on the contrary, is an ethics corresponding to the aspirations of the man who aspires to a perfect life.

All this will become clearer when we have examined the fundamental problem of ethics, of any ethical system, which is the problem of the moral imperative.

# Chapter Three

## *The Moral Imperative*

### I. EUDAIMONISM

GREEK ETHICS, like that of the Chinese, was as a whole distinctly eudaimonist.

Eudaimonism is an ethics of happiness; it identifies moral good with happiness, and makes the pursuit of happiness the aim of life.

It is, in short, spontaneous morality. It still remains the popular ethics; men seek to be happy—what else should they seek? Christianity has not eliminated that, and nothing will. Certain moral teachers may try to transcend the desire for happiness, but the mass of men always fall back into it. Nowadays social ethics may ask man to sacrifice himself to the good of the community, but this still consists in a collective happiness. The individual may have to renounce it for himself, but only in order to procure it for others. The 'Soviet paradise' which is so much talked of today, as much by its detractors as by its admirers, comes down to the happiness of men, and this paradise which everyone must toil to establish is a collective state where nobody will ever have to renounce his happiness again. It is the same with the happiness the American magazines picture, with their naive optimism about an affluent society where everyone will have all the good things he wants. It is a sort of transposition to earth of the popular picture of the Christian paradise, which is also a place of tangible pleasures, not very different from the paradise of Mahomet.

We are therefore up against a spontaneous conception, which does not seem to have raised any problems outside the Christian world. Man seeks for happiness; the idea of his doing otherwise does not even arise. All the exertions of the wise men have consisted in trying to persuade their fellows that happiness is to be found in virtue and nowhere else. Virtue is man's

69

development in accordance with his deep-lying tendencies or his nature.

All the same, man ought to mortify himself. The basis of mortification or ascesis is that he is a manifold and divided being, that his tendencies must be reduced to unity and that, with this in view, certain of them must even be thwarted, looked at in themselves. Nothing is more symptomatic in the history of wisdom than its agreement on this austerity. Even a thinker like Epicurus, for whom the moral rule was nothing but the pursuit of pleasure, ended up with a rule of physical austerity. It is true that this was nothing more than a calculus of pleasures such as was to reappear in modern times among the utilitarians, but this process brought out the fact that in many cases certain pains are superior to pleasures, because a man who has undergone them experiences a higher degree of pleasure.

The Stoics alone, at the end of antiquity, began to take a slightly different attitude. We shall be coming to them a little later.

On the other hand, it seemed so obvious to all these philosophers that virtue and happiness coincided that they found it hard to believe that anyone could do evil knowing what he was doing. There was universal agreement on this, as we have seen with Confucius. Plato wrote in the *Charmides*: 'When false beliefs have been eliminated and wisdom is taken for a guide, men act well and successfully, and since their action is successful, they cannot help being happy.' We might be reading Confucius.

We have already seen that this point of view still exists, despite the new elements introduced by Christianity. Men set out to arouse enthusiasm by proclaiming the beauty of an ideal or a cause, the enthusiasm being a mental excitement produced by beauty or goodness and inspiring a desire for action in accordance with them. This action may take very different forms. A man may sacrifice his life or his possessions, or simply speak in praise of the good thing, or go and see it or, as we saw with Kipling's poem, hang it up on his wall.

That man wants to be happy is thus the fundamental fact for eudaimonists, and they saw no need to prove it. Moreover, man must be helped to find happiness, and they saw no objection to that. They would have been stupefied that anyone should find this vulgar and should seek any other end.

What is more, they had no idea of an active God. Even where they did have some such idea, like the Chinese with their vague conception of Heaven, which varies from author to author, they did not feel themselves obliged to take the future life into consideration. The consequences of good or bad acts were confined to this world: a man would be more or less happy according to whether he behaved well or ill. They had no idea of an absolute; they never dreamed that a man could stake his whole destiny on a single act.

This attitude was accentuated in the Far East by the doctrine of reincarnation, which came from India, was passed on to China and is found to some extent in Greece, in Pythagoras: to some extent, and to the extent that we know Pythagoras. In any case, reincarnation runs counter to the absoluteness of ethics, for if the present life leads only to a later life whose nature results from it, nothing is ever irreparable.

In short, this ethics, which can be described as universal, comes down to saying: if you want to be happy and to live a fine life behave in such and such a way.

## II. The Stoics and the Order of Nature

The Stoics seem to have been the first philosophers in the Greek tradition to go beyond the idea of happiness and to envisage good as something distinct from it. Reacting against the Epicureans, who explicitly made ethics a methodology of enjoyment, they started from the idea of a cosmic order towards which everything is orientated and to which everything, including man, is subordinated. The primary fact was not the desire for happiness, but the spontaneous impulse of the being to follow the fundamental exigencies of nature. Pleasure and pain were simple accidents resulting from a man's behaviour.

Morality thus consisted in the fact of a being endowed with reason deliberately regulating his acts in accordance with the order of nature. The moral character of an act did not consist in its conforming with the natural order—or the cosmic order,

71

as the Stoics put it—for everything always conforms with nature; there is no alternative. What made an act moral was that the act conformed *rationally* with nature, that is that the reason accepted this order and complied with it. Here we have already an adumbration of Kant's distinction between the moral act and the licit act.

Hence the Stoics' ascesis, which focuses life on rational action and on the repression of the passions in order to set reason at liberty.

## III. THE CHRISTIAN CONTRIBUTION

Christianity profoundly transformed the character of ethics by its conception of God and of eternity.

In the first place, Christianity brought out as never before the idea of a God who is the creator and law-giver, author of the moral law. Man depends completely on God and must obey him.

This notion of the divine law was already present, we know, in the Old Testament. But the Jews had only a vague idea of the future life. They expected rewards and punishments in this world; the Book of Job has often been cited as a perfect example of their conception. But on the other hand, the transcendence and the personality of God assume such a prominence in the Old Testament that it is these that make the whole greatness of the book. God acts in the world, and he is the chief actor. His action is overwhelming. Man is driven to obey; there is no alternative.

On the other hand, we know, God's practical demands are very precise. There is a law. Good has thus a precise character, diametrically opposed to evil.

Hence the importance of duty: man must do what God commands. Duty is not a metaphysical abstraction, nor a dream of wisdom: it is the will of a master.

To this was added the idea of a future life. We know that this lacked clarity among the Jews, though it was sufficiently present to them for Jesus to be able to talk of it by allusion, without putting it forward as a new doctrine, opposed to what his listeners thought they knew.

72

In Christianity, the idea of future life is quite clear. What is more, it is more important than the present life. The present life is no more than a preparation for eternal life. It is a test. Man is on earth to show what he is worth, but the Kingdom is not of this world.

This last expression has a double meaning. The Kingdom is not of this world in the sense that it does not consist in the wordly goods to which men cling; on earth, nothing is final, everything points towards eternity. But in another sense, the Kingdom is already in this world, in the sense that the present life prefigures the eternal Kingdom and leads the way to it. The crown of everything may be in the next world, but the path that leads there is in this world. And no one will enter the eternal kingdom if he has not done his best to start building it here below, among his fellow-men, during their earthly life. When Christ talks of the Kingdom in the Gospels, these two meanings constantly recur.

Then again, life is a definitive test; eternity is at stake. This is in flat opposition to the doctrine of reincarnation.

What is more, eternity may be at stake in a single act. There is thus an absoluteness about the act. The difference between good and evil is not simply one of more or less but of being or not being.

Heaven and Hell are depicted in the most emphatic light; good and evil have the most radical consequences, since eternity depends on them. This is a central point in Christian ethics, which puts it in complete opposition to non-Christian ethics.

The doctrine that the nature of the future life is definitively fixed after a single life on earth illuminates this ethics with a light that is peculiar to it. On earth, nothing is final; a man can always correct a mistake, give up sinning, or make amends. But when life is over, nothing can be changed, and a man takes up his lodging in eternity as he was at the moment of his death. Hence the importance of the moment of death, the last act which freezes a man's attitude for ever. But we may die at any moment. Every one of our acts is therefore big with eternity.

The consequence is a sort of savage grandeur about the Christian sense of destiny, a dramatic Christian atmosphere which colours the whole of life. Any single act may win me eternal happiness or misery. Every one of my acts saves me or damns me. The act is an absolute.

This dramatic Christian outlook has more than once been contrasted with the sweetness and calm of pagan wisdom. The pagan wise man simply seeks for a balance in life. His attitude towards the ordinary man ranges from indifference to contempt or pity, but he suffers no anxiety about himself and his disciples. Christian anxiety and the tranquillity of the Greeks are in complete contrast, and some people nowadays tax Christianity with having made life impossible.

Christianity seems to have given birth to a new type of over-scrupulousness, that of the man who is afraid of not doing what he ought to and of being damned. Even if Christianity did not produce this type of men, it increased their numbers. But they are bad Christians. Scruples arise from fear, and this derives from the fact that a man sees in God first and foremost the master, lets himself be hypnotized by the thought of justice and sin, and does not abandon himself to love. Now as we have seen, love alone provides the key to Christianity. But there are all too many half-Christians; Christians in the sense that they accept the doctrines the Church teaches, and not Christians because the love of God holds no place either in their thoughts or in their lives.

In any case, the conclusion must be that the idea of good and evil held by Christians is strictly a Christian one and has no equivalent among non-Christians. This Christian conception has impregnated Western thought, which is consequently extremely different from the thinking of antiquity or of the Far East. And since a certain number of Western thinkers started trying to free themselves from Christianity and to re-think the problems of ethics in complete detachment from any Christian philosophical framework, they have been turning these questions over and over without ever succeeding in finding a stable position.

For it is by now impossible to leave Christianity out of account. It has profoundly influenced thought, and its influence is not confined to the Scholastic tradition. Descartes was a Christian. Kant was brought up in a Christian tradition, though he strayed away from positive faith. Many thinkers are still Christians today. And those who have struggled most

74

violently to free themselves from Christianity, such as Nietz-sche, Sartre and Camus, have Christianity at the back of their minds the whole time. They are obsessed by it, and their very anxiety to oppose it shows that Christianity is there. It clings to their body like a sort of shirt of Nessus.

Moreover, when we are tempted to contrast the dramatic Christian outlook with pagan serenity, there is one fact that should make us hesitate: the facility with which converts accept the Christian sense of good and evil. That suggests that there is something about the Christian conception which tallies with a spontaneous popular intuition. No doubt Christianity makes this explicit, but it confines itself to stating precisely what all upright men have an inkling of. We shall come across this again when we try to clarify the moral imperative.

After this exposition, there will be no difficulty in under-standing why Christian ethics, as it developed historically, should have laid such stress on the act.

Since the act has potentially a definitive character and any act may be irremediable, the essential thing is that it should be good. Every effort was therefore made to clarify the distinc-tion between good and evil acts. The main thing for a man is to be saved, and salvation is won through the state of grace which we enter through baptism and in which we remain as long as we do not sin. The root of the matter, therefore, is to stay in the state of grace, to avoid sin, and with a view to that, to know what sin is.

It is true that there are also degrees in virtue, and that it is desirable for a man to do the most good he can. So the question of perfection had also to be studied, and within the conception of good, the perfect had to be distinguished from the imper-fect. All this, however, was a minor matter. The main point was to be saved and to avoid sin. Whether a man sanctified himself more or less came in only at a later stage.

This explains how code morality developed in the Church, and how it came to be looked on as the main point of moral science, with wisdom morality falling into the background.

As Etienne Gilson has already remarked,[1] the isolated act

[1] *The Spirit of Medieval Philosophy*, English trans. by A. H. C. Downes, London, 1936, page 334.

had no importance for the ancients. 'With infinite pains they set out to model their interior statue of a man, they judged of a life only by its totality.' On the other hand, modern man, and this comes from Christianity, throws the whole of himself into the act. 'A single act may be a final triumph or an irremediable disaster.' And that has become so natural to modern man that he no longer realizes it is a Christian value.

It is important to note here that all this development is purely rational. It starts from certain ideas which are characteristic of the Christian view of life, but which are, however, separable from Christianity. That is why most people fail to see that they are Christian ideas.

Indeed, the doctrine of God as pure Act and that of a definitively settled future life are in themselves rational or philosophical notions. They have in fact been known through, or at least clarified by Revelation, but once known, they can be discussed without any reference to Revelation. These doctrines were presupposed in Christ's teaching; they were therefore true before the Christian Revelation and remain true independently of it. The real object of Revelation is the good news of salvation brought by Jesus; it is the positive fact of God's Incarnation in the concrete man Jesus at a definite moment in history, and the redemption of mankind brought about by him in a manner that was just as definite. The general doctrine of a transcendent God who is the creator, of the soul, of the future life and even of the divine fatherhood and the identification of God with love, all were true independent of Christ. They could therefore be discovered by human reflection, and in fact adumbrations of them can be found in a number of philosophies. But there was one thing philosophy could not discover. This was that God had determined to save man in this particular way, through Christ, that the Word has become incarnate and suffered, and that his spirit had then spread among his disciples by the peculiar and definite means that is known as supernatural life, or grace. That is Christianity, and it is quite a different thing from philosophy.

From the moral point of view, Christ summons men to follow him, and to follow him is to live with his life. Ethical thinkers asked themselves in what this consisted. To follow Christ is not just an abstract rule. He is a master whom men follow and on whom they pattern themselves; a spiritual master with whose spirit they become imbued. But most Christians do not worry about that. They are Christians because they have accepted the Christian teaching theoretically, but they do not understand that to be a Christian is above all to follow Christ. An effort is therefore made to discover the minimum to be required of them, and here we are back at code morality.

All this structure of teaching, it should be repeated, is rational. It does not come from Revelation, though it is linked with it. The abstract distinctions between good and evil and between the perfect and the imperfect are rational, that is to say philosophical, conceptions and are therefore subject to free discussion, as are all philosophical ideas. Now these conceptions turn ethics upside down. They are methodological instruments whose object is to systematize acts, and this concentration, even when it is brought to bear on the act to the neglect of the virtues or the orientations of life, is itself the fruit of an intellectual systematization. The line of Christ's teaching would be consonant with a different systematization.

We have seen that Christ was not concerned with these questions. His aim was to enlighten his disciples with regard to a pattern of life. Later on, men possibly devoted too much of their minds to a Christian rationalism. It was Christian in that it drew its inspiration from certain Christian positions, such as the importance of the state of grace. But it was rationalist in so far as its authors, having picked out certain trends in the teaching of Christ, proceeded to build an intellectual system inspired by their own views.

It is true that the fundamental conceptions drew their inspiration from the teaching of Christ, but that is not enough. The way a doctrine is expounded can change it, and a difference of emphasis can distort it as much as or even more than a mistake over a particular idea or formulation. If we want to construct an authentically Christian morality, we must start by immersing ourselves in Christ's teaching and his way of life. We must take his standpoint and only approach individual problems when we can constantly stay in this light of Christ's, stick to Christ, as it were.

77

The consequences of Christianity for ethics only made themselves felt gradually, without Christians themselves noticing what was happening. We are talking here of teaching. From the start, Christians were fully conscious that the Christian faith transforms life. The enthusiasm of the first Christians and their scorn for pagan ethics speak for themselves. Later on, Christians remained convinced that faith transforms life, and even leaned on this conviction too heavily, to the point where men were finally able to tax them with not having a transformed life at all, though they still claimed they had.

But though Christians may have believed that their faith transformed life, they did not realize that it transforms ethics, and even less that it transforms general philosophy. Ancient and medieval Christian thinkers had the greatest respect for Greek thought, and believed they were doing no more than carrying it on. Thus St Thomas's veneration for Plato and Aristotle limited his ambition to that of continuing their tradition of thought, and prevented him from being fully conscious of what he had modified in it.

There was thus a contrast which was going to have its effect in the field of ethics. On one hand Christians had the impression that Christianity transforms life. On the other hand, in the field of ideas they fell without resistance into line with the thinking of antiquity, which was pagan. This evolution led to what I am here calling moralism, which consists on one hand in isolating the moral point of view from others in thought and in life, and on the other in regarding it as the only important one. It was largely after the Renaissance that this trend of thinking began to spread. It reigned supreme in the eighteenth and nineteenth centuries, and it was only in the twentieth that people started to react against it.

## 1. The Aristotelian-Thomist synthesis

If we are to see how this evolution developed, we must start from the Aristotelian-Thomist synthesis achieved by St Thomas. Its characteristics are well known: ethics is based on a sound and coherent metaphysics. The true and the good are transcendental properties of being, and it is the same with the beautiful. They are mere differences in the point of view, accessible only to the mind; the only objective reality is being, but according as the mind considers it from one point of view or another, it appears under the form of the true or the good. The good is thus the same as the true. The good is *truly* good; the true is good in so far as it constitutes an end for the mind, and happiness derives from the possession of the good. There is no happiness outside of the good, and no good outside of the truth. All this forms a unity, and the synthesis is of a solidity and strength that leaves no room for any fissure. I have explained in another book, *La philosophie morale de Saint Thomas devant la pensée contemporaine,* the extent of the contrast between this mighty synthesis and the often blind gropings of the thinking of our time.

It is thus impossible that error should be good or that the good should lie in the untrue. The good lies in the truth that is lived or in the truth in so far as it is an end. It is impossible to be happy outside the good which is the true; no beauty is possible outside the good and the truth. A good life is a life which conforms with truth; it is at the same time a beautiful life, and there is no happiness outside this.

This synthesis is the firmest that has ever been put forward, but Christian feeling was to lead to the dissociation of moral good as the result of three main influences.

## 2.   *The primacy of moral good.*

Moral good, that is to say the good in human conduct, assumes an importance out of all proportion with the other forms in the eyes of the Christian, because it is on it and it alone that salvation depends. An intellectual or aesthetic mistake is of little account; it does not compromise salvation. But a single moral error may be enough.

It is true that theologians consider the k
truths, called 'necessary for salvation', to
man wants to be saved. But these are
truths, which do not demand any great in
it is enough to know their general tenor,
to trust to the Chuch. It is constantly be
shorter cathechism is sufficient for salva

have good will, God will help us to know these truths. There is therefore no problem. On the other hand, the moral life does raise problems.

The long and the short of it is that moral purity is the one thing necessary, for knowledge of what is necessary for salvation depends on it. On the other hand, virtue does not depend on intellectual knowledge, particularly when it bears on questions which do not directly concern salvation. An intellectual error has no importance, still less an aesthetic error, since they do not stand in the way of salvation.

It is therefore enough for a man to concern himself with moral good. He must master the fundamental truths, but it is enough to know them once for all, and there is no question of their being added to. It is not necessary in this field to engage in a daily stint of work, whereas the moral problem comes up every day and at every time of day.

The contrast with the ancients is clear-cut. For them the great problem was to know. Good followed from knowledge and evil resulted from ignorance. In the Christian world, knowledge raises no thorny problems; all the difficulty arises from the corruption of the will.

## 3. *Christian pessimism*

Christianity is a mixture of optimism and pessimism. It is pessimistic about man, for it believes him to have been corrupted by original sin; but this pessimism is never an absolute pessimism, like the Hindu pessimism. It would not be true to say that life is all suffering for the Christian as it is for the wise man of India. Original sin results in a certain fall from grace, but this is limited; it does not prevent all good, but prevents a man from attaining perfection.

On the other hand, Christianity is optimistic about God because of its doctrine that God is Love. God loves us; he wants to save us; he brings us salvation with a wealth of proofs of his love that makes doubt impossible. Complete perfection is open to the Christian through the gift he receives from God.

Nevertheless Christian pessimism about mankind results in a distrust of man. Man is an unhappy being who is a prey to the threefold concupiscence of his body and his mind. All beings are good in themselves as they come from the hands of God, but man perverts their primal innocence through the corruption he carries within him. Hence the notion of learning the danger of good things, which is fundamental for any understanding of Christian teaching. Temptation lurks in worldly possessions; the devil tempts man by bodily beauty; learning arouses and inflates intellectual pride. It is a favourite tag that learning is not necessary to salvation; it is even insinuated that an ignorant man is saved more easily than a learned one, because learning encourages conceit. And a pronounced undercurrent of distrust of the intellectual and the artistic takes form.

The undercurrent develops first and foremost in the thinking of Protestantism, which is more pessimistic than Catholicism; it is to be found in Luther and Calvin, then among the Puritans and Pietists, and on the Catholic side, in Jansenism, which is a distorted form of Catholicism. In the Catholic Church, this undercurrent has always come up against an opposing trend, which extolled intellectual culture and the arts, and modern liberal Protestantism has reacted too. All the same, the undercurrent is still strong; it became profoundly implanted in the Christian conscience in the form of the fear of sin. The first question many people ask themselves, just as much among pastors and teachers as among fervent believers, is that of risk. When risk is mentioned in this way, without further specification, it does not mean a risk of error, but a risk of sin.

The trend became accentuated in the eighteenth and nineteenth centuries, because the movements of emancipation, or of intellectual and artistic innovation, were linked with an anti-Christian trend, which was chiefly anti-Catholic. Anything that threatened to lead a man into sin was wrong. It was easy to slide from 'risky' to 'wrong', and to condemn in itself a thing that might be used for a good end, if rightly handled.

This trend also led men to isolate moral good from all other values and to seek it exclusively.

## 4. *Intentionalism*

Their concentration of attention on the act, which they

considered from the moral point of view, led Christian authors to emphasize the importance of intention, for this is what confers its moral value on the act. They thus distinguished the idea of *morals*.

The ancients reflected on the beautiful and perfect life. They examined it in itself. The moral character of any particular act seemed to them of little importance. It was life as a whole that mattered, as we have seen.

The Stoics started the process that Christians have completed. If morals depends on intention and if an act is only intentional on condition that it is free, since human autonomy expresses itself through free will, it is solely through the moral act that the value proper to man makes itself known. The *human* act is the free act, that is to say the moral act. That leads us back to the same conclusion: the whole problem of life is the moral problem.

This problem falls into two parts: first, knowing what is good and what is bad; then doing the good and avoiding the bad. The rest is without importance. If a good man turns out an ugly work of art, that matters little. St Teresa of the Child Jesus wrote sugary poetry: that has no effect on her sanctity. Making spelling mistakes is not of the least importance either. The only knowledge that matters is the knowledge of moral good; the only training that matters is the training of an upright will.

The result of all this was that for three centuries Christian thinking and Christian art stopped dead. Metaphysics and dogmatics stagnated; Christianity ceased to be a source of artistic inspiration. On the other hand, big strides were made by casuistry, that is to say moral reflection applied to acts as distinct entities. Apart from casuistry, Christian thinking ceased to be creative.

An excellent symbol of this state of affairs is what we shall call the 'Racine complex'. When he became converted at the age of thirty-eight, Racine, out of moral scruples, stopped writing. All his work, with the exception of two religious tragedies, written to order, was the work of a young man. Once he was converted, he never thought that he should employ his talent in the service of God, but only that he must avoid the risk of sinning.

This example shows what Christian thought and Christian life have lost through the abandonment, or at least the neglect, of the metaphysical heritage of the Middle Ages and the separation of moral philosophy from metaphysics. If the true, the good and the beautiful are indeed only different mental apprehensions of a single and identical being; if it is true that all truth and all beauty is good, and that the good is not to be found outside the true and the beautiful, the conclusion is inescapable. Moral value lies in a man's achieving the perfection of being which he is capable of achieving, and Racine's duty was thus to produce the beautiful works which he was capable of producing. If we are to use Christian language, we shall be forced to say that Racine 'sinned' gravely, that he possibly committed the gravest sin he was capable of committing when he refused to use for the service of God the talent that God himself had given him. It is thus an undeniable 'moral duty'—we must stress this—for a man to develop every perfection, in other words to take the place in the world he is capable of occupying and to produce the work he is capable of producing. Moral action is nothing but the application of free will to the pursuit of the good, which is an ontological value, and the good is the same as the true and the beautiful.

All this stems directly from the identity of being and its transcendental properties. Nevertheless the medieval authors who laid down the doctrine most unequivocally, St Thomas in particular, did not explicitly draw all the potential conclusions from it. That was because the human mind works slowly and it needs generations of thinkers to discover all the applications of a principle. It is all the more regrettable that, with the Renaissance, ethical thought became separated from metaphysics, and that metaphysical thought ceased to progress and ethics evolved alone.

## V. KANT AND THE CATEGORICAL IMPERATIVE

From the nineteenth century on, it has become impossible to discuss the moral problem without mentioning Kant. Kant thought of himself first of all as a metaphysician. As he saw it, moral philosophy did not in itself raise any serious problems, and when he developed his ethical ideas this was no more than a formulation of convictions he already possessed. Nevertheless, he seems to have had more influence on moral philosophy than he had on metaphysics.

But as I pointed out earlier, Kant is incomprehensible apart from his Christian background. He grew up in a pietistic environment, completely imbued with the self-evidence and primacy of duty. For him, ethics corresponded to an incontestable reality which he never dreamed of discussing. In an epitaph composed in 1782, when he was nearly sixty, he wrote: 'There is only one thing we can be certain of, our duty.'

This attitude led Kant to undertake an analysis of ethics, or of the character of the moral imperative apart from any question of its content. He was indeed forced to do so, since the consciousness of duty was for him the primary certitude, and most subsequent philosophers were to follow in his footsteps without realizing the revolutionary character of the position. We are at the opposite pole from the Thomist synthesis. There is no more question of being, or of transcendental properties. There is duty; we must start with duty when we want to think, even in metaphysics, and we must therefore discover what is the meaning of duty.

Everyone would agree, Kant says, that the only perfectly good thing in the world is a good will.

'Everyone would agree' ... The whole system collapses if it is doubted that everyone would agree. The ancients said: 'Everyone wants to be happy.' This statement was equally self-evident to them.

Now Kant's good will is the will to do what one ought to. It is not the will to do good, and Kant does not consider the idea of good on which the whole moral philosophy of antiquity was based. Not only does he not think of doing so, he is not even conscious that he is thus shifting the entire foundation of ethics. All this raises no problem in his eyes. Duty is a value accepted by everyone, and there is no need to hunt about for any other basis for ethics.

Now what is duty? It is what compels recognition in its own right, that is to say, by a categorical imperative, in contrast to what compels recognition by a hypothetical imperative. A good action which is done from a motive other than duty is not moral but simply licit. And as this idea of duty is purely a rational one, anything which is done out of sentiment is alien to morality. Duty expresses the rational objective; it is an end in itself, a categorical imperative, and it alone is an end in itself. In short, Kant's categorical imperative is the spontaneous vision of the absoluteness of duty.

I drew attention earlier to the similarity between this attitude and that of Catholic ethical thinkers who make the problem of sin the focal point of ethics. Thus it is not surprising that Kant's point of view was adopted without opposition by the Catholic moral philosophers of the nineteenth century as well as by the others, and that the Kantian analysis of moral value was regarded as a big step forward in moral philosophy. But it was to produce a reaction which is calling everything in question again today.

## VI. ANTIMORALISM

At the outset of this book, I remarked that the ethical teacher or the wise man is essentially a non-conformist. Code morality on the other hand is tied up with social conformity, and moralism generates a veritable stifling of the characteristically human values. The separation of ethics from life, and the exclusive concern with life's moral aspect leads to a diminution of vitality and a mistrust of values which are regarded as alien to ethics. And this mistrust stifles interest in the complete self-realization of man. When the doctrine of the transcendental properties of being was forgotten or reduced to suspended animation, it was a disastrous day for moral philosophy.

There was thus a reaction against moralism, and since moralism was regarded as identical with ethics, a reaction against ethics too. This reaction, which has been particularly vigorous in our times, is to be met with in varying degrees in other societies, linked with every sort of reaction against attempts to discipline thinking and living which stifle them instead of helping them to flower freely.

Now in every society where the moral rule is regarded as

fixed in its main lines, ethical scrutiny is brought to bear on more and more trivial questions. Men discuss whether it is virtuous or wicked to cut the hair or the beard, to wear a long or a short dress, to eat meat or sugar, to drink a particular drink or to sit on a particular seat.

These are indeed real problems which have got to be resolved and which inevitably arise. But though they may be real, they are minor details; and even if social life does make it necessary to codify these rules, they should yet be treated with the detachment their triviality deserves.

On the other hand these rules form part of ethics, indirectly, through social life, because ethics must take into account the exigencies of the social order. But when these scruples become absorbing, when they become, in appearance at least, the essence of ethics—and it seems easy for this to happen, where they are talked of a lot and the essential rules are not discussed, because they are regarded as raising no problem —a reaction is bound to occur. And since this reaction generally originates with young people, often with little tuition, and with no doctrinal synthesis behind them, it takes violent and often confused forms. Even if it is healthy in itself, it presents itself in a form as exaggerated as the abuse against which it is reacting, and seems all the more exaggerated since it runs counter to general opinion.

That is the explanation of Nietzsche's *Beyond Good and Evil* and Gide's *Immoralist* and many other writings. Among them we must not forget those of Lao-tse, who wrote more than two thousand years ago : 'The higher virtue is not what is usually called virtue : that is why it possesses the real nature of virtue. The lower virtue claims to be virtue : that is why it is not real virtue. The higher virtue makes no effort and expects no reward.'

This attitude is to be found in almost every age, as is a reaction against stereotyped metaphysics. In ethics, this reaction takes a naturalistic and a metaphysical form.

The naturalistic form consists in saying that man must follow nature without raising so many questions. It is an ethics of spontaneity or of instinct. We must trust man. That is the conclusion of the contemporary philosophers of 'absurdity', and in ancient times it was the attitude of the Cynics. History repeats itself. When the Cynics, like the atheistic Existentialists of our day, say that they will have none of morality and that good and evil are human inventions, they merely mean that they do not accept the code that society is trying to impose on them. This code does not seem to them to correspond to the real aspirations of nature, of *their* nature. It is a reactionary formula. What they are really seeking is what all free intelligences have always sought: the real formula of development in accordance with nature.

The metaphysical form of antimoralism is to be met with chiefly in the Far East, and it is from there that it has influenced the contemporary West.

One of the dominant notes of Hindu thinking, as is well known, is that Brahma, the supreme reality which we know under the name of God, is the absolute being and is undetermined. He is consequently devoid of all attributes and transcends all distinctions, including that between good and evil. In primitive Hindu thinking as we see it in the Rig Veda, which dates back more than a thousand years before Christ, Brahma is at once the being who dominates everything —our God the creator, in fact—and the transcendent being of whom nothing can be predicated.

> He who gives life and gives strength, whose shadow is immortality, whose shadow is death, who is this god that we may offer him our sacrifices?
> He through whom the snow-covered mountains exist, and the sea with the distant river, he whose arms are the spheres of heaven, who is this god that we may offer him our sacrifices?
> He who, through his might, cast his eyes even over the topmost waters, who gives power and generates the sacrificial fire, he who alone is god above all the gods, who is this god that we offer him our sacrifices?

And again:

> There was neither being nor not-being; there was neither the air around nor the sky above. Who is it that is moving? In what direction and under whose control? Were there waters and the profound abyss?
> There was neither death then, nor immortality. Day was not separated from night. Only the One breathed, with no extraneous breath, of himself, and there was nothing but him.
> Then for the first time desire awoke in him, and that was

87

the first germ of mind. The link of being, wise men discovered in not-being, wise men striving with their hearts full of intelligence.

Who knows, who can say whence creation was born and whence it comes, and whether the gods were only born after it? Who knows whence it came?

Whence creation came and whether it was created or not, He whose eye watches over it from the highest heaven—he only knows—and does even he know?

There we have primitive thought, at a time when it was expressed in poems. As in Greece, the systematic thinkers who were to be called philosophers only came later. But all Hindu thought culminates, in one form or another, in a rule of life designed to achieve union with Brahma. This is an unequivocally contemplative attitude.

This general aspiration can fit in with widely different metaphysical systems. Some of these deny all reality to the world or to man. Others allow an ideal or idealist reality; others again a material reality, but all direct their thought towards the same objective.

The rule of life thus becomes a rule of indifference with regard to everything. Now logically, indifference is incompatible with the difference between good and evil. He who believes in good has on the contrary a strongly preferential attitude.

We find the same outlook in Lao-tse, who has already been quoted. In contrast to Confucius, who is the ethical philosopher par excellence, Lao-tse is the most metaphysical of the Chinese wise men.

His metaphysics is based on the *tao*, the ineffable first principle, which is without either name or determinate qualities. The aim of life is to annihilate ourselves in the *tao*, but the *tao* is beyond good and evil, because there is no distinction in it. Good and evil are relations, since one only exists through the other, but the *tao* is above all relations. To distinguish between good and evil thus separates a man from the *tao*; it is the primary sin.

A similar attitude is to be found in Neo-Platonism. For Plotinus, the origin of everything was to be found in the transcendent and ineffable One 'of whom we can assert everything and deny everything'. It is true that the Neo-Platonists did

**88**

not go on from this to deny good and evil, because the Greeks are less extreme than the peoples of the Far East. But the principle is implicit there.

The same tendency appears among mystics of every faith, Christians included. Their anxiety to assert the divine transcendence without any reservation leads them to represent God as above any intellectual category and any qualification, and thus to deny that he can be called good, for to call him good would be to rank him among beings. God is thus above good.

We shall see to what extent these notions can be vindicated. Let us now end this long inquiry and try to get a clear idea of the way in which the moral imperative presents itself.

## VII. THE OBJECT OF ETHICS

We have seen that the stress laid on the notion of good, as the basis of ethics, comes from Christianity. We can find this idea outside the Christian world, but in a confused state. Christian thinking sifted it out with a clarity which reaches its culminating point in the Thomist synthesis. But the idea of good, when it is regarded as the primary idea, involves as many ambiguities as clarities.

### 1. *Primary intuition*

It seems that at the origin of every voluntary action is to be found the more or less confused perception of something which is strictly speaking inexpressible.

It is an intuition which is confused as far as the object is concerned, yet in other respects it is perhaps clearest of all, for the term 'inexpressible' does not mean 'obscure'. It is possible for an intuition to be clear and for words to obscure it.

To designate this inexpressible something, men have used such words as Absolute, One, Perfect, Tao, Pure Act, Being, or, in certain philosophies, I or Self.

But our mind works in such a way that as soon as we formulate an idea or use a word, the object it designates appears to be one thing among others. It takes its place among our conceptions; the very fact of being labelled by a word allots it a position among the objects of knowledge, gives it the appearance of something in common with our other objects of knowledge, and reduces it to dimensions proportionate to our mind. Whereas this Ineffable—one more word—contrasts with everything else so radically that it is not even incompatible with nothing, since it can be in everything and even be, in one sense, the being of everything, for all that it is different from everything.

We thus arrive at the following position. This ineffable something is, in a way, the thing we know best, because we find it in everything and it is, in another way, the basis of everything. Yet at the same time, we know it imperfectly, or do not know it at all in itself, because we cannot succeed in isolating it, in grasping it in itself or even in conceiving of it in itself.

Limited objects are the only ones that we perceive directly and our mind conceives clearly. But through each object or in each object we perceive another, and it is precisely this other that is the object of knowledge proper to intellectual knowledge.

It is the proper object of this sort of knowledge, because the difference between intellectual and sensible knowledge is that the inexpressible or the absolute appears as soon as the mind appears on the scene. Intellectual knowledge consists in referring sensible knowledge to the absolute. This is what the ancients called the Idea, and what is sometimes also called the universal.

What has just been said is commonplace enough. Plato said it long ago in terms which are constantly being quoted. But the very fact that it is commonplace is a guarantee of the universal character of the experience.

This inexpressible is also what the ancient Greeks used to call the Intelligible. Though it may be inexpressible or inseparable from what is not itself—by inseparable is meant inseparable *for us,* for as things stand, we do not know what this Ineffable may be in itself—this In-Itself is also what we know best, to such a point that we only know a particular object by referring this to it. We must even say, as I have just done, that the object proper to intellectual knowledge is to refer particular objects to this In-Itself. It is in this that intellectual knowledge differs from sensible knowledge, which stops short with the object.

Moreover, as soon as we pin the Ineffable down in a given word or formula, we reduce it to particularity and we cease to know it. To define the Ineffable is to lose it. And this antinomy is the despair of philosophers.

It is indeed the One of Plotinus, the Tao of Lao-tse, the Brahma of the Hindus, the Christians' God, the Absolute Thought of Hegel and the I of contemporary idealist thinkers. But when we try to express it, we immediately find ourselves asserting of it properties which we must then deny, because we can assert nothing of it without having to deny at once the limitation on our mind that the assertion involves.

On Newman's tomb is carved: 'The Name that can be named is not *the* Name.'

## 2. *Philosophy and ethics.*

Philosophy may be defined as an effort to express the inexpressible.

Why this effort? Why does not man accept the fact that the inexpressible is inexpressible, and why does he always start again, like a fly against a window-pane, trying to do what he has failed to do times out of number?

Why is it that positivism, with all its precursors from the Sophists and the Cynics down, does not succeed in satisfying the mind? The language it uses seems plain common-sense: 'Let's leave the inexpressible inexpressible: let us not worry about it, and let's turn our attention to what we can understand.'

I see four principal reasons for this apparently paradoxical situation. There are probably others, but here are those I see:

(a) The life of the mind is linked with that of the body; man, to use an expression in vogue nowadays, is a mind incarnate. Intellectual knowledge is thus tied up with sensible knowledge. I shall not attempt here to inquire what the body is and what the mind is, nor how they can be defined. I shall merely note that they are inseparable in man.

As a consequence, all intellectual knowledge is impure. Sensible knowledge obscures it. This again is commonplace,

91

the expression of a thousand year-old tradition. But in so far as intellectual knowledge is impure, the vision of the Ineffable is confused.

Confused it is, but man can purify his intellectual knowledge. That is what the philosopher is looking for: he is looking for an intellectual knowledge as pure as is possible.

(b) As we know nothing intellectually except in relation to the Ineffable, pure knowledge of the Ineffable is the condition of any purity of knowledge. It is the keystone of knowledge, or of science, in the wider sense of the word. All knowledge is distorted to the extent that knowledge of the Ineffable is impure. To purify this is thus the fundamental problem of the mind.

(c) Since life is experienced in successive and changing states of consciousness, man experiences moments of knowledge which are purer than others. In the purest moments of knowledge, he has a vision of the Ineffable which becomes obscure as soon as he tries to pin down these purer states of knowledge, by expressing them so as to be able to recapture them. The effort constantly fails, but it is as constantly renewed. On the plane of everyday life, that is the position of the people who write diaries. The real object of a diary, which takes forms that vary with individuals and their character, is always to pin down vital experiences.

(d) Man feels a natural desire to communicate to others the best thing he has. We shall confine ourselves to stating the fact, without seeking to explain it for the moment.

This is again a fact of daily experience. The parable of the lost silver piece bears witness to it. When the woman has found her lost coin, says Christ, 'she calls her friends and neighbours together; Rejoice with me, she says, I have found the silver piece which I lost'. It seemed to her that her joy would not be complete unless others shared it.

He who succeeds in expressing the Ineffable, more clearly or less unclearly than most people, wants to communicate his discovery. That is the origin of the first philosophical teaching and of philosophical literature.

But as the expression is always inadequate men still go on searching. Philosophy will never arrive at its end, for it stays on the same spot. The operation which it indulges is literally what is called in gymnastics a fixed position exercise. The philosopher circles indefinitely round the identical object, which everyone may possibly see in the same way, but which no one succeeds in expressing.

Doubtless there are contemplatives who do not feel this need for communication. They enjoy their vision and do not seek to express it. But they are not called philosophers.

\*　　\*　　\*

Let us pass on to ethics.

The passage is a very easy one, for once I am in the presence of the Ineffable, he is everything; there is nothing else.

At all events that is my impression. Everything disappears, as individual objects disappear under a blinding light. And in this everything that disappears, I myself am included. I have the impression that there is nothing else but the Ineffable, and that I myself too fade away, that the only reality in me is him. He is indeed thus the One.

Eastern philosophies try to express this more vividly than Western systems of thought. And yet nothing has changed; the world goes on and I go on, but the reality of the Ineffable so dominates everything else, that it is *as if* the rest had ceased to exist.

It is the phrase *as if* that is important and that brings about the link-up between the existence of particular realities and that of the Absolute. The kernel of truth in such phrases as 'Beyond good and evil' or 'Beyond being, beyond the true, the good and the beautiful' lies in the effort they represent to rediscover what men of former times called 'transcendental properties'. But they are clumsy phrases, formulations put forward by men who have no coherent metaphysics. And these same phrases, just because they are formulations, divide the One, reduce it to the level of our mind, and distort the vision of reality.

It is the same with everything that focuses the mind on man, such as the concern for happiness. When a man thinks of his happiness, he is thinking of himself, and the thought of himself is an obstacle to the presence of the Ineffable. It breaks up the unity.

But what difference is there between philosophy and

93

ethics? There is no essential difference. The ancients were right in combining them in the idea of wisdom. They have the same root and they lead to the same end. Only their approaches are different.

In the usual classifications, we are told: philosophy is essentially speculative; it is directed towards knowledge; ethics is directed towards action.

But what exactly is the difference?

When we talk of action, it is physical action we think of. Even when we talk of communicating ideas, we are alluding to writing or to the words that set the air vibrating. But the thing that is properly speaking intellectual is the thought itself, not its expression, that is to say the inner formulation of thought.

We must go even further. We know today that no thought can be formulated, even mentally, without a certain physical activity, a modification of the brain and nerve cells. When we think hard, we end up by being tired physically. The action proper to the intelligence is thinking in itself, apart from any formulation and any working of the brain. But this is impossible for men. Hence the anguish of philosophy.

When we try to picture to ourselves a pure mind, with neither a hand to write, nor a tongue to talk, nor a brain to reflect, we end up with the conclusion that its sole activity would be to think, and as we cannot conceive of a thought without expression, we cannot imagine what this mind would be. Mystics claim that something like this occurs to them at times, though they do not succeed in explaining it afterwards nor even in understanding it themselves once it is over.

But we must return to the human conditions of action. For man, the order of thought is distinct from the order of action, that is to say that thinking is a peculiar kind of action, different from what is generally called action, or what most men call action. The mind works differently in what is called thinking and what is called action. Hence the practical differences between ethics and speculation, which we must examine.

3. *The object of ethics*

There is no other perfection for man than to know the One,

94

to perceive that he exists and that nothing else exists, in the sense we have seen, and to shape his conduct on this.

'I am he who is; you are she who is not,' says Christ to St Catherine of Siena. As soon as we have seen this, we see that there is nothing else, or that the rest is unimportant in so far as it is separated from this. We see that the rest has no real existence outside this whole and that life can have no other aim but to pursue it, and we feel strongly that the wise men of antiquity were right in thinking that the lack of virtue proceeds from ignorance.

But man is subject to the law of the manifold, the law of space and of time. Ethics is the discipline through which he seeks to discover how to attain this more-than-knowledge of the One, that is to say, to disappear, in so far as there is within him something which resists there being nothing but the One. Inevitably we end up with the expressions of Hindu wisdom which have so often been described as pantheistic.

And that is all. There is nothing else to do in life. Ethics governs everything.

This pursuit of the One should thus govern every impulse of the mind and the body. The rule is simple, but it is complicated in practice because of the law of the manifold. We cannot live lost in the One. Certain wise men have tried, and it is once more in Hindu wisdom that we find the most systematic effort in this direction, but the result of trying to achieve this superhuman goal is to mutilate man. Man is not pure mind, and the application of the laws of human psychology to the pursuit of the One raises may delicate problems. That is why speculative philosophy differs from ethics, and theoretical ethics, or the philosophy of action, from practical ethics.

It is also possible to put forward the rule: man should realize the One in his life. But for man, to *realize* is a different matter from to know, because to act is a different matter from to think. And this despite the fact that man can only act in a human manner to the extent that his action is charged with thought, and that he is incapable of thinking without a certain action. These very phrases show that everything is complicated as soon as man is in question. The philosopher, bent on thinking as he is, often tries to sidestep this complication, but in so far as he refuses to accept the human situation, his thinking becomes distorted and he does not find the One he was seeking.

*  *  *

Human consciousness comprises a number of different states.

First we have abstract knowledge and experiential knowledge. There is a difference between an abstract exposition of the existence of the self and the consciousness of the self. In the same way, an abstract dissertation on the One does not automatically give rise to experiential knowledge of the One.

Experiential knowledge of the One is what is generally called rapture, and this term is more accurate. Some people may prefer the term 'unification' or 'reduction to the One'. But though these terms may be more expressive or more accurate once they are understood, they are also more abstract. Most people do not understand them. It is true that the word rapture also seems to them just as mysterious.

Nevertheless the word rapture is in current use to designate the state of a man who is absorbed in the contemplation of a work of art: auditive absorption where music is concerned and visual absorption where he is looking at a landscape or a picture. The term is an ordinary one, and it means that a man is so absorbed by an object that he does not think of anything else, and in particular does not think of himself. The man who is enraptured loses consciousness of himself and is conscious only of the object of knowledge. Applied to the One, the term thus means that a man loses consciousness of himself and the surrounding world and is conscious of nothing but the One.

Abstract knowledge is concerned with the universal, experiential knowledge with the individual. Abstract knowledge of a particular object consists in determining the universal ideas that apply to it. When we say that an object is of such a size, such a weight and such a colour, these are abstract, that is to say universal ideas which we are applying to a particular object. Experiential knowledge is quite another affair. I am conscious of an object even if I am incapable of saying that it weighs so much or is so many inches long. These details

96

improve my knowledge from certain points of view, but they do not necessarily improve my experiential knowledge, the existential shock which we discussed earlier. On the contrary, the scientist who pulls out his foot-rule or gets a pair of scales as soon as he sees an object sometimes experiences a less vivid existential shock than the unsophisticated character who does not worry about them. And the scientist's refusal to allow anything to be talked about without defining and measuring irritates the plain man.

That is why ethics expressed in abstract terms often gives the impression of being unreal. To call it unreal is to call it alien to the existential order of experiential knowledge. And this is individual.

Next, speculative knowledge differs from practical knowledge.

Speculative knowledge, or speculative philosophy, tries to express the One and that which is not the One.

For pure mind, in so far as we can conceive of it, that is to say for our mind, if it were purely mind, the expression of the One would lead immediately to rapture, or absorption, or unification. But man is plunged in matter. Perhaps he is also plunged in the limited, for the limited is necessarily manifold, and the immaterial limited must be subject to the law of all that is limited. It is difficult for us to define our ideas on this subject accurately, for we are so involved in matter that we cannot get a clear view of what a strictly immaterial knowledge would amount to. But if immaterial knowledge is itself manifold, that would possibly open the way to an explanation of the devil.

For this idea of the 'evil spirit', which is not peculiar to Christianity but is to be found in most religions in the form of a belief in a presiding genius of evil, assumes that even a pure spirit may not be automatically drawn to the One or the Good. It supposes that he retains a possibility of choice and of turning back on himself, and the devil is simply the pure spirit who preferred himself to the One.

All this may explain why a metaphysical exposition, however perfect it may be, never automatically produces unification or rapture. That is why ethics exists.

Since speculative knowledge does not in itself yield reduction to the One, we must seek the means of achieving it in another discipline. Ethics begins by explaining that we ought to aim at reduction to the One: we have here the metaphysics of ethics. It is a simple process, for it follows immediately from metaphysics. We have merely to posit the transcendental properties of being for the consequence to emerge. The fact that it is so obvious explains why this metaphysical idea does not bulk larger in ethical thought. On the other hand, the search for the means of realizing this unification sets innumerable problems, and it is these that keep ethical thinkers busy.

Christian ethics sees God as an active being, attending to the world, creating it and ruling it and placing man there with a view to a practical task. Thus unification with God implies an activity co-ordinated with his will and consequently a rule of action on the level of created things. But whatever the rule of action, the fundamental problem remains, how to purify the mind in order to attain an experiential or existential consciousness of the One.

Moreover, abstract or speculative knowledge of the One cannot be separated from experiential knowledge. We should distinguish between the two, in view of the human situation, but if we separate them, speculative knowledge goes astray. For it is impossible for an impure mind to perceive how everything is reduced to the One, and precise knowledge of the One involves knowledge of the way in which particular objects are unified in it. The impurity of the mind leads it to direct its attention to the particular, the not-One, as if it existed in itself, independently of the One, and we cannot attain a clear perception of the One except in so far as we perceive in what way it is the all in all. The ancients were thus right in thinking that speculative knowledge was linked with virtue as well as resulting in it. The conception of wisdom, as we have seen, combined the two values.

When we turn to history, we find that as a matter of fact philosophers generally are a little contemptuous of material values and lead what ordinary folk call an austere life. Intellectual pleasures are incompatible with sensual pleasures. It is rare for a philosopher to be a sensual man, and it is even rare for him to be worried by the ups and downs of life. Some philosophers are, and that is prejudicial to their thinking, as

98

can be seen with those I have called the 'tormented philosophers'. It can be seen in Kierkegaard, under the influence of anguish, in Nietzsche, under the influence of exasperation, and in Scheler, under the influence of sensuality. As soon as the philosopher thinks about his individual case, as soon as he wants to justify himself, his thinking goes astray.

All this explains why contemplation is the culminating point, not only of the greatest philosophers, but also of the purest souls, even if they have had little schooling. It also explains why this is even more so with pure souls than with thinkers, because the vision of the One is an existential and not a speculative phenomenon.

The intuition of the One comes spontaneously to man to the extent that he has a pure mind. The philosopher attains to it thanks to the purification resulting from speculative thinking which absorbs him completely, though he can only be absorbed through detachment from particular values, that is to say from the limited. That is why this intuition is rarely achieved by the professional philosophers of whom I talked earlier, those who teach philosophy professionally. The saint attains perception of the One through the purification of his soul. He is in no danger of being held up by concern for the ego.

The philosopher arrives at an abstract expression which the saint frequently does not even understand. But the saint arrives at an experiential or existential consciousness of the One which most philosophers do not attain to. That is why un-educated mystics sometimes produce philosophical expression of an exactitude which no one could expect from them, if their intellectual training alone were taken into account.

*　　*　　*

The contemplative bent is thus natural to anyone who succeeds in perceiving that the One exists. That is why contemplation is not specifically Christian.

We in the Western world have got used to linking the idea of God with Christianity. When a reaction against the Christian tradition took shape among intellectuals, they believed that the idea of God must be abandoned. And thinkers such as Hegel and Schopenhauer, who clearly had a perception of the

One, exercised their wits to find expressions which should designate the same being by other words, Absolute Thought or Absolute Will. On the other hand, Christians are sometimes disturbed at meeting with mysticism among the Hindus, the Chinese or the Moslems, and even more so if they find it to be more pronounced there than in most Christian circles. They fondly believed that the aspiration to unite oneself with God derived from the Christian revelation, and had never imagined that it could be found outside this. They become even more uneasy when they find in the eastern mystics terms identical with those of Christian mysticism.

In reality, mysticism *is* Christian, since the Christians' God is the One. But it is not peculiar to Christianity; it is common to all those who attain the perception of the One.

What is peculiar to Christianity is the fact of *God with us*, God made man, unification with God taking place in our human life. So, contrary to what many people believe, the specific type of the Christian is to be found more in a St Francis Xavier or a St Vincent de Paul than in a St Bruno or a St John of the Cross. It is not that contemplative sanctity is not Christian: it is Christian *too*. But we find among non-Christians types of wise men who approximate to it, once they have attained the perception of the One, whereas parallels to the apostolic saints are fewer. St Thomas's doctrine of the mixed life, which attributes the highest form of Christian perfection to a life of action steeped in contemplation, is Christian in the strict sense. For it is founded on the idea of a God who busies himself with men and summons them, not only to worship him and unite themselves with him in contemplation, but to *serve* him by saturating their whole active life in reduction to the One.

Outside Christianity, man's yearning for the One results in turning morality into a pursuit of rapture, or reducing ethics to a method of producing rapture. We find this with the Neo-Platonists, as well as in the Far East. In Christianity, there is a tendency among those who have mystical aspirations to regard this union with God as the ideal. But this is not the expression of what is peculiar to Christianity. When Christians have a hunger for God, the determination to put the whole of themselves into the search for him leads them to

100

focus their life on prayer, so as to attain purer and purer states of prayer, but that is only a stage. When the Christian unites himself with God, the creator appears to him as the God of love, and his very contemplation carries him back to the life of charity, charity to his brother-men. All the mystics are at one in saying that union with God in prayer leads to a life of love, where every manifestation of life becomes a testimony to love. The most authentic mystics never stop repeating that it is the whole of life that should be union with God, and that a man who does humble tasks with a great love is more perfect than the man who attains soaring heights of prayer, but does not display as much love in his life as a whole. Maritain went so far as to suggest, with this point in mind, a sort of rapture attained through work as the highest point of union with God. The Hindu, Taoist and Neo-Platonist wise men, however, hold aloof from action among men. There are indeed few Christians who attain this active rapture, and that is why a moderately pure contemplation seems to be a limit of perfection difficult to transcend.

This explains why in the Catholic Church the purely contemplative orders are regarded as those which make possible the highest form of perfection in this world. But it also explains why, when a contemplative attains the summit of sanctity, his concern for brotherly love appears at once. St Teresa of the Child Jesus gave in our own times an example of this which has had considerable repercussions. She entered the Carmelite order, which is an enclosed and purely contemplative form of life. But she ardently desired that her contemplation should be a power for good in the world, that is to say among her brother-men. And her contemplation was so steeped in charity that the Church proclaimed her patroness of missions, though she never left her convent, and was indeed forbidden to by the rule to which she had submitted.

\*     \*     \*

With regard to contemplation, as indeed in the whole field of philosophy, Christian thinkers attach great importance to the distinction between the logical and the ontological order. For them, that is to say, it is important to specify whether the

101

One is a mere mental conception, which means idealism, or whether it really exists in itself. This question hardly seems to worry non-Christians, and I think that this is for the following reason.

Even if the One were just a mental conception, the mere idea is so beautiful that the mind fastens on it as soon as it meets it. When we admire a picture, we do not ask whether the object it represents exists. Now the idea is to the mind what the picture is to the eye.

The One is thus so fascinating that the mind is absorbed as soon as it perceives it. Doubtless this is what happens with non-Christians. Christians are concerned with the difference because Revelation teaches them that the One is the active God of the Bible, and they want to identify the One which is a direct mental vision, and the God of Revelation, by a rational operation. They want to achieve this by a rational operation, that is by a chain of reasoning, and most of these chains of reasoning result in bringing out the importance of the *idea* of God rather than the divine *reality*.

From this point of view, Existentialism has done a service to Christian thinking by bringing out the importance of existence. A beautiful object which is real impresses me more than the representation of the same thing or the idea of beauty. But philosophers who live in the abstract are inclined to be content with the beauty of the idea.

When the mind has observed this aspect of the question, it seems that it must go even further. The intuition of the One in consciousness, which is a confused intuition for most people and only emerges into clarity for a few, is an intuition of reality or of what exists. In the West, Plato first, and then all those who followed in his footsteps have tried to explain this, but it is difficult to formulate.

We thus find many clumsy expressions for it. The argument of St Anselm, the rational inadequacy of which has so often been noted, is undoubtedly one of these clumsy attempts. But it is constantly being revived, because though it may be clumsy, it still corresponds to a real intuition. St Bonaventure and Descartes tried to reformulate it more adequately, and the Existentialist phenomenology of our days has tried again. If people are always coming back to it, it is because they see that underneath it lies a reality, the reality which is hardest of all to formulate in clear terms.

Thus it seems that it is necessary to distinguish the fact of seeing from the rational statement by which we try to express our intuition. When we put ourselves on the level of spiritual being, we no longer clearly perceive, as has been seen, the difference between thinking, willing, existing and acting. Moreover, Christian metaphysics agrees that for God, all these are one and the same thing. For God, to create the world is merely to think of the world existing. The world exists from the moment that God thinks of it as existing. To think of the world as existing and to will that the world shall exist is the same thing in God. God willing is equivalent to God acting; but God willing is also God thinking that he wills or thinking that he is acting. And acting, for God, is to think that something is.

God is thus indeed the indistinct and indeterminate One of the Neo-Platonists, the Ineffable of the Hindus and the Tao of Lao-tse. Indistinct does not, as the common usage would have it, mean 'vague', but 'in which there is no distinction'. Indeterminate does not mean 'inexact', but 'in which there is no determination', for there is only determination if there are limits, and there are only limits if another being exists. First primal Being is necessarily everything that Being can be.

Then again, as we have also seen, the spiritual being, so far as we can know it, exists in so far as it thinks and does not exist otherwise. Thinking and existing thus amount to the same thing for it, as do thinking and willing. This is what Hegel tried to express when he said that Thought comes first. He felt he ought to react against the philosophy of being by saying: 'It is not being that comes first, but thought, and there is no other being but thought.' He believed that the philosophy of being assumed that we must first accept being and then thought, and certain statements by philosophers who put forward a philosophy of being might have led him to this false conclusion. His upbringing and the outlook of the circle to which he belonged had prevented him from understanding the idea of the primal One in which everything is included. The same is true of Schopenhauer when he says that the Will comes first.

It is true that a certain philosophy of being does give this impression, because its partisans, without realizing it, start from an abstract conception of being derived from human knowledge bearing on particular objects. They then try to ascend to the First Being by purifying the notion of being derived from particular objects. But in the particular being, being is independent of thought, because there are beings without thought.

This last expression merely means that these beings, if we consider them in themselves, are devoid of thought: we first posit being, then we note that among beings there are thinking beings, and thought comes to seem a secondary idea. But from another point of view, there is no being without thought. For the being which considered in itself is without thought, only exists because there is a thought elsewhere. It exists in so far as it is an achievement or a work of this thought; it is thought by this thought; outside of this thought, it is inconceivable, and there is no being in it except to the degree that the thought thinks it. This is exactly what Christian metaphysics says; it has been said by all the mystics of all nations, and if Hegel believed he was saying something new, it was because he was somewhat ignorant.

And I do not know whether I myself have succeeded in expressing clearly this fundamental idea, the hardest to describe in the whole range of human knowledge. It will never be completely described; I have merely submitted my contribution.

It now remains to inquire in just what way the relationship of man with the One presents itself in practice. That will be the object of the next chapter.

## VIII. MORAL OBLIGATION

Before we tackle the question of practical ethics, or of the paths to morality, we must see where the imperative fits in. Since Kant, ethics has generally been represented as the science of duty. Now for anyone who has the vision of the One this problem does not arise. It is therefore easy to understand why it has scarcely been raised outside the Judaeo-Christian world.

It seems as if the notion of duty arises when the moral rule is imposed on minds which do not understand its meaning. The content of the moral rule, that is to say good, the expression of the will of God, seems to them to conflict with *their* good. The problem before ethics is then to decide why one good must be sacrificed to the other.

The idea of obligation would thus appear to derive from two facts. Firstly, God demands obedience from men who do not understand what he wants, and secondly, in Christianity, for ordinary people the idea of good becomes distinct from that of salvation, even disconnected from it and occasionally even opposed to it. We have here the classical opposition between the sacrifice of wordly goods, which are regarded as real, good things which really yield happiness on earth, and eternal happiness.

We are talking of a purely external obligation. God is stronger than man and imposes on him obligations of which man understands nothing. 'His ways are not our ways': we must bow our heads and accept. The means of pressure God uses is the threat of eternal punishment if I refuse to obey. I have not got to ask myself whether what he demands from me is reasonable; I have simply got to obey. God is a master; the ethics which follows from this is a slave ethics.

The conception of duty thus derives from an internal conflict between the propensity to pleasure and the moral imperative. Hence the idea to which Bentham gave such publicity, but which is a commonplace of ethics, that if men were only shown that the moral rule is the source of happiness they would all observe it. Moral depravity is simply the result of ignorance. But the idea of divine sovereignty has made a virtue of blind obedience, an idea which is often stressed by religious minds. It is more virtuous to obey without understanding, because by this we show our submissiveness to God: we shall come across this again. Camus replies to this attitude by rebelling. In his *Rebel: An Essay on Man in Revolt*, the climax of a tradition whose development he recalls, he describes simply and clearly the attitude of a man who will not conform to a rule whose cogency he does not see.

From quite a different point of view, contemporary psychologists, studying the birth of the feeling of obligation in children, find that it starts with the awareness of an authority imposing a law from outside. The young child seeks his own good instinctively; for him the good is that of metaphysics. The feeling of obligation arises when he is told that he cannot perform an act which seems to him to correspond to his good, or to pursue an object which he regards as good for him.

\*　　\*　　\*

Now this slave ethics falls into the background with real Christians, the more so the more perfectly Christian they are, and is replaced by an ethics of love for the One who reveals himself and gives himself to us in Christ.

The Christian who surrenders himself to love does not think about obligation any more. He seeks for good and he seeks God in a union with the divine will. The question of obligation no longer arises for him. He even feels he is misunderstood when he is asked whether he is obliged to do what he is doing, and he is hurt if people insinuate that what he is doing is being done out of duty.

This is what lies behind, among other things, the vow of choosing the more perfect which is to be found in some of the lives of the saints. This vow is a naïve and philosophically inaccurate expression of the idea of 'beyond duty'.

It is philosophically inaccurate because it is based on the popular belief in the existence of a perfect way. As things happen, however, good is manifold and can be attained in a number of ways between which a man can choose, and perfection is to be found not in each individual act taken separately, but only in the general trend of life. This is, of course, the attitude of wisdom morality. But ordinary people believe that we can compare the particular good in each act considered in itself, and each time choose the most perfect.

Of course, if a man wants to pass judgment on Christianity, he should concentrate on the doctrine of Christ and on the disciples who do their best to follow him, that is to say good Christians. The mistake of Nietzsche among others, and of all the rebels whom Camus parades before us so confidently, was that they judged Christianity by the states of conscience and the testimony of bad Christians, that is to say of those who receive the law of Christ like a yoke imposed on them by fear.

The line generally taken by the masters of Christian spirituality is that obligatory things must be done out of love and not because they are obligatory, and that they would have to be done, even if they were not obligatory. 'True ethics makes nonsense of ethics,' said Pascal in one of those trenchant phrases in which he excelled. Another expression of this state of soul, naïve this time, is that of saints who declare that they are ready to go to hell if by doing so they could give glory to God. Rationally speaking, the expression is self-contradictory, since hell consists in hating God, and a man cannot give glory to God by hating him. But the thing these saints see in hell is that it is a place of misery, and they want to protest against the idea that they are serving God out of self-interest, in order to be happy.

This idea of the gratuitousness of love has often been expressed by Christian mystics. Here is a Spanish text of the sixteenth century, which is sometimes attributed to St Teresa, sometimes to St John of the Cross, but is probably the work of an anonymous author. In any case, it expresses admirably what Christian love is:

> It is not the heaven you have promised me that makes
> me love you, oh my God.
> It is not the terrors of hell that stop me offending you,
> it is you, Lord,
> It is to see you nailed to the cross, vilified, covered
> with stripes, insulted, dead.
> . . . It is ultimately your love.
> So that, even if there were no heaven, I should love you,
> And even if there were no hell, I should fear you.
> You need give me nothing to make me love you,
> For even if I did not hope what I do hope,
> I should love you exactly as I do love you . . .

\* \* \*

Christianity has rendered the world the service of putting the problem of the moral imperative in clear terms. This problem arose gradually as casuistical ethics developed. But it never asserted itself with the acuteness it does now till the day when men with a Christian upbringing lost real faith and asked themselves what duty was founded on.

In the Middle Ages, the Scholastic authors talked little of it; St Thomas, among others, only referred to it occasionally. He had a complete philosophico-theological system where everything hangs together, and in it man is bound by the divine law, expressed on one hand by Revelation and on the other by the voice of conscience, in which the will of God is heard.

But Kant, who was impregnated with the self-evidence and authority of the moral imperative, and who also regarded the philosophical system as indemonstrable, analysed moral consciousness without any presuppositions. It was thus that he came to base the whole of morality on the imperative of duty.

Now what can the absoluteness of duty be based on except the absoluteness of good, and what can the absoluteness of good be based on except the Absolute itself? Kant, who wrote in the classical age, could only conceive of ideas that were clear and distinct. But nowadays we realize that clear and distinct ideas result from the clarification of confused ideas and that they spring, as it were, from the soul of confused consciousness. We understand that though the sense of duty may be clearly perceived in certain communities, under the influence of ideas generally accepted as going without speaking, it always reposes on the confused intuition of the One, which is unconscious with many people for lack of an adequate spiritual development. Kant had within him this intuition of the One. He was determined to reach it by philosophic reasoning but he was convinced of it before starting. The chain of reasoning he based on duty was no more than a formulation; but he got to God, and he knew in advance that he would get there.

In short, the feeling of duty may be defined as 'the consciousness of the repercussions of the intuition of the One on our practical life'. Obligation considered in itself corresponds simply to the coercive character of the One in relation to the intelligence.

When the mind attains to the intuition of the One, it sees that life has no more meaning outside the pursuit of reduction to the One. The words 'has no more meaning' signify 'becomes unintelligible'. Now the intelligible is the law of the intelligence. The intelligence calls for the intelligible as the body calls for food.

This seems to be contradicted in our times by the philosophy of absurdity which had already been adumbrated by Nietzsche and which is trumpeted abroad by thinkers like Sartre and Camus. But they themselves unintentionally parade proof of the law of intelligibility, because after having declared at the top of their voices that everything is absurd, that nothing is intelligible and that nothing can be explained, they end with a rule, that is to say, a coherent ethical theory. At least they try to do so, and when we finish reading them, we are astonished at the traditional character of what they finally put forward. They end up, to cut a long story short, by saying that man should follow his nature. And we cannot help asking ourselves whether it was necessary to start by tearing everything down to get only to that.

The Scholastic tradition is that man, under the compulsion of the good in itself, is compelled to seek it. He would be unable not to seek it. He may be mistaken about what is the good but it is the good he seeks. He thus feels himself compelled to want everything that leads to it. It is a moral compulsion, that is to say one that constrains the mind, as against physical compulsion which constrains a man by material means, and leaves no room for free will, that is to say choice. The moral compulsion derives from the fact that it would be a contradiction for man to desire an object which would divert him from the good in itself, which he desires in all circumstances.

We are thus back at the traditional position. It could not be otherwise.

Chapter Four

# *The Ways to the Good*

WE NOW have to define the way which must be followed to attain the reduction to the One which is the object of ethics. To define this way is to determine what makes for reduction to the One and what stands in its way. We shall thus be able to sketch out the main lines of the system.

What is called an ethical system is itself a reduction to unity. We must reduce every particular action to unity, so that they may all contribute to the reduction to the One which is the final object of life. It is metaphysics that puts the One forward, and we have seen that ethics arises from this intuition of Being. This primary intuition which lays down the end is the object of metaphysical ethics. We have seen what it amounts to. We must inquire how to introduce it into life.

## I. THE TWO WAYS OF ETHICS

We have seen that ethical reflection offers us two starting points: the practical assessment of acts and the perception of the Ineffable. The first corresponds to what may be called the practical attitude of mind; the second to the contemplative, the contemplative corresponding in the order of action to the speculative in the order of knowledge.

### 1. *The approach from the moral sense*

This interests minds not given to speculation, who are stimulated by contact with the exigencies of action and who react spontaneously to the intuition of the moral good realized in acts. This sense of the moral good realized in acts may be called the sense of the rightness of life, but it may also be

110

called the sense of the balance of life, of the unity of life, of the healthiness of life, of the beauty of life or of the perfection of life. In any case, what characterizes these minds is that the first question they ask themselves is what should be done.

A passage from the *Enchiridion* of Epictetus expresses this point of view perfectly. It is entitled 'The three parts of philosophy', and here is how it starts. 'The first and most indispensable part of philosophy is that which deals with the putting into practice of theories: for example, not to lie. The second is that which contains the proofs: for example, by what principles it is proved that we must not lie. The third is that which confirms and explains the others: for example, how we can be certain that a given argument is a proof; what is a proof . . . what is true and what is false?'

We are dealing here with minds more concerned with the demands of practical life than with abstract principles. This is the case with most men, and those who are known in history as ethical teachers are minds that take just this attitude. This will be easily understood in view of what has been said previously on the link between the mind and sensible knowledge.

Nowadays, we meet with this attitude in the West in a certain number of thinkers separated from Christian traditions, who for that very reason are obsessed by the moral problem. Christians are less so, because for them religion points the way. They have a practical problem, that of how to realize the ideal, to which the best of them devote themselves, but they have no moral problem in the sense of a problem of knowing where moral good lies; at least it only arises in relatively unimportant cases of application. But minds that have lost the Christian faith are confronted with the moral problem in all its immensity. There are novelists who have devoted all their writings to it. Most of the novels of Georges Duhamel or Aldous Huxley, for example, are devoted solely to this question, or portray characters who are concerned with nothing else.

If we go back in history, Chinese philosophy and Greek philosophy provide outstanding instances of this characteristic. Confucius, of whom I have spoken more than once, is probably the most representative type, both by his personality and by the influence he exerted. He was not curious about metaphysics. The Chinese traditionally accepted a natural religion which was based on a belief in Heaven, a term which stood for a somewhat vague entity, which might be a personal God, or the material heavens, or Nature; sometimes, indeed, it was nothing other than the moral principle. Where Confucius is concerned, there has been much discussion on the meaning he attributed to Heaven, and it is generally thought that at the beginning of his career he regarded it as a person and a providence, but that this conception progressively grew blurred, doubtless because he took little interest in it. At the end of his life Heaven was for Confucius the principle of moral good, and though he did not deny its personal character, he was not concerned to assert it either, still less to prove it. It was enough for him that man should do good, and good appears in actions.

Things were much the same with the Greeks, though their approach was very different. The ideas that engrossed Plato and Aristotle, the two greatest metaphysicians of antiquity, sprang from the city-state and culminated in it. The starting point of their thinking was the polity or the organization of a perfect City, and it was to find the rule for this that they embarked on the great digression which was to lead them through all the processes of logic and metaphysics. Philosophy was a form of reflection whose aim was to ornament life; it took its place alongside rhetoric and music. It was immersed in the material world and only with difficulty rose above it from time to time. In this respect books on metaphysics which isolate from their context the passages where purely spiritual and speculative inclinations come to the fore give a misleading impression of the real character of their teaching and the nature of their interests.

In the *Symposium,* for instance, Plato presents a set of dinner guests who agree to speak in praise of love. It is chiefly a question of homosexual love, but the dialogue leads to the statement that the most beautiful thing in love is the union of souls, and Socrates goes on from that to the love of beauty in itself. In the edition I have before me, Socrates's discussion of beauty in itself takes two pages out of eighty. Later on, students saw nothing else but that in the Symposium, and a whole system was extracted from it. Whereas in Plato, the passage was no more than a peak where he had momentarily halted.

In the same way, in the *Republic* there is a discussion of the Good which has often since been reproduced and used as a text, but this discussion also comes up incidentally. Plato is talking of education and political power, which he wanted to see handed over to philosophers. If good is to hold sway, it must be known, and that is where the discussion in question comes in. With the great Stoics of imperial Roman times thinking turns away from the problem of the city, because men were then living under an absolute monarchy. Ethics thus became individualistic, but remained focused on man and his life on earth.

The starting point of this whole trend of thinking is definitely to be found in practical life, as it confronts men on earth. It was not until the nineteenth century that Western thinking joined Hindu thinking in the idealistic outlook which turns the mind directly towards the One. The passage from Plato on the Good is very characteristic:

> You have often been told that the idea of good is the highest knowledge, and that all other things become useful and advantageous only by their use of this. You can hardly be ignorant that of this I was about to speak, concerning which, as you have often heard me say, we know so little; and without which, any other knowledge or possession of any kind will profit us nothing. . . .
> Of this, then, which every soul of man pursues and makes the end of all his actions, having a presentiment that there is such an end, and yet hesitating because neither knowing the nature nor having the same assurance of this as of other things. . . .
> (Plato, *Republic* VI, trans. Jowett, p. 767, two volume ed, New York, 1937.)

Plato then goes on to a comparison of the Good with the sun, which makes everything visible but cannot be looked at directly itself.

Man's capacity to perceive spiritual values becomes purer as his specifically human characteristics develop, but up to now these specifically human characteristics have been little enough developed in most people. The external aspects of civilization should not mislead us over this. The fact that

113

a man wears a jacket and tie, is well-spoken and drives a car does not necessarily mean that the human characteristics are developed in him. On the contrary, a concern with material good immerses a man ever deeper in the material world.

In any case, an object that is to command the attention of the ordinary man must be such that it can be expressed as a value for life, that is, it must appear capable of helping him to live, and to live better. This term 'to live better' has a material and a spiritual aspect. Most men appreciate the spiritual aspect only in so far as they discover it in material things, and all the more so if the material aspect is easily grasped.

In this respect, Christian experience is undoubtedly that in which these human characteristics display themselves most strikingly, and the Catholic Church, which represents the most explicit and best organized aspect of Christian life, provides invaluable evidence of this.

Nothing is more spiritual than Christianity. The distinctive point of its teaching is the introduction of the divine into everything that is human, and indeed into everything, through the doctrine of creation. What is more, the Catholic Church includes bodies of priests and religious whose mainspring is purely spiritual. If they have given themselves to the Church, it is solely with a view to the Church's specific aims, sanctity and the salvation of souls. Yet we find that most of them only become enthusiastic about the spiritual objectives to which they have dedicated their lives—only, that is to say, apprehend these spiritual objectives intensely enough to arouse their enthusiasm—in so far as these spiritual aims are translated into material values; for example if they have a church or a school to build, or succeed in drawing packed congregations, or can produce impressive statistics about attendance at the sacraments. Those who are not concerned with these things are as often as not relatively lukewarm. Those who rise to purely spiritual cares, such as the life of God in souls, with nothing material behind them, remain exceptions, despite the clarity of Christian doctrine and the origin of their vocation.

In every Catholic country where nationalist movements

114

have arisen, the clergy has played a big and sometimes a leading part in them. There is a double reason for this. Priests are idealists, sensitive to spiritual values, and disinterested where material values, particularly money, are concerned. But on the other hand, the national cause is bound up with ethics through its connections with justice and other virtues, and most priests grow enthusiastic more easily over religious values when they are seen to be involved in natural human values.

This experience, which we encounter throughout the history of the Church, is a striking manifestation of the incapacity of most people to be drawn to the spiritual in itself. If the phenomenon is so marked in the Catholic Church, what must it be with people who have no clear spiritual doctrine, and who know nothing of the God who was made man and the divine love revealed by Christ? We can understand in these circumstances that the aspiration to the One in most people takes the form of a moral judgment, inspired by particular and immediately realizable objectives.

What is rarer is the awakening of the sense of the good in itself, as applied to a man's own person, that is, the search for good in itself, and not the intellectual attempt to justify a particular good that he desires. The phrase, 'to justify a particular good that he desires', means that the man sits down and thinks with a view to linking the particular good he desires with the absolute good which men cannot help desiring or to the One of which they have only a vague idea.

On the other hand, this moral correctness is much commoner when somebody else is concerned. Europeans are shocked by the unfairness of the Negro question in the United States, whereas Americans do not notice it or justify it. But Americans are equally shocked by class differences and the poverty of the people in Europe or South America. We condemn hate and violence in other people, without realizing that we ourselves are guilty of both in other fields. In the words of the Gospel, we see the speck of dust in our neighbour's eye and are not aware of the beam that is in our own. All ethical teachers have said the same. The wise man tries to rise above it, but wise men are rare.

Nevertheless, this universal experience shows that most men have the sense of the good within them, and that this sense makes itself felt, as long as personal cupidity does not come into play. We can therefore understand why purification from cupidity should be the primary objective of the wise man, and why this is a universal tradition.

\* \* \*

As the moral sense grows more delicate, the moral act is seen as an absolute value, and even as the absolute value par excellence. As long as moral value is not respected, the mind cannot be at peace. Good is an absolute and must be done unconditionally.

It is not just a question of doing good ourselves; good must prevail everywhere. I have already noted how all ethical teachers are concerned, not merely with their personal good, but with that of everyone. Even the most eudaimonist of them, Epicurus for example, feel the need to surround themselves with disciples and to teach what they believe to be the recipe for good. In Bentham's utilitarianism, this propensity attains its high water mark, undoubtedly under the influence of Christianity. Bentham wants to be the benefactor of the human race. Ethics is taken to be the prescription for happiness, but it is not enough for him to seek happiness for himself; he will not rest till he has made all mankind happy. They all show the same missionary spirit. Confucius, Plato, Epictetus and Sakya-Muni all surrounded themselves with disciples and opened schools of virtue. Objective good is not attained till all have attained to it.

In short, Kant expressed an accurate idea when he laid down that the rule of duty is so to act that what one does can be applied to all men.

\* \* \*

The conclusion that emerges from this analysis is that all teachers, those who reduce ethics to duty as well as those who reduce it to good or to happiness, see that the moral problem is to reduce life to unity. Not all of them have reflected on it;

but the moral sense is the sense of an order, of something that is one, of an equilibrium which reduces the multiplicity of acts to a rule.

Nevertheless, at first sight, this reduction to unity is not necessarily a reduction to the One. Deeper reflection enables us to see that reduction to unity implies reduction to the One or leads to it, but that not everyone attains to this, because the human intelligence is dull and slow, because man is lost in the manifold, to which practical life is subjected, and the mind is lost there. Our attention is consequently absorbed by the manifold, and even by very special aspects of it. Again, the case of Confucius is exceedingly symptomatic, for he found in the Chinese tradition a very distinct sense of the One, but did not linger over it. The question was of little interest to him.

With some philosophers, the conception of the One comes up incidentally. I cited earlier a passage of Epictetus which expressed his preoccupation with immediate objects. On the other hand, in his *Moral Discourses* we find the following passage, which is in quite a different vein:

> If we had an honest judgment, what else ought we to do, all together and each separately, but extol God, sing his praises and offer him thanksgivings? Ought we not, whether we were ploughing the land or eating our meals, to sing a hymn to God? ... What can I do, old and halting as I am, but hymn God? If I were a nightingale, I should do as a nightingale is meant to; if I were a swan, I should behave as a swan. I am a reasonable being: I must hymn God ...

The historian who wants to reduce the thinking of Epictetus to a coherent whole may find some inconsistency here. It is of little consequence: he had not systematized his ideas. We simply see that he did rise from time to time to the vision of the One.

But most men are too deeply involved in the manifold. They are absorbed by the aspect of the manifold with which their life is occupied; and if this is true even of wise men, what can we expect of ordinary people? Engineers, doctors or tradesmen are absorbed by their profession. Married people and parents are absorbed by the thousand and one distractions of family life; even priests, as we have seen, are absorbed by the

117

day-to-day cares of their ministry. Thus they do not on their own attain to the idea of reduction to the One. Or if they do, it is only in the form of a vague idea in the background of consciousness, and they are unable to express what they see in this way, or even to realize what they have seen.

They will only express the idea of reduction to the One if they are provided with a ready-made phrase, and even so such a phrase will remain a mere abstraction for many of them. All the same, it is easier for a man to understand a given phrase than to discover it himself. That is the role of religions and, from the moral point of view, of those who use the second approach, to the consideration of which we shall soon be coming.

\*       \*       \*

The counterpart of the moral sense is a moral tradition which will be found down all the centuries.

We can take as our starting point the doctrine of *synderesis* (conscience) which was long attributed to Aristotle, was revived in the Middle Ages and culminated in the philosophy of St Thomas.[1] Synderesis implies the self-evidence of the fundamental data of morality. St Thomas embodied it in his philosophical synthesis.

In his teaching, the first principles of knowledge are self-evident to the mind and form the starting point of speculative philosophy. St Thomas considers that there should be a similar certitude in the field of action. The first principles of action are therefore self-evident: they do not have to be discovered or proved.

But St Thomas and all the authors of his time spoke of synderesis as if it were a matter of course, and never stated what these self-evident first principles were. We sometimes get the impression that the synderesis they asserted so force-

[1]Aristotle does not talk of *synderesis* in the moral sense of the word. St Jerome, who quotes him, and through whom his doctrine on this point came down to the Middle Ages, talks of *syneidesis*. A copyist's mistake turned this into *synderesis*, and this mistake was reproduced in all the manuscripts, and became the basis of the medieval doctrine.

fully has no content, and that it is, as it were, an empty receptacle. Its proponents never give anything but general and abstract rules, such as that men should do good and avoid evil. Now this rule is useless as long as we do not know what good and evil consist in.

To this St Thomas adds his doctrine of prudence, which is also incorporated in the main body of his philosophy. For him, the mind does not apprehend the individual, which is the object of experiential knowledge. Consequently as soon as a man is confronted with an individual case, the general ideas applicable to it suggest themselves in such numbers that his mind is unable to analyse them all. And since in such individual cases he has got to make a decision quickly, the virtue of prudence is involved.

Prudence is a virtue which results from a simultaneous balance of mind and will, and itself springs from the corpus of moral virtues. Thanks to this balance, in which daring is matched with prudence in the ordinary acceptation of the word, with courage, which St Thomas calls the virtue of fortitude, and with restraint which he describes as temperance, the prudent man has an intuition of what is the proper action in the particular case. St Thomas does not use the word 'intuition', which is a modern expression, but that is what is in his mind.

Thus, to the extent that his prudence develops, the wise man need no longer think out each particular case. He ceases to resort to casuistry, for the aim of this is to suggest solutions for particular problems to those who do not spontaneously see the solution, because they are wanting in prudence.

This doctrine comes into prominence again with the Renaissance, in the form of an ethics of common-sense. Since the intellectual unity of the Christian world had been disrupted by the Reformation and free-thought, thinkers concerned with action came more and more to feel the necessity of giving ethics a solid foundation, which should be independent of speculative controversies. They thus asserted with increasing insistency the self-evidence of the moral rule. If a man wants to know what he should do, he has only got to ask himself; he will find the moral rule graven on his conscience. The English and Scottish common-sense school in the eighteenth century

119

and the eclectic spiritual philosophers in France in the nineteenth believed they had found in this self-evidence of the moral rule a means of keeping out of controversies. The positivist and relativist reaction of the second half of the nineteenth century started from the denial that anything whatever is imprinted on the conscience.

All the same, thinkers concerned with conduct clung to the idea that ethics is something self-evident; they could hardly do otherwise, unless they were ready to agree that, before doing anything, a man must engage in reflections and inquiries which seemed to them incompatible with the exigencies of action. Right down to our day, this attitude remains that of the legal theorists, the object of whose thinking is the social order. A man cannot tackle the problems raised by this unless he is at ease over the question of principles.

Often, however, this self-evidence is only an apparent self-evidence. It means what is self-evident in a certain environment, or self-evident through the customs with which a man is familiar, customary ways of thinking as well as of acting.

As a result of all the controversies of the last century, contemporary thinkers are trying to put forward a new formulation which will revive the tradition but adapt it.

In France, Le Senne has advanced such a formulation in the theory of *'proversive'* morality. We have already seen that he draws a distinction between ethics and morals. For him ethics consists of fixed rules, while morals represents something above these rules, which is generally called the moral sense, that is the mind's aspiration to the good.

Now, says Le Senne, moral rules never apply exactly to practice, because they are abstractions. But morals is 'proversive', that is to say it is directed towards the future, towards that which does not yet exist but is going to be summoned into existence by the action of man. Action thus creates values, and we can only assess moral value when we are engaged in action and apprehend all the elements of it through experience. We need not completely abandon the moral rules that codify the experience of the past, but we should be constantly retouching them as experiences of action bring out new elements.

In short, according to this conception, ethics is never

complete. It develops. The mind discovers it in action.

Alongside this, a certain number of German authors, Catholic theologians in particular, have put forward a *circumstantial ethics*. Reacting against what they regard as the exaggerations of casuistry, they feel that moral rules cannot provide practical solutions for every concrete case. The aim of morality is to allow man to 'fulfil himself', and he can only succeed by constantly 'inventing' new values in terms of concrete circumstances, which are themselves always new. Some of these authors so stress the original character of each experience that they create the impression that rules serve no purpose; others are more moderate.

If we are to understand these theories, we must see them in their setting in the contemporary atmosphere. Our age is experiencing a reaction against a practical morality governed by rigid rules. On every side, attention is being directed to the difference of viewpoints, or the complexity of actions which assume different aspects according to the point of view of the observer. The difference arises from the fact that no one considers an action from all the available points of view, and this is merely due to the limitations of the human mind, which is incapable of apprehending reality in all its richness. People go so far as to say that if we are to pass judgment on a set of circumstances, we must have experienced them. We do not know what poverty means unless we have been through it; we do not understand what it is to be hungry if we have always been well-fed. In the same vein, married people claim that unmarried men should not be allowed to busy themselves with the ethics of marriage, and we sometimes hear statements so extreme that it might be thought that a judge should be divorced to give a fair judgment in a divorce case, and that he should have been a thief to try thieves.

The truth there is in this theory corresponds to the Thomist doctrine of prudence. It is true that to pass judgment on a situation we must put ourselves in the shoes of the person concerned, and there we come up against the danger of academic ethics, the ethical teaching propounded by pure intellectuals who live in abstractions and are not interested in actual men. Prudence, this balance of virtues, assumes, among other things, love. It assumes that if we are to concern ourselves with anyone else, we must love him, want his good and seek this without any regard to ourselves. It assumes therefore that we do not seek facile solutions, by which we sidestep principles, and leave our unfortunate charges to flounder about in their difficulties. Finally it assumes that we do not react emotionally against phraseology not perhaps completely adapted to the times, but which still contains a great deal of truth. When we analyse the thinking of men like Nietzsche and Sartre, we see that many of the expressions they use result from a state of emotional reaction against principles which daily irritated them. This is to muddle things. It leads us back to the fundamental idea of wisdom, which lays down that if we want to behave well, we must have sound principles, but which also lays down that if we want to have good principles we must behave well.

If we pursue circumstantial morality beyond the Thomist doctrine of prudence, we end up by confusing the rule of good with the subjective elements of responsibility. Now these are two very different elements. When a man steals, the first question is whether he *has* stolen, whether his act genuinely constitutes a theft. The next question to arise is that of his responsibility and the excuses he may have; but these are two different questions. The statement that ethics is created in the course of action involves the danger that the individual man, who has to decide on the morality of his act without any previously established principles, may find the good in what he desires, and may thus make his desires the rule of good instead of making the good the rule of his desires.

It is true that the perfectly prudent man has an intuition of the value of an act as soon as he is confronted with it. That is why wise men are worth consulting. The wise man is he who is endowed in a high degree with St Thomas's virtue of prudence. But as we know, wise men are rare. Most men are a prey to desires which they resist with difficulty, and which disturb their mind as much as they tempt their will. That is why it is important to determine as far as can be the way in which the general rule of good is applicable to everyday cases.

A legal saw, which is true in ethics, lays down that a man cannot be judge and party in the same cause; just because if a man is a party, his desires and personal interest cloud his mind. If married people claim to be the only judges of the ethics of conjugal relations, everyone will exalt into a rule what suits his own desires. It would be the same if tradesmen were to set themselves up as judges of what constitutes honesty in trade.

That does not mean that experience cannot make its contribution. Those who live through the problems of conjugal life or the problems of trade see elements which might escape the man who is approaching them from an abstract standpoint. That is why practical ethics should be worked out by a collaboration between teachers who have the principles at their fingertips and practical men who try out their application. Prudent teachers have always realized this. When Lessius, in the seventeenth century, had to write a treatise on the casuistics of justice, he started by taking a course of instruction on the Antwerp Bourse so as to discover the way in which problems came up in practice. But he did not deny the value of principles; he merely thought that to know how principles applied, we must have a clear understanding of how practice looked, that is to say we must as far as possible consider the truth as a whole. Nowadays, this attitude has become general. We realize that applied ethics should be determined by collaboration between practical men and theorists : conjugal ethics by collaboration between ethical teachers and married folk, business ethics by collaboration between them and business men, political morality by collaboration between them and politicians and so on. The fact that this attitude is no longer confined to particularly enlightened teachers such as Lessius, but has become habitual, represents progress, and if our times have achieved it, we must congratulate ourselves. But that has nothing to do with a circumstantial ethics which would deprive principles of any significance.

2. *The way through the sense of the One*

A few men, as we have seen, have a very lively sense of the One. This sense may to a certain extent be identified with the religious sense, but to a certain extent only. It is perhaps the perfection of the religious sense; but it has its deviations. The religious sense is the sense of the beyond, the perception, that is to say, that beyond the tangible world there exists a higher reality which must be taken into consideration.

But since the human mind is not pure mind, most people conceive of this higher reality in terms of what they meet on earth, in terms of man in particular. The gods they believe in are many and fierce, actuated by all the human passions, choleric and egoistical and violent; and this conception results in religions of fear and of interest. Man looks on the gods as beings like himself, but more powerful than he is; he flatters them to try and win their favour, as he would flatter a powerful man on earth. He does not try to serve the gods, but to make use of them. He does not try to know what the gods want, but merely to impose on their benevolence so as to get from them what *he* wants.

Here again, the Christian religion is the most interesting in history. No other religion has developed to the same degree the idea of a perfect God who is at the same time Creator and Providence, busying himself with men, guiding them and desiring their happiness. Yet within this perfectly pure religion there comes into being a practical religion which is very different. The psychological content of the idea of God held by most Christians is by no means that of the God of the Gospels, and they have not the least desire to comply with his law. God to them is first and foremost the Almighty, who will punish them if they displease him. They must therefore try to please him to win his favour, but they do not even think of submitting their desires to an opinion drawing its inspiration from what God proposes. They cling to the carnal; they cling to all the good things of this world. The only problem for them is to win from God the help he is capable of giving to obtain the good things they desire, and to obtain these good things without being punished for it.

Only a restricted elite manages to rise to the idea of the Father God who can be angry only with moral evil and who only asks for love. Nevertheless, even in the Old Testament, the prophets were constantly inculcating this idea, and it is at the very root of the teaching of Jesus. Despite this, after twenty centuries of Christianity, when a genuine Christian propounds this idea and applies it, he amazes people.

The sense of God, which we are discussing now, comprises

124

two points of view which do not always coincide, that of transcendence and that of perfection. We shall study them in succession.

*　　*　　*

### The sense of transcendence

We might talk of the 'Abraham complex'.

When God ordered Abraham to sacrifice his son, Abraham saw no moral problem in it. Jahweh had spoken; he obeyed.

Since then, ethical thinkers have sought of a way to justify him; but for him there was no problem. Good is what God commands. If he had not lived three thousand years before Nietzsche, he might have said: God is above good and evil.

Since then, there have been endless discussions of the question. We know that, for Descartes, good is good because God wills it and not for any intrinsic reason which compels recognition even from God. Those who have a strong sense of the divine transcendence would regard it as more or less sacrilegious to say that God was bound by anything.

The picture of God in the Old Testament often recalls this conception. Jahweh is above all the sovereign Master. When he has spoken, there are no further problems; it is not for man to judge his master. The Abraham complex is the sense of the creature, the sense, that is, of his complete dependence on the Almighty.

To my knowledge, this idea is not expressed anywhere else with such emphasis as in the Bible. It is, however, to be found elsewhere, with different variations, from the moment men reach the idea of a transcendent God intervening in human affairs. In the primitive Greek tradition, for example, we meet the idea of a divine fatality against which men can do nothing.

In legends like those of Prometheus or Oedipus, men are tossed about by a fate which expresses an arbitrary will of the gods. Man does not grasp the reason for it, but he must submit: he is forced to. Since the Greeks did not have as strong a sense of the divine transcendence as the Jews, they revolted. It was a vain revolt, because this fate dominated them, but they revolted all the same.

Prometheus complained that his fate was contrary to *dikè*;

125

Oedipus was indignant too. Abraham, on the other hand, had not a word of complaint. God had spoken, and he obeyed at once without expressing the least sorrow. To have expressed sorrow would have been to insinuate that God was wrong. In the same way Job, overwhelmed as he was with misfortunes that nothing seemed to justify, praised the name of God. Whatever God does, whatever God commands, may his name be praised.

\*     \*     \*

## The sense of perfection

The Jews had a lively sense of the divine transcendence, but they were at the same time a primitive people. They seemed too crude, most of them anyway, to conceive of perfection. Jahweh was first and foremost the Master.

Nevertheless we find almost everywhere the sense that God is the Perfection. It appears in the prophets. Greek philosophy progressively wends its way there, by long and roundabout routes, and ends up by expressing it in clear language, with the Neo-Platonists. On the other hand, this idea is familiar to oriental thinking, in India and in China, but at the price of a misunderstanding of the relations between God and the world.

This Perfection is expressed by something beyond what we call perfection. But it remains perfection, that is to say, it corresponds to what we call perfection, but transposed to the plane of the ineffable.

God thus ordains morality, that is, God being the perfect One, we cannot reach him; in so far as he is to be reached, we cannot please him, in so far as the word 'please' has a meaning where he is concerned, except to the degree that we respect the moral law. But what does morality ordain?

If God expresses no wish, morality can have no other object than to absorb us in him. In terms of earthly values, this leads to an ethics of pure detachment. If God speaks, we must do what he wishes. Now outside Christianity, God does not speak.

The difficulty is to link the One with life and life with the One in a completely harmonious manner taking into account all the elements of reality. Systems of ethics which take only practical life into consideration and relegate the One to the background are often commonplace, attaching too much importance to the human character of the act. Those which are focused on the One run the risk of being bloodless, not taking account of the human situation. In the absence of any manifestation of the divine will, the sense of the One leads in practice to ethical systems of pure renunciation, of which I shall be speaking later. But if the One manifests a desire, that desire becomes moral law.

We are still not at the end of our mental exertions, however, for the desire expressed by God never takes the form of a concrete rule applying automatically to all the circumstances of life. We have got to inquire how this law fits in with the One, and first and foremost to discover what the phrase 'fits in with the One' means. Fitting in implies that there is a presence and a contact. Just how can we make contact with the Transcendent?

\*　　\*　　\*

Besides those who reach a clear and metaphysically accurate notion of the One—clear in the heart of obscurity, as we have seen, but still clear in a certain sense—there are many people who have a confused vision of the Absolute or the One, without realizing that the One is what the metaphysicians talk about, is what their abstract and incomprehensible phrases refer to.

They therefore seek the One and find it in all sorts of things —the State, the Country, the Race, Humanity or the Beautiful —which they exalt into absolutes and spell with a capital letter. This amounts to the making of false gods. The delusion of such people results simply from the fact that since they have not attained to a sufficient intellectual purity and accuracy, they formulate their thinking in a way which is in itself absurd. But they do not see the absurdity of it because they are absorbed by immediate ends. And all this has repercussions on ethics.

The most notorious example of this attitude is to be found today in Communism. Communism sees the supreme good in the Socialist society, or the good of the human community, realized in the triumph of the proletariat. In short, it identifies the One with this earthly well-being of the human community. Communists consequently apply to this end everything that Christians say about God. Man should submit to it completely. No other human value can hold its own against this supreme value. Every other value is subordinated to it. Family and country have no standing unless they serve the supreme good of the Socialist society; justice is the service of the Socialist society; the commandment to love means to love the Socialist society and everything that is useful to it, and so on.

## II. The Problem of Reduction to the One

We have seen that all the thinkers who attain the notion of the One define it in the same way, despite the fact that they declare it to be indefinable. The Hindus call it Brahman or Brahma with a short a, a neuter word, as opposed to Brahma with a long a, which designates a personal God. It is 'being in itself, one, absolute, neuter, indeterminate, devoid of every contingent quality, the inconceivable supreme being, the Incommensurable, the Not-born, the Unfathomable, the Unintelligible'.

Christians talk of it in very similar terms. Scholastic philosophy made a great effort to clarify the ideas involved, to scrutinize the words that had been accumulated and only to retain those that were mutually consistent. But we have seen that as soon as a certain precision is reached, we are confronted with the danger of a limiting conceptualism. And other thinkers, the mystics, counter with the opposite procedure, that of seeking a more accurate conception by accumulating conceptually contradictory terms.

At the same time, all those who attain the idea of the One immediately conclude from this that it is desirable, that it is the Desirable. Some make a formal assertion of the fact; others try to avoid phraseology which applies to our relations with sensible objects, but they then lapse into the inexpressible or the ineffable.

128

In any case, they are agreed in considering that the One relegates every individual good to the background, to the point where it is as if the rest no longer existed and as if man had no other aim in life but to discover the One.

It may seem astonishing that no one says: since we cannot know it, don't let us worry about it. Those who do talk like this are in reality those who have not arrived at the realization that it exists.

We thus find ourselves face to face with a One with whom we do not find ourselves face to face, since the phrase 'face to face' has no meaning here. This One is absolutely inaccessible, and at the same time it has become the only conceivable aim of existence. What does all this mean?

The aim of life is therefore to identity ourselves with the One. In one way, when we search our hearts, we find it is within us and we see that it is the only reality or the essential reality of our being.

We see? We see nothing! We are no longer there to see, because we have disappeared and there is nothing left but it. In the phrase of the anonymous English mystic of the Middle Ages, we are engulfed in the 'cloud of unknowing'. We are beyond good and happiness.

All the mystics of every religion and every school of wisdom talk in the same way. In view of the texts already quoted, we shall only cite this song of a Moslem mystic, in which no Christian will find anything to quarrel with:

Love came and delivered me from all the rest; he lifted me up in his mercy after he had laid me low. Thanked be the Lord for having melted me like sugar in the water of his union.

I went to see the doctor, and I said to him: 'O erudite man, what can you prescribe me for the malady of life?' He prescribed me abandonment of quality and extinction of my existence, that is to say to escape from everything that *is*.

As long as a man is fasting, he does not attain the pleasure of drunkenness; as long as he does not abandon his body, he does not attain the life of the soul; as long as he does not annihilate himself in the love of the friend, as water annihilates fire, he does not attain the Being.

On the day when man and woman appear before the throne of judgment, their faces yellow with fear at the accounts they

129

have to render, I shall appear with my love in my hand, and
I shall say: My account should be settled according to this.
(Omar ben al-Farid, d. 1235)

\* \* \*

We have already seen that in these circumstances, ethics
turns to the search for exalted contemplative states. Let us
specify for the last time the shade of difference that Christianity contributes.

The God of Christianity is indeed the primal One, the
Brahma of the Hindus, the Pure Act, the Great Being of the
American Indians of former times. Now a man has only to
realize that the One exists for the desire to unite with it to
awaken in him. This leads to all the forms of mysticism, and
we have seen the extent to which they resemble each other.

Christianity adds to this the idea of creation.

This idea is to be found in a number of primitive cos-
mogonies, but with no precise doctrine. It was unknown to
the Greeks in the great Classical period: God and the world
existed, and they did not ask themselves how this double
existence hung together. The doctrine of the emanation of
beings in Neo-Platonism is nearly that of creation, without
having its clarity.

In Hindu thought, it is not known whether Brahma concerns himself with the world, and in Chinese thinking,
Heaven is more of a governor than a creator.

In contrast, the idea of creation dominates the Bible, and
Christian thinkers have systematized it strictly. As we have
seen, it is a complete causality, involving a presence in the
creation of the Creator, who gives it a depth greater than
anything created can achieve independently of him.

This presence of the Creator in the creation is of the order
of the ineffable, since nothing that we experience can give
any idea of it. Even the word 'presence' is only true of it in an
analogical way, that is to say that we are dealing with a
phenomenon which corresponds more closely to presence
than to any other notion derived from our experience, though
it is entirely different. In any case, through creation, the
divine reality is in us in such a way that if we retire within
ourselves, we find God there as the essential reality of our

130

being. A reality so essential, as we have seen, that the mind feels driven to say that it is the whole of reality or the sole reality.

And yet the notion of creation assumes that the creator God brings creatures into existence in so far as they are not-him. In so far as it is a creature, the creature is therefore not God, since it is because of this that it is what it is. At the same time, it is God, since it only exists as far as God exists, in so far as and only in so far as God thinks of it as existing. We have seen all this, but it is so little known, that it cannot be stressed too much.

Over and above all this, in Christianity, comes the supernatural order. Christ brought Divinity anew and even more totally to this life of the creature, already penetrated with the divine.

'How more totally?' it will be asked. 'Is there anything more than total? Is not total all, and is there something beyond the all?'

As far as these things can be explained, supernatural life represents a hold by God on that which, in creation, distinguishes the creature from the Creator. God takes on himself, in the creature, what is properly speaking created, so that even this becomes him. 'I am the vine, you are its branches.' The life that circulates in us is from now on the life of Christ, and the life of Christ is the life of God himself.

If union with God in creation is something ineffable, as it is, union with God in the supernatural life is, as it were, a thing beyond the ineffable, or a super-ineffable. But can we institute degrees in the ineffable, since the word means that which cannot be expressed? All these notions plunge us into a reality which is completely beyond us. It is thus not surprising that words are powerless to express what the mystics perceive and that, in particular, they cannot make plain the difference between Christian and non-Christian mysticisms, between the state of union which is a perception of the One, the consciousness of being a creature, and that which is a consciousness of supernatural union. Since the perception that the One exists is enough to demand the strongest terms for its expression, there are no stronger ones left over to describe other states.

131

But if Christian teaching is true, if Christ has really brought the divine life that he promised, the content of Christian mystical union must be different from the others. That does not prevent it from being true that, as experience shows, it will always be impossible to compare mystical states, which are all in the domain of the ineffable. We cannot compare two ineffables; we note them, and we interpret them in terms of the doctrine we believe to be true.

Nevertheless in the doctrine of creation as well as in the Christian doctrine of supernatural life, God expresses his will by a law. This is natural law in the order of creation, and a law of supernatural love in Christianity, the latter taking over and integrating the former, which it transforms when it does so.

Moreover, as we have also seen, the doctrine of creation and redemption makes all man's life a life in God. Union with God cannot therefore be identified with perception of the union. In it, mystical states become states exceptional by nature, subject to the good pleasure of God, and cease to be an end for man. The end is to live in God through Christ, drawing inspiration from his spirit and fostering his life within us by all the practices of the Christian life. The prayer through which the Christian immerses himself in the contemplation of the uncreated love goes hand in hand with the action through which charity expresses itself, and it is impossible to say which produces which. It is an endless circle in which there is no beginning.

All this gives Christianity a very special appearance and makes it the doctrine with the most complete hold on life. Other faiths may see more or less clearly, in an intuitive way, the link between life in all its human aspects and the transcendent One. But since they lack a precise and co-ordinated doctrine, their attempts at explanation are always full of gaps. On the other hand, the popular version of Christianity has developed a religious imagery which obscures the fact that the Christian God is the primal One, and prompts the reaction of those who feel they must call themselves atheists, because they think it necessary to challenge the idea of God which they confuse with the popular imagery. They then find themselves committed to a line where the obstacles are insurmountable, as we see with Hegel, Nietzsche and the rest. We have already remarked that the weakness of many philosophers is to cling to words whose meaning they believe to be necessary—whereas meaning corresponds simply to usage in a particular group or society—and not to try to go beyond the word to pin down the idea.

On the other hand, in Christian circles, concentration on the supernatural life has diverted attention from the divine presence in creation. Since union with God in creation represents a stage of union outstripped by supernatural life, little interest has been taken in it. There has thus been nothing to hinder the development of a popular conception which turns the Creator into a craftsman, the great architect, who makes a world which, once it is made, detaches itself from its author, just as the objects of human activity detach themselves from man, exist without him, and continue to exist when their author has disappeared. Most Christians think of creation in this way, and therefore never think of a continued creative presence, which is none other than the very reality of the creature.

This false conception of creation was also the butt of the reaction against the doctrine of creation. When Hegel said there was no reality but Thought, he was seeking to rediscover the doctrine of creation, which he did not know. From another point of view, when the Hindus—who were not reacting against Christianity because they did not know of it—thought that the world was illusory, that there was only Brahma, and that earthly appearances were only a thought or a dream of Brahma, they were seeking for the creationist doctrine which the Judaeo-Christian tradition is alone in expressing precisely. But motives of an affective order prevent many people taking the Christian doctrine into consideration, or even taking any pains to become acquainted with it.

## III. THE ELIMINATION OF OBSTACLES

If the whole of ethics comes down to reduction to the One, it also comes down, in one way, to the elimination of what opposes this. The obstacles can be reduced to the various

133

forms of attachment to things other than the One, and these forms of attachment in turn can be reduced to two: attachment to the sensible, that is to say to matter, and attachment to the self. In one way, ethics thus centres on detachment.

As soon as we agree that the aim of life is so to act that there shall be nothing but the One, we must agree that to be concerned with the self and with sensible objects, otherwise than as instruments for attaining the One, is an evil thing, indeed the evil thing par excellence. First comes the sensible, that is to say the material world, then the self, with a series of satisfactions which are not all of the material order, but which are linked with the sensible. There are satisfactions of pride and of vanity, and all the satisfactions through which a man enjoys asserting himself and being conscious of having some power and worth of his own, independently of the One, all the satisfactions which spring from human intercourse. All this must therefore be done away with.

But we cannot do away with it, for to do that we should have to stop living. To live is to assert oneself: life is constantly bringing us back to ourselves. It might seem at first sight as if suicide, the only way in which a man can escape from himself, was the way out. But suicide is not a solution, as the Buddha, Schopenhauer and many others have observed, for suicide implies an illimitable will to self-assertion. There is probably no act through which man asserts himself more. We must therefore manage to live as if we were not living.

The search for a method which will result in there being nothing but the One, even though we are still ourselves, forms the essential object of what is called practical ethics. This point is common to all ethical systems, as soon as they acknowledge that man should submit himself to the One; the others, as we have seen, are merely systems stemming from a reaction, which lapse into incoherence. In our own times, Communist ethics is an outstanding case in point. It goes all out to constrain the individual to a complete detachment from himself and all his desires, in exactly the same way as more metaphysical systems, only it replaces God by the Socialist society. The end in view bears another name, but the organ-

134

ization of life so as to attain it is the same. Here we have the problem of ascesis, or the fight against oneself.

## 1. *The asceses of emptiness*

A certain number of ethical theories attempt to resolve the problem by creating within man the completest possible emptiness. This is the logical trend of Hindu morality. Not all thinkers have pushed it to its conclusion, but some have succeeded in doing so.

We know that it has been the constant tradition of Hindu wisdom that the world and man are only appearances and that life is sorrow because it is a pursuit of emptiness. To abolish sorrow we must abolish the desire to live and the taste for living. There is therefore nothing which we must not renounce. The wise man practises total renunciation, and since nobody knows whether Brahma concerns himself with the world, for we cannot have any idea of him, there is no saying where we shall end up through this renunciation, on what shore we shall land, or even whether there is a shore. The climax of renunciation is *nirvana,* and we do not know what it is or whether it is anything.

This common conception gives rise to a series of methods for the disintegration of the ego, or the self, as they say in India, all characterized by the most complete renunciation.

The extreme form of this ascesis is the doctrine of Yoga, which summons its adepts to return to the divine Unconscious by the destruction of their factitious personality, so as to get back to the primitive simplicity of the soul 'without consciousness and without personality, such as it was of old, when it lay sleeping in the depths of the divine abyss'. To attain this state, yogis practise a method in which there is an element of physical technique—physical immobility, control of breathing, and so on—whose aim is not to attain consciousness of the One, but pure and simple unconsciousness. To Western eyes this seems a degrading method, because Western minds conceive of no other end but the exaltation of the self or its reabsorption into something greater than itself. Here, however, we have a reabsorption of the self without any absorption in something else. It is merely a question of reaching a state of unconsciousness. This results in a sort of acrobatics of annihilation of which the fakirs are the best known example. There are bogus fakirs who are mere conjurers, but there are also genuine fakirs who take this work of annihilation seriously and who go to the most amazing extremes.

In contrast to this is primitive Buddhism, which is in agreement on the end to be pursued, but seeks it through a purification of desire which rules out all violence. The Buddhist's ideal is a serenity of the soul which results from perfect indifference. The only desire which is good is that for *nirvana*, which is neither existence nor non-existence. This point is made in a very ancient text, which is pre-Buddhist incidentally, but in which Buddhism sees nothing to quarrel with. The son of Katyayani, this says, does not meditate on earth, water or fire; he no longer meditates on anything. And the gods venerate the son of Katyayani, saying: 'All homage to you, excellent man, for we do not know on what you are meditating.'

The perfect indifference of the Buddhist leads him to agree to anything that other people want. He thus attains a sort of kindness, which derives more from indifference than from love. The Buddhist is compassionate and merciful, but this comes through not-willing, not through willing. The only feeling towards others that is capable of strengthening this detachment is compassion. For compassion for those who cling to appearances and thus revolve in the cycle of sorrow which is life is the only feeling that fosters detachment, or the consciousness of non-existence, to the point of not even being conscious of non-existence.

The two examples just given correspond to a trend of thinking which is very general in India. The people look up to these wise men, who do not concern themselves with them.

\*   \*   \*

In China, the philosophy of Lao-tse results in a not dissimilar conception.

Lao-tse, as we have seen, focuses life on union with the Tao, and that is a union which is not a union, because we are beyond the expressible. The means of attaining to it is to return

136

to primitive simplicity. Lao-tse's virtue is a 'virtue of child-hood', in reaction against the complications and subtleties of civilization. His utterances sometimes recall those of Christ, the way of spiritual childhood of St Teresa of the Child Jesus, and the naturism of Rousseau and Tolstoi. We are again confronted with a human tradition which reappears periodically in different forms.

The wise man goes back to the simple and natural life of the child. His ideal is the new born baby, who cannot yet distinguish good from evil. The new born baby is, of all men, the nearest to non-being. Man approaches the Tao when he returns to not-being.

Like the Hindus, Lao-Tse suggests physical means of diminishing the self, though on more moderate lines. The wise man controls his breathing, damps down his activity, obliterates himself in the common herd. He cultivates weakness and deliberately lessens himself. He is insignificant and ignorant; he shows no curiosity and shuns the idea of learning. He is without will and naive. 'He seeks to remain colourless and indefinite, neutral like the little child who has not yet felt his first emotion, without intention, without plan, without aim.'

One of the elements which strikes us as most disconcerting about this Taoist ethics is that it is applied to politics. In social life, the wise man does his best to do nothing. 'There is nothing that cannot be settled by the practice of not acting.' The wise man is excited about nothing: 'as regards love of the people and solicitude for the State, he confines himself to not intervening'.

Taoist philosophy is thus not a mere abstract doctrine; it is applied and it has exerted a considerable influence on public life in China. In contrast to the Confucians, who practised a morality mindful of conforming to nature, the Taoists practised a morality of indifference. This explains certain disconcerting phenomena in public life in the old traditional China, such as the calm and systematic negligence of so many officials, which filled Europeans with indignation and ill temper.

But every such ethics of emptiness is supremely anti-social. It diverts men from seeking the good of their neighbours. And

137

every such ethics is a victim of an internal contradiction, for when a man flees from himself, it is still of himself that he is thinking. If the aim of disintegration is for us to escape from unhappiness, it is still a form of happiness that we are pursuing. What is lacking in these ethics is love. But love demands an object to love, and love is only noble if its object is something greater than itself.

## 2. *The dualist asceses*

The opposition between the body and the mind makes a strong impression on those who are concerned with moral life. Many of them have no eyes for anything but this. We can observe this among other things in the practice of Christian ethics as it is to be seen throughout history, despite the fact that Christian ethics transcends the problem from many points of view. When we talk of renunciation, the only interpretation most people attach to it is renunciation of material enjoyments. The body is regarded as the enemy of the soul rather than as its servant.

In the early centuries of the Church, the Desert Fathers gave the impression that their principal objective was to subjugate the body, and what struck people most about them was their self-mortification. All of them said, however, that this was not the essential thing, and all the Christian spiritual writers were to repeat it. But that was what struck ordinary people more than anything, and mortification occupied a place in their lives which their biographies stress. In the eyes of ordinary folk, the saint is a man who mortifies himself a lot and who prays a lot—in the first place a man who mortifies himself a lot.

The opposition between body and mind is so apparent that it has drawn the attention even of materialists. A wise man such as Epicurus, who maintained that there was no other pleasure but that of the belly, went on to try and show that physical pleasure must be sought in a mental satisfaction, that is to say a non-physical satisfaction: the remembrance of pleasure and the expectation of new pleasure. And he explained that this non-physical pleasure was physical all the same.

It is even easier to understand why the Pythagorean and

Platonist traditions, which flourished in the first centuries of the Christian era in various schools, should identify matter with evil. The reason was that matter leads to separateness, since it is characterized by multiplicity. Happiness lies in the One, the immanent *logos*. We must discover it in ourselves; the obstacle is our material separateness.

We are thus once more confronted with a very general and persistent human tradition. Its most thorough-going expression is to be found in the Manichaeism of the end of Antiquity, which derives from ancient Mazdaism and gave birth to the medieval Cathari. It will be a good thing to say a few words about this trend of thinking, which is little known to anyone but specialists, but which is characteristic, because it pushed dualism to its logical conclusion.

The starting point is Mazdaism, the religion of ancient Persia, which was reformed by Zoroaster about 600 B.C. This Mazdaean religion was the purest of Antiquity, and is so close to Christianity that we sometimes ask ourselves whether it was not subject to Jewish influences.

Many authors who have prejudices against Christianity's claim to be of divine origin believe they have found an answer to this claim in the presence of Zoroastrian influences in Christianity. They do not ask themselves whether the influence may not have worked the other way round.

In any case, Zoroaster is thought to have lived about 600 B.C. This was perhaps the greatest age of human thought, the age of Confucius and the Buddha. The Greeks only came later, and Christ represents the consummation of what men were seeking.

Nothing is known of the life of Zoroaster; there are no dates we can be sure of. He was probably a contemporary of the Babylonian exile of the Jews, which settled them in the Euphrates area. We do not know where Zoroaster came from; perhaps one day we shall discover he was a Jew.

His doctrine was to have an unquestionable influence on the Jews, as did Hellenism later on. The story of the Three Wise Men at the opening of the New Testament seems to indicate that there were spiritual contacts between the Zoroastrian world and the Jewish world.

The Persian tradition differs from the Hindu in that it

accepts the reality of the material world, and from the Greek in that it assigns an origin to the world. The Greeks started off from the existing world and did not ask themselves where it had come from.

Zoroaster ascribed the origin of the world to a good creator-God, Ahura Mazda, whom the West was later to call Ormuzd. But this good God came into conflict with a principle of evil, Ahriman.

Both are primal. The question of their origin is not raised. And they fight each other. At first sight, Ahriman appears to be as strong as Ahura Mazda. Nevertheless it is certain that Ahura Mazda will end by winning. At the end of time, he will send a Saviour, and the world will end with the final defeat of Ahriman.

Meanwhile, however, the struggle is a bitter one. Virtuous men are the allies of Ahura Mazda; the wicked are the allies of Ahriman. Every virtuous action smooths the path of Ahura Mazda and brings the coming of his kingdom nearer.

At the end of antiquity, Zoroastrianism gave birth to Manichaeism, named after its founder Manes, who lived in the third century A.D. Manichaeism accentuated the difference between good and evil, identifying them with light and darkness, the soul and the body. After Ormuzd had created a good spiritual world, Ahriman created Adam and Eve, and thus plunged the spirit or the light into the darkness of matter. The procreation and multiplication of the human race led to the gleams of light becoming more and more scattered, thus losing their luminosity. Evil was thus identified with the body and with matter. Good consisted in a man's spiritualizing himself, and the result was an ethics of pure austerity.

In the Middle Ages, Manichaeism was revived by the Cathari, who condemned sexual relations absolutely, within marriage just as much as outside it. To bring a child into the world was a crime: it was to become an accomplice of Ahriman. A pregnant woman was literally possessed by the devil.

The result was an ethics which was impracticable for the masses, and the difficulty was avoided, as is always the case, by an ethics in two degrees. The 'elect' (in Manichaeism) or the 'perfect' (among the Cathari) led an extremely austere life. The ordinary devotees, the 'auditors' (in Manichaeism) or the 'believers' (among the Cathari) sinned, but could make their peace on their deathbed, by means of a rite by which the perfect transmitted their own purity to them. Consequently, the great virtue of the believers lay in giving alms to the perfect, whom they housed and fed. It seems that sometimes, when a believer who had made his peace appeared to be in danger of recovering, he was persuaded to let himself die of starvation, for fear of losing his purity again.

In the medieval struggles against the Cathari, Catholics were incensed by certain attitudes of theirs which seemed immoral from a Catholic point of view. The reason was that they did not understand the logic of their enemies' position. An instance was when the perfect stayed with believers who were living with a mistress, or even with more than one mistress. But for the Cathari, to live with a mistress was a less serious depravity than marriage, and the gravest sin was to want children. On the other hand, the perfect were genuine ascetics, and their austerity gave them a great prestige. It even formed a contrast with the high living of bishops and abbots and was one of the great attractions of the Cathari, all the more so since the believer could confine himself to admiring the perfect without imitating them.

In any case, the interest of these doctrines is that they show what dualism leads to when it is pushed to its logical conclusion. They are 'types'. And as the tendency towards dualism is universal, it is a good thing to find it in its pure state if we are to understand it. We must take it into account, for example, if we are to understand how the sin of the flesh has become the sin *par excellence* for the great mass of Christians, whereas Christ's thinking takes a very different line. We need to remember it to understand why in Stoicism passion is evil in itself, and why in large sections of historical Christianity, in Luther, in Calvin and with the Jansenists, original sin corrupts completely: the achievements of historical man, as we know him, are thus corrupt in themselves. All this would be inexplicable if there were not in the depths of the unenlightened conscience an impression that matter is evil and that the body, the mainspring of man's material life, is also the mainspring of evil.

## 3.   *The asceses of balance*

Ascesis can finally be understood as an experience of balance, and the basis of a general philosophy of the goodness of nature, particularly if this is founded on the idea of a creator-God. This ascesis of balance assumes an optimistic general view of the world, which regards goodness as a distinguishing mark of nature or of the existent.

We find it, in particular, in Confucian ethics, which rests on the unequivocal assertion that nature is good, together with the notion of Heaven, which is providence or a moral rule. We meet it again in the Greek tradition, especially in Aristotle. Finally we see it in Christian ethics, and it is through Christian ethics that it has exerted its influence on Western thought, stamping it with that air of vigorous optimism which characterizes it as a whole.

Since Christian ethics dominates our world, I am going to stick to that. We need only recall that Chinese ethics so much resembles what Christians call natural ethics, that the first missionaries to China, in the seventeenth century, were amazed at what they found there and considered the Chinese to be 'naturally Christian'.

\*     \*     \*

The Christian must master his passions if he is to put himself at the service of God. He must master them, not kill them. We must not destroy anything in nature.

Although teachers of ethics sometimes make remarks which seem, when taken in isolation, to contradict this principle, we may link up with this fundamental conception the repugnance shown in the Church to anything that mutilates the human being. We have here a sort of instinct, whose rational justification is not always convincing, but which points to a certain intuitive view of what the Christian conception of life implies.

One of the most curious manifestations of this is the Church's opposition to castration. In the first centuries, a certain number of fervent Christians, who found great difficulty in remaining chaste, took it into their heads to castrate themselves in order to remove the temptation. The Church forbade the practice. Even if a man discovered from experience that

142

he could not succeed in being chaste, he must not mutilate himself in order to respect morality. He must expose himself to temptation. Since we know that, for the Church, sin is the gravest thing in the world, this attitude is very symptomatic. No doubt the present-day opposition of the Church to sterilization and cremation should be linked with it, possibly also the Church's condemnation of contraception. The formulation of arguments to justify these attitudes is sometimes faulty. But the point of view, and the unity of this point of view applied to such different questions, should be understood as stemming from a very deep-lying intuitive attitude.

Nevertheless, since the passions are strong, popular preaching does not always correspond to this attitude and sometimes gives the impression that morality comes down to little more than the mortification of the passions. In the same way, a certain number of saints, especially in the Middle Ages, seem to have wrecked themselves by their mortifications : examples are St Francis of Assisi, St Catherine of Siena and, later on, St Rose of Lima. They advised others against these austerities, however, and justified their own action by saying that they were the greatest sinners on earth and had to employ the strongest measures to curb their passions. In any case, it can safely be asserted that from this point of view they do not represent the authentic Christian tradition, for we find nothing similar in Christ and the Apostles.

Christian ascesis thus proposes a conception of ascesis which consists in giving to the service of God all we have received from him. In this conception, ascesis retains its original meaning of a struggle, but it is merely a struggle to master the passions.

This mastery of the passions which turns the Christian into a perfect man strongly resembles, considered in itself, the Greek ideal of which we shall be speaking in the next chapter, and that of Confucius.

*　　*　　*

Christian ascesis also possesses a specifically Christian characteristic, which accentuates its severity : the penitential aspect.

Penitence is an expression of regret. Now the Christian acknowledges himself to be guilty. The idea of transgression, the idea that all men are sinners and that we are therefore sinners ourselves is one of the elements which go to make up the moral atmosphere of Christianity. In our times, it results in a marked contrast between Christian ethics and non-Christian Western theories. Thus the Christian must expiate his sin. Ascesis, which is a struggle against ourselves designed to harden us, has penance as its counterpart.

The fervent Christian throws himself into it enthusiastically. Penance occupies a considerable place in the communal life of the Church. And it is indeed penance, rather than mortification. Thus, in the liturgical year, the practice of penance is laid down at periods when the Christian is asked to reflect more earnestly on the fact that he is a sinner, principally in Lent.

Since many unbelievers today make fun of penance, people sometimes put forward certain secondary characteristics of the practice in order to justify it. Thus it is urged that the ritual fasts are good for the health. As an argument for popular apologetics, that may go down today, but it was not the reason why these particular penances were instituted. The primary reason was genuinely that of penance, and the Church's prescriptions can only be understood in terms of Christian doctrine and outlook as a whole.

The penitential aspect of ethics becomes more important as concern for sin increases. Now we have seen that popular Christian ethics comes down to little else. We can therefore understand why the bulk of Christians sees little but this aspect of ethics.

Today the sense of the need for penance is growing less, because it is characteristic of a state of sturdy faith and of loose morals. Today a sturdy faith without a Christian life that corresponds with it is becoming rarer and rarer. When we meet a case of this kind, we have the impression that we are up against a Christian of the old days. A man of the twentieth century who does not live a Christian life loses his faith.

But though this penitential aspect may emphasize the role of mortification, it does not modify its fundamental character.

The Christian should train himself, not wreck himself, and he must use all his natural gifts in the service of God.

\*　　\*　　\*

Finally, ascesis should free man from himself, and on this point, Christian ethics lays a very special emphasis.

For ethics to comprise a clear idea of a liberation from the self that shall be an absorption in the One, it must also include a clear idea of the One and of the relations between the One and man. If the One does not manifest itself as an active being we shall inevitably end up with an ascesis of emptiness. On the other hand, when the idea of the One is lacking in clarity, ethics is focused on man and renunciation can extend to anything, except the self.

In moralities like those of Zoroaster and Confucius, which are based on a more or less clear conception of God as creator and providence, we have a foreshadowing of the Christian conception; but Christianity's revelation of divine love gives an unparalleled prominence to divine action. After this, Christians looking back to the purely philosophical notion of creation may recognize the presence of God in this, but in fact men did not discover it before they possessed the revelation of love.

In the teaching of Christian ethics as it has developed historically, we find two very different trends which are difficult to harmonize.

Firstly, there is the specifically Christian idea of the absorption of man in the divine love. This trend does not seek to demolish the human personality. On the contrary, it seeks to arouse it for the better service of God; but it is angled towards self-forgetfulness. Its principle of perfection might be formulated as: 'For God and others'. The self disappears.

There is nothing here of pantheism, of monism or of idealism, simply the complete absence of a human good or happiness considered in isolation.

Alongside this is the influence of Greek thought.

Christianity developed in the West. That is an historical fact; it might have been otherwise if the circumstances had been different. In the East, Christianity would have found traditions of thought that fitted in with it better. But since Christianity did develop in the West, it came under the influence of Greek thought, for the converts to Christianity had been trained in this. Christian thinking thus fell into line behind Greek thinking.

Now Greek thinking was focused on man. The idea of God only appeared in it adventitiously; it remained in the background and retained an extremely abstract character, and the notion of the relations between God and the world was vague. The Neo-Platonism of the end of antiquity seems only to have arrived at the contemplative conception which is peculiar to it among Greek philosophies under the influence of Judaeo-Christian circles in Alexandria.

When Christian thinkers started to philosophize, they did so under the influence of the rather narrow rationalism of the Greeks and, from the thirteenth century on, of Aristotle in particular.

It is true that the Christian thinkers who revived the trend of thinking that had come down to them from the Greeks transformed the system through the predominant position they attributed to God. When St Thomas tackled the moral problem, he started from the notion of the final end, and this is in God. But later, when it came to analysing actions, the Schoolmen returned to the structure of thought which antiquity had bequeathed to them.

They then elaborated the rational system which we find today in treatises on moral philosophy. Man inevitably seeks his good, in accordance with the ontological principle: *Bonum est quod omnia appetunt*. Man wants his good. He inevitably wants it; he is incapable of not wanting it. Even when he seems not to want it, he still wants it. When he forgets himself, it is because he sees his good in forgetting himself; the contary is inconceivable. A man who commits suicide sees his good in committing suicide, and so on.

There is obviously a clearcut antithesis between the spirit of the two attitudes. The first is an intuitive attitude of moral generosity. The second rests on a logician's type of reasoning, which sees everything in terms of reason, rules out anything that is beyond reason, and does not even suspect that there are realities which elude reason, still less that these realities are possibly the essential realities.

To say that a man who forgets himself sees his good in it all the same is to lapse into a rather summary psychology. He undoubtedly may see his good in forgetting himself, if he thinks about forgetting himself, but in that case he is not really forgetting himself. If he really does forget himself, he does not think of it any more, for the characteristic of forgetfulness is that a man no longer thinks of the object he has forgotten.

The logician distinguishes between being, truth, goodness and beauty, and then goes on to assert that the only difference between them lies in different points of view of the mind. We are thus distorting these ideas when we treat them as separate realities. Yet we do so without wanting to, as soon as we talk of them separately. This point has already been referred to.

Again, when it is said that man seeks *his* good in *the* good, the good of the man and good in itself are being distinguished only to be identified the moment after. But that brings us to the heart of the mystery of knowledge.

Knowledge is a unity of the known and the knower and a presence of the known in the knower, but it is quite as much a presence of the knower in the known. When we say that man seeks his good in the good, we are distinguishing and separating the two. The mind holds to the idea that the good is something other than the good *of the man,* or that the good of the man is something other than the good.

In one way this is true, for every good is not a human good, and what is more, every human good is not good for all of us. But human good is nothing but the good in so far as it applies to man. *My good* is *the good* in so far as it applies to me. There is thus no need to think of my good as a distinct entity from the good and then to inquire how they fit in together.

And to this we must add love.

Traditional psychology locates love in the will, and distinguishes the will from the intelligence, though love is inseparable from knowledge and a man cannot love without knowing.

Love is a tendency towards fusion, that is to say towards unification, a tendency towards fusion or the achievement of

147

fusion. The formula of love is: there are no longer two, but one. Now as there are no longer two but one, and to the extent that this is realized, the thought of self is no longer opposed to that of the other. A man's own good can thus no longer be distinguished from that of the loved one, and if the unification is realized by absorption into a greater than himself, the good of the loved one becomes the good of the lover, but in a different sense from that of traditional philosophy. It would be more accurate to say that the good of the lover disappears with himself. A rationalist will never understand that.

Christian thinking has always been poised between the rationalism which it took from the Greeks and the intuitionism which it draws from Christ. Mystics have tried to express love, the forgetfulness of self in love, the unity achieved by love. Logicians have had them condemned because their expressions are open to criticism, and have retorted to them in chains of formal reasoning. The content of treatises on moral philosophy does not generally strike any sort of Christian note; it is Greek intellectualism. And it pulls Christian ardour up dead by insinuating that the purest impulses of charity are just self-seeking.

We are thus back at the idea of the renunciation of self, which is much more important than that of the renunciation of material goods. Abstract reason has not in its pride taken a single step in the direction of reduction to the One.

Renunciation of self is simply, in Christian ethics, the negative aspect of the presence of the One. God invades what man vacates. To forget myself is the condition of my thinking of God; to the extent that I forget myself, my thought can focus on God, and the presence in me of God expresses itself in my acts. To the extent that I lose consciousness of myself, consciousness of the divine reality can invade me.

This train of ideas would lead us to conclusions resembling those of Lao-tse. The difference is that our God is an active God, a creator who wants me such as I am and wants my human activity; he is a God of love who wants to invade me with the love that is in him and wants me to transmit this love to the world. But to return to ascesis, the substitution of the divine will for mine transforms my acts only in so far as these are impure. It thus purifies my life; it refines it; it purges it of

148

everything that runs counter to God's plans; it only destroys the evil.

We are now at the starting point of the study of the methods of ascecis, which I need not enter into for the moment. These methods involve a training and a discipline which are often similar, in individual cases, for the Christian and the non-Christian. Christian ascetic authors took many texts from Greek moral philosophers who were pagans, and if they had known them, they would have taken even more from the Hindu and Chinese wise men. But the thing that matters is not any particular text, but the general spirit which forms its setting; it is the system that matters. The idea of the God of love revealed by Christ gives everything Christian a coherence which is not to be found elsewhere.

# Chapter Five

## *Ethics and Society*

WHEN WE were inquiring into the origin of ethical reflection, we found that it had a specifically individual character. The moral philosopher is a non-conformist. Ethics is founded on personal reflection, and on consciousness of personality and of independence of the environment. The philosopher passes judgment on accepted opinions.

All the same, this formula is still ambiguous, for though he may pass judgment on accepted opinions, what he is judging is a moral rule accepted by those around him. Morality is a fact; we find an established morality in any human community, and the moral fact is indeed one of the characteristics of man. Morality thus existed before ethical reflection; it is independent of reflection. What is specifically individual is ethical *reflection*. When we say that the moral philosopher passes judgment on accepted opinions, we mean that he passes judgment on *morality* as the community imposes it. But that shows that every human community has a body of rules which forms an ethical system.

What has just been said and what has been stated earlier is in flat contradiction to what many of our contemporaries are teaching. In the ethical literature of our times, ethics is often represented as a product of social life, and most authors cannot conceive of ethics outside social life. They believe that the isolated man would never have any idea of an ethical theory and that the very conception of a moral rule comes from society.

But in that case, the moral philosopher becomes a conformist. This present-day conception runs counter to the whole of tradition, which has always put the moral problem from the point of view of the conscience, that is to say the point of view of what is most deep-seated and most personal in man. Moreover, the tendency today to link morality with social pressures is prevalent principally among those who have come under the influence of the sociological school of thinking. And as ideas are very incoherent outside this school, the sociological conception of ethics has considerable prestige.

We have sufficiently stressed earlier in this book the point that morality is a social fact as well as a fruit of reflection, and that it is indeed a social fact before it is reflected on. But to limit morality to the social fact is to confuse two facts. The existence of a moral rule in the social community is a fact; but the reaction of those who take up a personal attitude towards this fact is another. If morality is simply the good in so far as it presents itself to the free will, it is obvious that the moral problem confronts the solitary man just as it does the social man. Possibly he will not use the word 'moral', but he will have the idea of moral value, that is to say of the value of an act in so far as it is an object to be pursued by the free will, and that is the good.

The solitary man observes that he becomes ill if he eats too much, and that over-eating is thus an evil for him : hence the rule of temperance. Temperance presents itself to the free will as an end or a good. The question is whether this is enough to give the human attitude what is called a moral character. We shall be going into this in the next chapter.

We can already note that the rules of ethics laid down by society have the same character as we have just observed with temperance. They amount to saying : if you want to be happy and respected, do this or that. That is to say they have a character which used to be called eudaimonist and which is today known as utilitarian. They correspond to Kant's hypothetical imperative, and we know that Kant denied the moral character of an act performed because of a hypothetical imperative. According to him, the fact that an act conformed with duty did not make it moral; it had to be done out of duty. Others, on the contrary, as we have seen, consider that the most purely moral character is to be found in the act performed without seeking any advantage from it—which runs counter to utilitarianism—but also beyond duty, since this represents only a secondary aspect of morality. And we have seen the labours of those who declare that they would do good or serve God, or love the object which they see as expressing the good, God or the human community or anything else, even if they were not obliged to. We thus find three conceptions: one which focuses ethics on happiness or utility, a second which focuses it on duty, and a third which focuses it on the good. As this chapter is concerned with social morality, the question we must examine is that of the specifically moral value of utilitarianism.

To say that eudaimonism or utilitarianism is not morality is to play with the meanings of words, and we have seen that there are always disadvantages about that. In fact, eudaimonist or utilitarian systems are discussed throughout the history of moral philosophy. Christian ethics itself is steeped in utilitarianism: we have seen the part the fear of punishment plays in practical Christian ethics. Sociological ethics scarcely conceives of a different kind of ethics. Now this utilitarian notion is certainly not dependent on social life, as is shown by the example of temperance cited above. What can be linked with society is the fact of calling this moral, distinguishing it from other forms of action or of intention; but these distinctions are a minor affair. They are questions of form, not of substance, *formalia* and not *realia*. In this respect Kant, who had such a fundamentally individualist conception of moral value and who set such rigid bounds to it, was a product of his environment. He had no suspicion of it, but it was the influence of his environment which explains the origin of his thinking, and in particular why he allowed no moral value to anything that was not tied up with duty. This explanation, it must be added, sheds no light on the value of this conception. In any case, if we want to take the whole of moral reality into account, we must start from what exists, that is the three moral conceptions and the three moral attitudes which I have just described.

We can, however, dismiss the sociological thesis right away, in so far as it refuses to consider anything in ethics but social influences. We shall have the opportunity of saying more about this later on. We must allow for it nowadays because it is of considerable importance, social again, on account of the position held by some of its champions. But even this is a sociological fact belonging to the sociology of ethics, and has little doctrinal value.

\* \* \*

The question of the relations between ethics and society is more complicated than it appears at first sight, because the very notion of society is full of ambiguities.

In the strict sense, society is a community of men living an *organized* common life with a view to a common end. What constitutes society is thus organization, and what induces this is the end. But men's life in common has other characteristics, and the word society or the word social are used in more general senses.

Thus we talk of 'social events', and of 'society', meaning any sort of gathering, even unorganized. We say that man likes society, meaning simply companionship. We also say that a man has a sociable nature when he likes to mix with his fellow-men, but that is quite a different matter from belonging to an organized society. I have entitled this chapter: 'Ethics and Society', because the word society is in vogue today. It would possibly have been more accurate to call it 'Ethics and human communities' or 'Ethics and life in common'. The ambiguities of the word 'society' are a frequent source of confusion in many contemporary books. 'Sociological' literature is full of them.

The first question which this chapter will tackle will be to examine the moral philosophies which have in fact developed in human communities, to see whether they present constant characteristics, and to pinpoint such agreements and divergencies as we may find in them.

The primary interest of the question is a psychological one. The fact that different ethical theories have developed in different social communities in no way proves, as certain sociologists believe, that there is no moral truth. The question of the moral fact and of moral truth are different questions, which should be approached from different angles. But the question of the moral fact and of the social development of ethics is an interesting one. For if we discover a general agreement on certain points, we can draw the conclusion that certain truths are probably regarded as self-evident, take this as

153

a starting point, and go on to ask how this self-evidence can be explained.

The second question this chapter will tackle will be to inquire to what extent a man must take other men into account, and in particular to what extent he must take into account the convictions and ways of thought obtaining in his community. This inquiry must be directed even more particularly to the question of how far a man must allow for the necessities of social life, or even of social utility or common utility.

Here principles come in. The moral convictions obtaining in a community are a fact; how far does this fact compel our recognition as a source of obligation? We have here a series of questions over which the greatest confusion reigns, and the confusion is often due the fact that we do not distinguish society in the strict sense from the unorganized social environment.

## I. ETHICS AS A PRODUCT OF THE HUMAN COMMUNITY

The moral philosopher, let us repeat, is a non-conformist, but at the same time his reflection is not pure invention. His reflection is concerned at once with existing ethics and existing morals. Ethics consists of the rules whose observation or violation cause a man to be praised or blamed. Morals means the behaviour of men in relation to ethics. Morals are more good or less good according as they conform more or less to ethical theory.

What we are concerned with in this book is ethics. Nevertheless, we shall see that from certain points of view morals have repercussions on ethics. We, however, shall discuss morals only in the light of their conformity to ethical theory.

### 1. *The ethics of the good man*

We find among every people a non-systematized ethics which expresses itself through a collection of precepts which nobody worries much about unifying. 'Do this, don't do that,' it says. Why? This question is considered impertinent.

And in every civilized people, this ethics is expressed in a literature which is not so much moral reflection as moral testimony, a testimony to what men regard as the moral rule. So we find manuals of ethics, and we also find ethical judgments interspersed in ordinary writings. Epics, plays and histories depict a type of hero who is looked on as a model or a type of villain who is regarded as a bad example.

Now the thing that strikes us at first sight is the uniformity of these ethical theories. We can safely say that, except for a few details, the type of the good man is the same everywhere.

Egyptian texts of various periods of antiquity have been discovered which give us fragments of what may have been a course in ethics. The Greek and Chinese ethics have been known for a long time. All of them see the first characteristic of the good man as his mastery of himself. This leads him not to give way to his passions. The good man is moderate in everything, in eating and drinking in the first place, and then in his speech. He makes little display of his feelings. He does not laugh, he does not shout, he does not let himself be carried away about anything. He contents himself with little and does not run after worldly goods. He is a good husband and father, but he is firm and strict, and does not let himself be ordered about either by his wife or his children. All moral teachers condemn a disorderly life.

The good man's attitude to his fellow-men is first and foremost one of respect, with frequently a touch of utilitarianism. He must keep his word, comply with the law, help the unfortunate and display kindness to all. Sometimes it is even stated that he must love his neighbour: 'Always do good . . . If a man does you harm, repay him with good', said the Egyptians (quoted by Duesberg, *Les Scribes Inspirés*, vol. 1, p. 107).

All this is generally steeped in a sort of utilitarianism, which expresses itself through promising happiness and holding out the prospect of pleasing the gods and being looked up to, while in monarchical or aristocratic societies it is mingled with advice on how to please the powerful.

From the individual point of view, these are ethical theories of courage and dignity; from the social point of view, they are theories of mutual respect and good breeding. Greek ethics is the one giving least importance to family virtues. On the other hand, friendship bulks large in it, and this friendship

155

does not exclude homosexuality. Moreover, chastity as such has little place in these systems. They generally contain stern warnings against debauchery and courtesans, on account of the dangers to which they expose men's health and fortunes; but the ideal of chastity does not appear in them.

Jewish ethics differs little from the others. The wisdom books of the Bible have been compared with Egyptian ethical works and they have been found to be very similar. We noted earlier that this Old Testament ethics is extremely utilitarian. The greatness of Confucius probably lies in the fact that he was the wise man who pushed to its furthest point this ethics of self-mastery, moderation, and kindness to and respect for others; an attitude that was always steeped in an equally moderate and unobtrusive concern for self-interest.

India stands out as an exception to this whole moral tradition, for it has always been dominated by an ethics of extremes. The Christian world too presents a character of its own, of which I shall be speaking in a moment, even though the 'ethics of the good man' is enunciated there alongside Christian ethics properly so called.

This unanimity over the 'ethics of the good man' seems to imply that it is self-evident to man. Sociologists explain it through the influence of society. But this explanation explains nothing, for the question is why this self-evidence comes out as soon as men start living together.

What makes it even more obvious that the truth of these principles is self-evident is that attempts to justify them are so often unconvincing. That is the case especially with the justification by success. It is far from being obvious that virtue leads to happiness in the sense men attach to this word. As a matter of fact, one of the most shocking things in this world is the unhappiness of so many virtuous men and the happiness of so many wicked ones. All the same, moral teachers of every country and of every age go on repeating tirelessly that the good man is blessed by the gods and that they will make him happy. But since these arguments are so often bad, it is all the more impressive to see the same assertions being constantly made.

Furthermore, this ethics in no way corresponds to the reduction to the One of which I talked earlier. The latter

156

unifies the whole of life in terms of an absolute. The ethics of the good man is an ethics of unobtrusiveness and balance, which aims at moderation even in virtue, which must not be shown off, and rejects the absolute, because it regards this as going too far. In short, it tries to reconcile multiplicity and unity through balance. Nothing will thus be pushed to its conclusion, but every virtue will be balanced by a suspicion of its contrary. Men must display generosity and altruism, for example, but always with a lurking thought of self-interest, very unobtrusive, but constantly present; and a man will pursue his own interests, but always with a certain concern for dignity and nobility. The most decisive form of censure will be to say: 'That's going too far'. The absolute is thus fundamentally repugnant to this attitude.

Moreover, it does not stop men getting the 'moral shock', from reading Kipling's *If* or the Sermon on the Mount; but it does stop them from putting them into practice. If the 'good man' were to find somebody trying to do so, he would think this was a little too much, and would regard him as slightly unbalanced, or at least devoid of common sense.

The ethics of the good man corresponds, in short, to an 'art of living' inspired, not by philosophical considerations, but by public opinion. Nowadays, it has assumed a somewhat novel form in sociological ethics.

The old tradition is carried on through 'arts of living' of every kind, and it would be interesting to bring out the evolution of ideas in them and the growing prominence of certain prejudices, especially social prejudices. But more characteristic of our age is the sociological evolution.

For sociology, ethics is first of all a fact, and this tallies with what has been said above. But many sociologists stop at that. Starting at the position that ethics is a fact, they conclude from it that there is no moral problem, and that all that has to be done is to establish a moral science which shall explain how ethical theories originate, develop and disappear. Now this attitude misinterprets the nature of the moral fact, for the moral fact is that men believe that there is a moral rule. The moral fact thus raises the moral problem: if men believe there is a rule, we must inquire whether they are right or wrong, and if they are not in agreement on this rule, we must inquire who is mistaken. If some men believe that the sun revolves round the earth and others that the earth revolves round the sun, we cannot avoid raising the question who is right.

Sociology thus ends up by trying to establish an art of living, in a different way from that of the ancients, but with the same scope. Basing themselves on an array of scientific observations, sociologists inquire which are the rules which 'succeed', this term meaning 'which make man happy', or 'which yield good results'. This new art of living is baptized 'science of behaviour' or 'moral science' but the novelty of the words and the methods should not mislead us into believing the idea is new. It is simply the old ethics of the good man, tricked out with an array of scientific observations which the ancients had never thought of. And its objective is naively eudaimonist, for what aim can this ethics set itself but to make men happy?

No doubt concern for society introduces a note appropriate to the times. Since men's happiness depends on life in society, individual men must be persuaded to allow for the exigencies of social life. But here again, there is no question of proving; since men are subject to the pressure of the social environment, this must reflect the exigencies of life in common. If it is socially desirable that men should sacrifice themselves for the community, an environment must be created which imbues its members with the conviction that they must be ready for this sacrifice. That is not a question of reasoning. If everyone around the individual says that men must sacrifice themselves for the community, if children grow up with this conviction, if those who do not do it are the objects of universal censure, everyone will be convinced of it. The moral question is not a question of proof, but of education and propaganda.

The ethics of the good man thus pursues its course in new attire. But social ethics assumes yet other forms. Before examining them, however, I think it will be useful to say a few words about the relations between the ethics of the good man and Christian ethics.

## 2. *Christianity and the ethics of the good man*

In Christian society, the ethics which most people profess

and practise corresponds fairly closely to the ethics of the good man which we find among every people. Most people believe that is what Christian ethics is, and they do not know that there is anything else.

Christian thought has classified this ethics under the heading of 'natural ethics', as opposed to supernatural ethics which derives directly from Revelation. But it never laid down just what each of these moral standards comprises, and most Christians are hardly aware of the supernatural standard. They know theoretically that there is one, but they have no clear idea what it covers, beyond questions of religious practice. When cases of application are put up to them, it is easy to see that in their eyes Christian ethics, to which they are committed by believing themselves to be Christians, is nothing but natural ethics.

How is this possible? It can be explained, I believe, in two ways.

First of all, in order to enhance the value of Christianity, non-Christian ethical theories were disparaged to the point of caricature. This is an apologetic attitude, that is to say the attitude of a controversialist. Non-Christians were represented as being depraved, and necessarily depraved, and Christian ethics as deriving entirely and solely from Revelation. A great number of Christians were thus trained to believe, not only that all non-Christians were depraved, but also that they themselves only respected ethical standards because they were Christians, and that outside Christianity the moral question did not arise. Many Christians have the impression that it is solely because they are Christians that they are not thieves, debauchees and so on, that if they had not faith, they would have no motive for being virtuous, and that ethics has no meaning outside Revelation. As a result, some Christians actually come to entertain a certain complacency over immorality, considering that it is in it that human happiness lies, and that they are making a great sacrifice for their faith by renouncing all those good things which appear to them real good things and real doorways to happiness.

They are thus extremely upset when they meet non-Christians who are virtuous, honourable, chaste and respect their fellow-men; and there are some whose faith is disturbed.

159

Now a study of non-Christian ethical ideas leads us to realize that natural ethics extends further than is generally admitted in theory in Christian circles. I say 'in theory', because in practice, Christian ethical literature is full of quotations from the pagan Neo-Platonists and Stoics, which amounts to saying that such utterances do not imply that their authors were Christians. Even in the Middle Ages this was avoided, by the spreading of legends such as that of a correspondence between Seneca and St Paul, or by attributing to St Dionysius the Areopagite the *Treatise on the Divine Names*. But we can no longer content ourselves with that today. I have already recalled how, when the Jesuits arrived in China in the seventeenth century, they were amazed at the Chinese wisdom, declared the Chinese to be 'naturally Christians' and as a result hoped for a swift and massive conversion.

For two centuries, the number of non-Christians in Western countries has been growing, and they do not seem to practise a morality different from that of Catholics, in a certain number of fields of moral life at least. The field where the Christian religion plays the most visible role is that of the family. When it comes to professional honour, respect for truth and equity, and political controversies, there are no appreciable differences, and we even find non-Christians with a higher morality than that of certain devout Catholics who practise the family virtues.

Even in the domain of devotion, certain Christians are sometimes impressed by seeing Moslems pray, and they get the impression that the average Moslem is more faithful to his duties of religious observance than the average Christian. Moreover, there appears to be no intrinsic difference between the prayers of certain Christians and those of non-Christians. They demand the same favours, often in the same terms. The difference is extrinsic, that is to say the prayers are addressed to God by another name, and the phraseology is different in so far as it is prescribed to the faithful. But what the two sets of men ask of God is the same, and they employ the same methods of pleasing him. I have known Christians extremely upset at finding in a Buddhist temple a form of worship which expressed itself in exactly the same way as that in a sanctuary of the Blessed Virgin.

Then again, the practical ethics of the vast body of Christians disregards almost completely certain moral values on which Christ insisted, and which he even gave as the signs by which his disciples would be recognized.

An example is the forgiveness of wrongs and the love of enemies. Here are the words of Jesus: 'You have heard that it was said, Thou shalt love thy neighbour and hate thy enemy. But I tell you, love your enemies, do good to those who hate you, pray for those who persecute and insult you, that so you may be true sons of your Father in heaven, who makes his sun rise on the evil and equally on the good, his rain fall on the just and equally on the unjust. If you love those who love you, what title have you to a reward? Will not the publicans do as much? If you greet none but your brethren, what are you doing more than others? Will not the very heathen do as much? But you are to be perfect, as your heavenly Father is perfect' (*Matt.* V, 43-48).

The interest of this text lies in its precision. Christ points to three signs by which his disciples will be recognized: they will love their enemies, pray for their persecutors and greet their enemies. Yet most Christians do nothing of the sort. They love only their friends, they do good to nobody but them and they pray not for, but against their persecutors. The other precept of the Sermon on the Mount, prescribing the turning of the left cheek to the man who strikes us on the right, has become almost a subject of derision in many Christian circles.

And all this is not confined to lukewarm Christians; it is true of fervent Christians also. The idea of forgiving wrongs is not taken into consideration, and though cases of it are cited in the lives of the saints, that is because it is regarded as a sign of sanctity, that is, of exceptional virtue. In short, what Christ put forward as one of the signs by which the Christian would be recognized is not the practice of the mass of those who are looked on as Christians and who give themselves out as such.

If some readers think this is exaggerated, I can assure them that what is asserted here is the fruit of a wide and well organized experience.

Nevertheless, even the forgiveness of wrongs is not specifically Christian. We find it in every ethics that has any nobility, though it is generally inspired by other motives; but we have

161

seen that a distinction must be made between precepts and their motivation. It seems that there is a self-evidence in certain precepts, which are later vindicated no matter how, sometimes none too convincingly. The universality of most of these precepts considered in themselves obliges us to lay down what constitutes the specific character of Christianity.

We have already discussed this, but the question comes up again at every turn. When we adopt the standpoint of natural ethics, it stares us in the face that what constitutes Christianity is faithfulness to Christ the Saviour. Christ reveals the divine love to us with a precision and an eloquence undreamed of before he came. And he is talking of love in every sense of the word: the love which is in God, the love of God for men and the love of men for God, the last-named being identifiable with the love in God and the love of God for men, because it is the divine life in man. Christ therefore summons men to a divine life through which they are associated with himself, his love and his work. And this association is expressed in the supernatural life, which is not in itself conscious, but which constitutes a reality that transforms the soul and has its repercussion on natural ethics, by giving strength to practise it better.

Yet this union with Christ the Saviour is known and understood by only a small fraction of Christians, while a much smaller fraction ever begins to put it into application. Most Christians are Christians because they have been baptized, and baptism introduces a man into the supernatural life and constitutes a summons to go forward in it. But most people do not respond to this summons; they do not even know there is one. Think of the millions of baptized Christians who receive no religious instruction, or who receive it in such unsatisfactory conditions that they never become aware of the summons which the Christian faith constitutes.

That is the reason why there can be Christians in whom the spirit of Christ does not manifest itself. If we wanted to know whether it really did not manifest itself anywhere, there would have to be much more searching social investigations than have been undertaken up to now. In the past, the question has never been examined except with a view to polemics, either to justify Christianity or to attack it, and it may be that

Christians are unfaithful to the spirit of Christ over some points and faithful over others. There is no doubt that there is something peculiar to Christian countries, and that among these, there are differences between Catholic, Orthodox and Protestant lands. Moreover, not everything we find in these countries is ascribable to religion; many elements can also be ascribed to the natural character of the people and the pattern of its history. The determination of the importance of each of these elements would demand extremely painstaking inquiries, and these have not even been started.

But all this explains why so many non-Christians do not become aware of the life of Christ in Christians, or the doctrine of Christ in the life of Christians. When an unbeliever becomes converted, it is usually because he has met Christ by associating with a Christian or a Christian group, or by reading books in which the Christian spirit genuinely asserts itself. Christians are responsible for the faith. It is a deposit which has been entrusted to them. To the extent that the Christian revelation is misunderstood, it is partly at least the fault of Christians. It may be that non-Christians refuse to regard Christianity objectively. That is to be seen as early as the Gospels, in the part played by prejudices, intellectual arrogance and triviality of mind. But if non-Christians are to regard Christianity objectively, Christians must start by presenting it as it is.

\*     \*     \*

We have discussed the Christian conception of natural ethics. This very form of words indicates that Christianity makes no claim to do away with it. But what is the Christian idea of ethics as a whole, and what are the relations between natural and revealed ethics?

Christ is constantly referring to natural ethics as to a rule whose value he acknowledges. Respect for the life, property and reputation of others, respect for chastity, and the worship of God are values he does not question.

Christianity was later to exert an influence on natural ethics in two ways.

In the first place, on the intellectual plane, it clarified it.

163

The Catholic Church in particular asserts its mission to define the precepts of natural ethics, as natural truths which serve as a starting point for Revelation. And the historical influence of Christianity has worked towards a precise definition of natural ethics, such as was unknown previously. The labours that Catholic theologians have undertaken to specify the exigencies of natural ethics represent the most thorough inquiry that has ever been made in this field. Nothing comparable to the edifice of Catholic moral theology is to be found, either in the schools of philosophy, or in other religions.

Secondly, the Catholic tradition has applied itself to unifying natural ethics and Revelation.

In order to do this, it has distinguished the theological virtues from the moral virtues. The theological virtues are those whose direct object is God, and which derive, directly also, from Revelation. They are located on the plane of the absolute. From the point of view which we adopted earlier, the theological virtues express reduction to the One. There can be no excess in them. The more intense faith, hope and charity are, the better it will be. We can never believe too much, and we can never love too much. With these virtues, there is no question of a golden mean or of moderation. We must abandon ourselves to them completely.

The moral virtues are quite different. The name which has been given them is an ambiguous one, for the theological virtues are 'moral' to the highest degree; they might be said to represent the pinnacle of morality. But the term 'moral virtues' was borrowed by medieval authors from the Greeks, and particularly from Aristotle, by whom the moral virtues were contrasted with the intellectual virtues. The notion of intellectual virtue fell into the background; men spoke rather of 'intellectual qualities', and thenceforward moral virtue was contrasted to theological virtue.

In contrast to theological virtue, moral virtue is essentially a virtue of balance. Whereas the theological virtues unite a man directly with God, the moral virtues bear on human action in so far as it develops man harmoniously so as to make him capable of the theological virtues. The object of these virtues is thus man and not God. But while God is the absolute, man, for his part, is a composite, mixed and changing being,

164

and if his development is to be assured, all the exigencies of his nature must be taken into consideration. The moral virtues are thus characterized by balance and moderation; the rule of these virtues is 'neither too much nor too little'. Whether it is a question of temperance, which regulates the way in which a man treats his body, of justice, which regu- ates the way in which he treats his fellow-men, of fortitude or courage, which regulates efforts and impulses, or of pru- dence which prescribes the golden mean in everything, all these virtues make allowances for human diversity. In them we meet once more the ethics of the good man, but purified of its interested character, because it is linked with the theo- logical virtues, which cover it, as it were, with their wings and lay down the general sense of life.

All the same, this distinction between the theological and the moral virtues does not exhaust the question, for though excess in the theological virtues may be impossible, there may be ill-timed manifestations of them. Faith, hope and charity may manifest themselves at the wrong moment, or in a clumsy way. The manifestations of the theological virtues are human acts. They are thus subject to the laws of human action, and this occurs in space and in time, is tied up with other men in its social manifestations, and is obliged to take into account what these men are. It is easy to see what a delicate job the clarification of these notions is.

\*　　\*　　\*

Yet the activity of Christianity is not confined to this doctrinal work. On the contrary, it represents no more than a preparation, a working up of raw materials with a view to proceeding to action afterwards. The objective is to induce Christians to *live* in accordance with ethics; the aim is to trans- form moral life. Some people may adopt the easy way out of *saying* that Christianity purifies conduct, and accepting this *a priori* as something that should be so and that should not be called in question, without worrying their heads about what happens in reality. But historically too, in the reality of the centuries, the Church has never stopped seeking the true sanctification of Christians.

165

The task has constantly been thwarted by a thousand and one difficulties. But if we look at it down the centuries, we shall nowhere find such a continuous, general and systematic effort. If we want to remain objective, and if we stick to the facts as history depicts them, we shall be forced to agree that no school and no religion has shown an efficacy on the moral plane that can be compared with that of Christianity.

But this efficacy is not shown in the over-simple way that most people would like, that of a point-by-point correspondence between faith and ethics. Christianity works as Christ foretold it would, like a leaven. In Christian civilization, moral conceptions grow clearer and morals improve, generally speaking. Looked at in detail, morals improve, sometimes from one point of view, sometimes from another, with lapses, and no correspondence can be established between faith and morals in individual cases. That is easy to understand, for the outwardly visible results of grace depend on the character of the man who receives it. A man who possesses grace, but who has natural failings, a violent character, for example, may outwardly display less virtue than another who has a well-balanced character, but who has no faith. We cannot isolate the supernatural life like a chemical element and measure its effect. But when we observe the action of Christianity on the historical plane, we must admit that it is the most active instrument of moral improvement the human race has ever known.

To understand the nature of the relationship between natural and revealed ethics in Christianity, we must again note that we do not know exactly what Revelation has added to natural ethics. Christ does not make the distinction. Sometimes he says: 'You have heard that this was said . . . I tell you that', and seems to contrast his teaching with that which his audience already know; but he only does so incidentally. Moreover, all his teaching is incidental. Its direct object is the orientation of life; it is a wisdom morality, as we have seen above, not a collection of precepts, a code morality. And when we try and systematize Christ's ethics, it is impossible to determine exactly what is specifically supernatural.

We have already observed that if we look at life closely, the natural extends further than Christians generally believe;

166

but in Christianity many natural precepts take on a complexion which is peculiar to them. Thus we have seen that chastity as such is not much stressed in the ethics of the good man, such as it is found in most civilizations. In Christianity, on the contrary, it is extremely strongly stressed, in conjunction with marital fidelity and the sanctity of marriage; and no one could say what is specifically supernatural in this group of ideas, that is to say what could be prescribed leaving Revelation out of account. We can merely say that we are faced with a group of ideas linked with Revelation.

It is the same with the practice of charity. We find in every ethical theory a series of precepts which are related to it. They all say that we must do good to our fellow-men, that we must be kind-hearted and compassionate and that we must practise mutual aid. The theological doctrine of charity considered as a supernatural virtue is quite distinct from all this. But in practice, when it comes to exercising charity, it is hard to define just what the theological virtue adds to the natural virtues.

All this explains even better why in Christian societies men should be apt to practise the natural virtues without worrying much about what Christianity ought to add to them, and should even feel confident that these natural virtues become supernatural when they are practised by Christians. This is actually true from a certain point of view, since moral virtues transformed by grace become what theologians call infused virtues. But still it is not true that this transformation manifests itself automatically in the practice of these virtues.

It follows from all this that the practice of Christian ethics, as it is to be seen in history, puts the accent on natural ethics more than Christ did. Christian ethics more often than not looks like a purified natural ethics. In the preaching of Christ, the aspects of the break with the world are in the foreground. 'If any man has a mind to come my way, let him renounce self, and take up his cross' . . . But Christians later elaborated a two-tier ethics. The first was the obligatory ethics which applied to everyone and amounted to little more than a purified natural ethics. The practice of the theological virtues was restricted to certain limited activities, of a specifically religious character, and the aspects of breaking with the world put

167

forward by Christ became no more than an invitation, to which Christians were free to reply as they pleased. It is this that gives rise to the criticism we sometimes hear that the Christian's is a 'middle-class' morality. All the same, the aspiration to an ethics of absolute self-devotion still survives. A certain number of Christians dedicate their lives to it and are held up as an example.

But the fact that Christian ethics as a whole, as it is generally propounded, is first of all natural ethics also explains why non-Christians are willing to listen to it, and can adhere to it without acknowledging Christ as the Saviour. It explains too how such non-Christians sometimes attain to a moral perfection which most Christians do not reach, and that certain of them can get the impression that Christianity is not necessary for the achievement of moral perfection, even for the contemplative life or the sacrifice of a man's self to his neighbour. Hence again the desire manifested by active Christians nowadays to emphasize what is specifically Christian.

All this does not prevent Christianity from being a leaven in the world, nor does it mean that the non-Christian who achieves genuine moral perfection without believing in the Christian faith has not come under the influence of Christianity, indirectly perhaps, but none the less really. It does not mean either that this non-Christian might not attain an even more harmonious perfection if he were a Christian. All this is full of nuances, and it is easy to lapse into oversimplification. It is none the less true that there are many bad Christians, and that a non-Christian who hungers for perfection can, thanks to Christianity, find a purified doctrine of natural ethics which was unknown before.

Thus the development of historical studies which is characteristic of our times, together with the comparison of Christian with other teachings, allows us and also obliges us to define the scope of the Christian revelation. In the old days, Christian authors used to cite the pagan wise men of antiquity, Aristotle, Cicero or Seneca, without hesitation, and did not bother to mark what Christ's revelation had added to or modified in their teachings. Right up to our own times, many Christian authors have treated the Sermon on the Mount as the essential document of Christ's teaching, though no Gospel text contains more maxims which are common to the wise men of every nation. The sermon after the Last Supper in St John is more characteristic, but much less known. Many authors go so far as to treat the Ten Commandments as the fundamental expression of Christian ethics. Whereas the Ten Commandments are not even Christian, but serve as a preamble to the Jewish Law and express the fundamental ideas of natural law, and their popularity happens to derive from the fact that they correspond to what men say everywhere. All this, coming from Christian authors, shows how hazy the notion of Christian ethics is. If we in our age succeed in clarifying it, we shall have taken a big step forward, not only in the understanding of Christian doctrine, but in moral thought in general.

## 3.  *Ethical theories of honour*

The next forms of social ethics after the ethics of the good man are the theories of honour, which are situated on a lower plane, where the dependence of ethics on morals is more clearly apparent.

They are class moralities. In every social group, certain attitudes are vital if life in the group is to be possible or easy. Consequently these attitudes inspire moral rules which are regarded as fundamental. They express themselves through a conception of honour which often plays havoc with the rules of theoretical ethics.

Thus in military circles, the most essential virtue is physical courage. The soldier will therefore be dishonoured if he is a coward, not if he is a debauchee or a thief. In business circles, on the other hand, respect for an agreement entered into in the circumstances necessary for the exercise of the calling, respect for an agreement or for a signature, is the indispensable condition of life in common. The business man will therefore be dishonoured if he does not 'honour' his signature; he will not be if he lacks physical courage.

And these ethical ideas are unequivocally class moralities; they often impose obligations towards those who form part of the class concerned, not towards outsiders. The gentleman, for example, is bound to respect his word if he has given it to another gentleman, not—in the old days, at any rate—if he has given it to someone of a lower class. And it matters little what theoretical ethics or the law have to say: a gambling debt is sacred if a gentleman has incurred it to someone of the same station; on the other hand, there is nothing sacred about a business debt. In reality, if gambling debts have acquired this sacred character, it is because we are dealing with a social class in which gambling plays an important part, which would not be possible unless paramount importance were attached to debts incurred in the course of it.

This ethics of honour can thus be explained by an instinct for collective defence. Life in the particular class would not be possible if these rules were not observed. We find this in every class. Stockbrokers, for instance, scrupulously respect their plighted word among themselves, and will honour obligations running into thousands on the basis of a mere couple of words, with nothing in writing, whereas they are by no means so scrupulous where their clients are concerned. There is a class morality even among prostitutes and robbers. The latter will respect justice when it comes to sharing out the swag, or respect promises they make among themselves, because life would be impossible otherwise.

It is not hard to see the origin of these ethical ideas. They focus ethics on the attitudes necessary to the life of the class. They tally with what Marxists say of ethics, but the Marxists are wrong when they think that there is no other kind. Ethical theories of honour are second class theories, and though they may serve as an instrument of defence for certain circles, they often run counter to true ethics.

Indeed, in complicated situations, they concentrate all their attention on an aspect which is not always the principal one: for example, physical courage, discounting any question of brutality or injustice. Again, they focus on certain manifestations of virility, or acts which are regarded in this way, such as getting drunk or indulging in physical love, assuming that this manifestation of virility is the sign of a virility which extends to the whole of life. They pay no attention to the disadvantages which these manifestations of virility involve. Now the immorality of such behaviour is not due to the fact that it is a sign of virility, but to other more important factors. Theories of honour pay attention only to one aspect of behaviour, secondary in itself, but important in the given class or group because of the customs that obtain there. In the cases we have just cited, the accent is on virility, with no question raised as to whether there are not other ways of demonstrating it, which might be more effective and better co-ordinated with the development of man.

We have just cited some particularly coarse examples of an ethics of honour in order to bring out its character as strikingly as possible. But such ethical ideas are to be found everywhere, because they are due to the exigencies of social life, and men all live in society. Every social group attributes primary importance to what life in common within it demands: thus there come into existence a gentlemanly morality, and medical, legal, commercial, working-class and farmers' moralities. We have seen above that the ethical teacher or the wise man is essentially a non-conformist. He is therefore always inclined to disregard or to despise the ethics of his own group. He is then looked on as lacking a sense of honour; he is looked down on in his circle, and if he goes too far, he is barred from it. In our Western society, officers and gentlemen could formerly be barred from their own class because they refused to fight a duel.

Based as they are on a social defence reflex, these theories are as often as not incoherent. It is no use seeking for unity in them, for that comes from the intelligence, and they are pure products of collective instinct. When they reach a certain intensity, they become clan moralities, moralities of a group shut in on itself, and are only obligatory towards members of the group. This will be found in every self-contained group. The nearer the group comes to being self-contained, the more demanding become the rules of life peculiar to it. To understand that, we can look back at the example cited above of the gang of robbers.

4. *The confusion between morals and ethics*

We are coming now to the lowest level of social ethics. In most human communities men consider that good consists in what is done. When something is done by everyone it must be good. If something is never done by anyone, it cannot be a duty. What everyone disapproves of must be wrong. If an

171

ethical thinker teaches that something which everybody does is wrong, he meets with an unanswerable retort: 'But everybody does that', and the matter is settled. Or if he declares an act to be a duty and is told: 'But nobody does it', the matter is settled just as decisively. In other words, practice is the touchstone of the rule, and not the rule of practice.

It is thus that in some circles, everybody defrauds the tax-collector; in others it is an accepted thing that young people behave dissolutely, or that in schools the pupils all lie to their masters. If somebody concerned with moral value expresses his disapproval, or says he means to behave differently, people laugh at him, call him simple-minded and soft, and even try to 'teach him a thing or two', and consider they are doing him a good turn by doing so. Or if they do not venture to contradict the moralist, they say that is all very well 'in theory' but it is not 'practical'. For most people, the moral rule is a 'theoretical' rule, and they mean by this that it has no relation to reality, or that they do not see how to translate it into facts. They will say: 'That's all very fine; maybe it's true; but if you come down to hard tacks, people just can't live like that'. The reason being that for most people, it is impossible to live any differently from the way those around them live. If we want to know whether the moral rule is being applied, and how, and how far, we must look at what is being done.

This tendency to confuse ethics with morals is so strong that most men seem to find it impossible to rise to the conception of a moral rule inspired by the exigencies of human development, and to work out rules for its application which will allow them to pass judgment on what is done in their circle. Hence the importance of providing an environment where the moral rule shall be applied and the necessity for those who are concerned with moral development to take care of the moulding of such an environment.

Here once more, the Catholic Church provides an unrivalled field of experience, because no other community has such an unambiguous code of ethics. Yet even the Catholic clergy, for all that they are charged with teaching ethics and supervising its application, have a tendency to mould their judgment to suit the practice of their environment. Thus there are Catholic schools where the pupils habitually tell lies and

cheat in their school work, and where a tolerance born of the
general practice creeps in; the masters end up by saying:
'That's not lying, it's pulling a fast one'. In frontier villages
with a population of smugglers, the parish priest ends up by
ceasing to protest, and it is the same with regard to poachers
in the country, or forms of fraud or theft which are habitual
in certain circles. And if a theoretician recalls the rule, he is
told: 'If we make a sin of that, everyone will be a sinner'. It is
impossible to count what everybody does a sin.

In the Catholic Church, this attitude does not apply to
chastity. On this point, the Church has never ceased to assert
the moral rule against all comers; with little success, it must
be added. The Church's efforts have not prevented the
Christian world from showing an indulgence towards licenti-
ous living that contrasts with the Christian rule; an indulgence
which is expressed in the opinion that though the Church
may be right 'in principle', chastity such as it calls for is too
difficult to be demanded of the masses. We could paint an
extremely varied picture of the forms of sexual licence which
have been allowed in circles that are in other respects
Christian. And here the contrast is clearcut, because the
Church has always unflinchingly upheld its teaching. But its
case stands alone: outside the Christian world, the confusion
between ethics and morals comes up again in matters of sex
and in other fields. All that is necessary to realize this is to
look at the forms of adultery and polygamy allowed in other
communities.

But when it comes to values other than sexual values,
Catholic teachers themselves show an inclination to allow
for the customs of the environment and not to put too heavy
a load on men's consciences. When something seems very
difficult, the moral teacher will hesitate before declaring it
obligatory; and yet this difficulty often has a social origin. It
is difficult to tell the truth in a circle where everybody tells
lies. If that were made a sin, everybody would be a sinner.
Moral teachers are merciful; they hesitate to put Christians
in a position where sin becomes inevitable.

This attitude results from a confusion of levels, but its fre-
quency, we might even say its universality, not only among
the unreflecting masses, but among professional moral

173

teachers, shows how hard it is for a man to distinguish between these levels.

Nevertheless, the confusion of levels is obvious. A first question arises over the objective or intrinsic value of an act or of the exigencies of nature. Another question, which comes up on quite a different level, is that of the grounds for excuse the sinner may have. If a sin is very common, it is possible that a given individual may not be a sinner, because it is not subjectively possible for him to resist the influence of his environment. It is possible that, for lack of intellectual training, he may not even be capable of seeing that the act is a sin, but that makes no difference to the act's intrinsic value. Theft does not stop being theft because I live in a world of thieves, any more than adultery stops being a sin if everybody around me indulges in it. The distinction between the two levels is clearcut, but human experience shows that men who are capable of thinking about principles on the level of principles, without letting practical considerations come in, are extremely rare.

\*    \*    \*

Confusion between ethics and morals results in putting an end to any moral endeavour. If ethics only tells us to act like everyone else, mediocrity becomes the rule. The idea of sacrifice for the sake of good will not even enter peoples' heads. This attitude is to be found more or less in any social environment where the masses have no other rule than 'what is done'. We have seen earlier that the moral teacher is essentially a nonconformist. Confusion of ethics with morals is, in a way, the end of ethics.

5.  *Salvation rites*

Social ethics are facile, for on one hand they avoid demanding from men more than they are willing to give, and on the other they appeal to self-interest. All the same, they do not satisfy men; this again is a matter of experience recorded by history. The first of the forms we saw yields only a very limited happiness; the second and the third merely provide excuses, but assure no sort of development. None of them prevents men being unhappy, and there are many unhappy

174

people in the world. What is more, men are afraid of death. They know their days are numbered. In so far as the idea of moral good emerges obscurely in their consciousness, they realize that they have not attained to it and that they are incapable of achieving it. They have attained neither to good nor to happiness, but it is principally the idea of happiness that acts on their minds. Hence the aspiration to salvation in another world, which shall be obtained otherwise than through virtue.

In response to this aspiration, doctrines and practices have sprung up almost everywhere, which are more often than not known under the name of mystery religions or salvation rites.

We know a good deal about the Greek mysteries, of which the most celebrated were those of Demeter at Eleusis. Their object was to enable men to link themselves with the goddess through a certain number of rites which plunged the initiate into a sort of trance or rapture and also guaranteed him an eternity of happiness.

Under the Empire, a certain number of eastern mysteries spread through the Roman world, those of Isis, Serapis and Mithras, which had much the same characteristics and the same end. The most moving of these salvation religions is undoubtedly *Amidism*, a refined form of popular Buddhism.

We know that in the course of the centuries, Buddhism gave birth to a series of popular creeds, in which the Buddha becomes a God who is prayed to. Amidism, which is more or less contemporary with Christianity, is the religion of Amitabha, or Amida. He is a god of mercy, who has infinite merits and has promised to apply them to any sinner who calls on him. This is salvation as it was to be found later in certain aberrant forms of Christianity.

Amidism thus promises paradise to its devotees, and gives lengthy descriptions of the Pure Land, where Amida admits his faithful after their death. There is a striking similarity with the descriptions of paradise in popular Christian literature. The *bodhisattva* who surround Amida are like the angels and saints of Christianity, and among them is a goddess of mercy, Avalokiteshvara, who answers the prayers of mothers and

175

saves children. For a man to be saved, it is enough for him to hate his sins and to have faith in Amida.

We know very little of the origins of Amidism, and we do not know how it became grafted onto Buddhism. Certain authors believe Amida to be of Iranian origin, and see in him 'the Buddhist transposition of some "luminous" spirit of the Persian pantheon'. That would be interesting, for Iran was the meeting-point of all the ancient eastern and western religions. In certain traditions again, Amitabha is the word of Sakyamuni, the founder of Buddhism; in others, he becomes incarnate under the name of Sakyamuni. But the point of interest lies elsewhere: the universality of these salvation religions and their similarities show that they answer to a profound human need.

Again, magic partly works in the same sense. In the Hellenic world once more, gnosis gives an intellectual form to what the salvation rites bring in sensible form. Gnosis sought to unveil the secret of salvation, and it played a big role at the end of antiquity. All this forms a very confused trend, but it is very important for an understanding of the popular conscience. And all this is found again in Christianity, not in the thinking of Christ, nor in the authentically Christian development, but in the aberrant forms of Christianity.

Christ's teaching runs clean counter to these salvation doctrines and rites, because Christ links salvation with virtue, and no doctrine has gone so far in linking the worship of God with morality. The only way of pleasing God is to practise virtue. It only needs a glass of water given to one of these little ones, but it is the charity that counts. Christ only talks of rites and set phrases to express his scorn of them. It is not he who says: 'Lord, Lord ...' who will enter into the Kingdom.

All the same, Christianity is also a salvation religion. In one way Christ is indeed first and foremost the Saviour, and he too teaches that we cannot save ourselves by our own efforts; salvation, and the grace that leads us to it, are free gifts of God. But we do not obtain this free gift through rites and set phrases; we get it through the free gift of ourselves, in faith and charity. This gives Christianity a richness of content quite different from the pagan salvation rites, and it is

176

easy to see why it supplanted the other salvation religions wherever it found them.

But Christianity suffered from many aberrations in the course of the centuries, because historical Christianity results from Christ's impact on men, and expresses the way in which men season the teaching of Christ. I have already spoken of certain deviations. We can find manifestations of them in the cult of the Blessed Virgin in the Middle Ages. Christian people were then very uncultured. To spread the cult of the blessed Virgin, an attempt was made to inspire absolute confidence in her. It was explained that, however disorderly a man's life was, if he retained a minimum of devotion to the Blessed Virgin she would intervene to protect her servant at the hour of his death.

This conception can be interpreted in two ways. The first is that a minimum of devotion to the Blessed Virgin is followed by a protection on her part which guarantees that a man will end his days by repenting of his sins. The other is that the protection of the Blessed Virgin relieves a man from the necessity of repenting, and that she will save whoever has paid her homage, no matter what his sins or the hardness of his heart. This second interpretation is at odds with Christian thinking, but all the same it comes out in certain medieval stories. It is a relation of the salvation rites, but it is a pure aberration from the Christian point of view. Moreover, we no longer find it in the Marian devotion of our times, as this is expressed, for example, in the great centres of pilgrimage, Lourdes and Fatima.

Later, the notion of the salvation rite came up in more than one form of Christianity outside the Catholic Church, for instance in the Lutheran doctrine of salvation by faith.

Christ's doctrine on this point is a finely shaded one, and the Church has produced a series of definitions in the course of the centuries in order to preserve the balance of his tradition. Man cannot save himself by his own efforts; grace is a free gift which man cannot merit in the strict sense. God gives it to whom he will, but man can nevertheless draw down the divine good-will by doing what he can. He prepares himself for grace; he responds to grace; grace is constantly associated with works, though it is not possible to determine exactly what this relationship is.

177

Luther reacted against the Catholic tradition; moreover he was temperamentally violent and liked extreme expressions. He declared that, according to St Paul's teaching, man is saved by faith alone, that works are without importance and are irrelevant to salvation and that sin therefore does not matter, since faith alone leads to salvation. Hence such violent expressions as the *Pecca fortiter; crede fortius,* which recall the salvation rites. Later, Luther and his disciples produced a series of explanatory propositions, and Lutheranism evolved. But the fundamental idea that salvation does not depend on works was an influence in favour of seeking God's approval in other ways than doing good.

Aberrations of the same kind are to be found in Russian Orthodoxy. Certain sects place the whole accent of the Christian life on contrition. The man who pleases God is not the man who practises the loftiest virtues, it is he who repents most wholeheartedly. Now sinning violently may lead to deeper contrition. We should thus distrust the man who has not sinned ... These sects draw their followers from a rather uncultured public. We find members of them who have devoted all their lives to God and who indulge in uproarious sins with a sort of ostentation which is followed by a contrition just as uproarious.

These conceptions are no more than deviations from Christianity, but they show that the salvation rites correspond to a deep-lying human trend, and that this trend comes to life as soon as men stray away from a pure idea of morality. Their persistence in Christianity could be interpreted as showing that it has failed; but we should note that the salvation rites come to the surface in Christianity only when it becomes corrupted. Social ethics, on the other hand, do not satisfy the mind, and there the salvation rites occur as the result, not of a deviation, but of a gap. This brings us to the wise men's ethics, which raises the moral problem in all its purity.

## II.  THE WISE MEN'S ETHICS AS AGAINST SOCIAL ETHICS

The moral ideas which develop spontaneously in any social environment stress the things which concern relations between men, respect for others, men's outward attitude and so forth. Now we have seen that the wise men's ethics works the other way round. The wise man is a non-conformist. His rule of action is within himself.

Most wise men are intellectual aristocrats, who despise the masses and keep away from them. Almost all of them express this contempt. 'Every time I have mixed with men, I have come back from it less of a man', says the author of the *Imitation of Christ*, taking over a text of Seneca's : 'When I mix with men, I come back from it less human.' The Chinese wise man Vighna says in the *Ka-kiu-king*, in the third century B.C. : 'Since the ignorant crowd of mortals cannot attain salvation as a body, the wise man holds aloof from them and follows his own path, as happy as the elephant from the herd who has recovered his freedom.' We could find any number of similar texts.

The wise man generally shows his contempt by living as he pleases, without worrying about what people say. The ordinary man is extremely concerned to follow normal practice, because he wants to be well thought of in his circle. The wise man is a law to himself. The common herd regards him as a madman or a superman : a madman because he does nothing like other people and responds to motives which they do not understand, and a superman because they realize that he is above the things which interest the masses, is not excited by what excites his fellow-men and does not share the absolute judgments of the man in the street. He may also shock people and stir the authorities to action. More often than not, he is surrounded by a group of admiring disciples, while the man in the street regards him as an eccentric. In Plato's *Symposium,* his disciples' admiration for Socrates leaps to the eye in the portrait of him which Alcibiades paints at the end of the dialogue. That did not stop him from being condemned to death in the end, because the authorities regarded him as a bit too much of a non-conformist.

Thus the almost universal trend of moral thinking tends towards a wise man who is detached from men, an anti-social wise man, in short. The wise man's life is first and foremost an inner life.

179

## 1. *The three types of wisdom*

Before dealing with the wise man's relationships with society, I should like to describe the different types of wise men. It seems to me that there are three: the saint, the hero and the ascetic. This is what I mean.

The aspiration to sanctity results from a man's discovery of the One and his desire to lose himself in it. The saint is the man who succeeds in this to such an extent that people who look at him from the outside can gain the impression that he has achieved this end. Asceticism, mastery of the self and outward good works are all nothing but means to achieve union or the expression of union. The saint thus renounces everything, but this is in order to possess Him who is worth more than anything. God alone has value; the rest is only smoke, as the Bible says, or appearance, as Hindu wisdom puts it. No man can have two masters, says Jesus. He has to choose between God and the world; one rules out the other.

The type of the saint is predominant in Christianity. It is also to be found in India and in Neo-Platonism, and even among the Moslems. In Christian literature, the saint is the *man of God*. The pure type is to be found in St Benedict, for example, or before him in the Desert Fathers. Among the Moslems, the saint is the *sufi* or the *marabou;* in India he is known under different names according to the sects. In any case, everywhere and always he is the man whose life is concentrated on God.

Tagore writes:

> That I want thee, only thee—let my heart repeat without end. All desires that distract me, day and night, are false and empty to the core.
>
> As the night keeps hidden in its gloom the petition for light, even thus in the depth of my unconsciousness rings the cry—I want thee, only thee.
>
> As the storm still seeks its end in peace when it strikes against peace with all its might, even thus my rebellion strikes against thy love and still its cry is—I want thee, only thee.

Next the hero.

The ethics of the hero is the ethics of those who do not see outside man the One to whom they can give themselves. Man must thus achieve an absolute within himself. Kipling's poem

180

*If* puts this formula of the hero into words. The hero bears witness to human nobility, and the essence of this nobility is that the mind towers above every event. Man is not the master of events; he lives in a world that is not within his control. What is within his control is his mind and his will. The hero is always master of himself.

Greek literature is permeated with the ethical ideal of the hero. The hero is the expression of human nobility. He is social because he lives in the midst of comrades, like the Homeric heroes or those of the Greek tragedies, and one element of human nobility consists in a man being looked up to by his circle. In the Greek tragedies, the chorus, one of whose principal tasks is to sing the praises of the hero, is also one of the essential components of the work as a whole. The perennial value of Greek literature undoubtedly lies in the fact that no other body of writings has brought out to such a degree the human value attained in its pure state by the hero.

Nevertheless, the hero sometimes seems different from the wise man, because he has a more popular character. Achilles could not be called a wise man. The hero is the product of the instinct for the absolute in man, but those who are portrayed in literature only approximate to the type, though they bring it to life and thus lend it prestige. In *If*, Kipling provides an absolute description of the hero, and we have seen that it produces a pure form of what I have called the 'moral shock'.

In antiquity, the Stoics tried to find a metaphysical expression for it, that is to say to link the notion of the hero to a system. In our times, it comes up on every side, particularly in Existentialist philosophy, because this claims to have brought out a conception of life which is spontaneously revealed without any systematic reflection. Nietzsche had earlier tried to provide in his superman a type of the hero borrowed from the Greek. But he failed because his romanticism impelled him to frenzy, whereas the hero is characterized by the composure with which he regards life. It was through this composure that he became the master of circumstances, and composure was the one thing Nietzsche lacked.

The Stoics, on the other hand, regarded composure as the

supreme virtue. They called it *apatheia*. The wise man was the man who never lost his head.

The type of the perfect hero may be the man who never loses his head and keeps his temper in every storm, but it should be added that this hero is not to be met with, any more than the perfect saint. The saint who gives the impression of being completely absorbed in God has personally the impression of being far away from him. The type of the Greek hero is Heracles, who is a legendary character. Another type is Achilles, who is depicted as being subject to emotional disturbances. Furthermore, later on the Stoics, after working out the theory of *apatheia*, declared that nobody attained to it perfectly. It was an ideal to be pursued, but man never attains to it. He attains to it to a greater or less degree, and that is why we must define the ideal and work towards it, but we must be under no illusions either.

The hero therefore pursues as an absolute the assertion of human nobility, and he gives the 'moral shock' in its pure state, because moral value in him is to be seen in itself, without mixture with or dependence on other values. In the saint, it is not self-realization that predominates, but God. So humility is not one of the hero's virtues.

All the same, the hero does not necessarily deny God. He is not interested in metaphysics, but people uninterested in metaphysics accept current ideas, and these take account of God without making him a touchstone for conduct. I spoke earlier of the popular religions. On the metaphysical or religious plane, the attitude of the hero is the usual attitude of his own society. Atheism assumes an active interest in metaphysics.

The Greek hero's attitude to the gods is thus that of the man in the street, with his surges of rebellion when the gods impose a fate which seems to him unjust. This represents a fundamental contrast with those whom I earlier called the 'tormented' philosophers of our day, who are active atheists and who at the same time as they declare their atheism try to put forward a theory of the autonomy of man. Since they acknowledge no subordination, they want to make man the creator of the moral rule and, with that in view, to make him independent of the cosmic order. But as man is a subordinate being, they can only end up in failure.

Not only do they end up in failure on the level of facts, but they are forced to acknowledge it on the level of theory. This last phenomenon is symptomatic, for theory seems to be able to stand up to a lot, as long as it is not applied. Now Nietzsche already in *Beyond Good and Evil* ended by saying: 'The corruption, the hounding to the abyss of superior men, of souls of an unusual kind, is the rule.' They reach 'a complete inner despair. . . . This martyrdom may one day result in the superior man turning bitterly against his own destiny and trying to destroy himself . . . to kill himself'.

All the same, the aspiration to the autonomy it has asserted still survives today in the atheistic school of Existentialism. As we noted above, it must always fail, but the attempt is constantly being renewed. This attitude is due to trends of thinking alien to ethics, and it will not last for ever, but it has lasted for nearly a century now. 'God is dead,' said Nietzsche, a statement which reveals a concern over metaphysics. Men have been repeating it since then in a hundred different ways; and there are some who take pleasure in likening them to the savage who finds the arrow he has shot at the heavens falling back on his own face.

The tradition of the old-time hero with his rather tough serenity reappears in our times in minds with no metaphysics. We saw that in Kipling's *If* there was no allusion to the next world, but there was no denial of it either. The writer's attention was simply fixed on life in this world, and this attitude corresponds to the state of mind of the masses.

The hero is thus essentially centred on himself. That is what gives him a touch of toughness, even if he is kind. If he is kind, it is in order to assert his nobility, for none of his attitudes is alien to nobility. In this he contrasts with the saint, who is absorbed in the One, who disappears and might be said to think of nothing but forgetting himself. The hero does not even think of thinking of anything but himself. . . . He may renounce many good things, devote himself to difficult tasks, and choose a tough life, but it is merely in order to prove his value to himself. That is just as true of the Stoic philosophers as it is of the heroes of Greek tragedy, Nietzsche's superman and the hero of Kipling.

\* \* \*

Now we come to the third type of wise man, the ascetic. The pure ascetic is a product of a pessimistic ethics. If happiness is unattainable, the only thing for the wise man is to withdraw into a sort of renunciation which is neither a search for God, nor even a search to assert himself, but a simple flight from sorrow. Pessimistic ethics is also negative.

India is the favourite home of such negative ethics. Primitive Buddhism is probably their most perfect expression, because Buddhism is gentle. It does not seek to extinguish desire by violent methods, but by a discipline of the senses and the mind which progressively empties a man of all desires, just as much the desire for knowledge as the desire for material goods or social success.

The active temperament of the Western peoples has prevented negative moralities from spreading in the West as they have in the East. Nevertheless, Epicurus tended in this direction. His ethics was a doctrine of disenchantment. He sought for happiness, and happiness for him lay in pleasure; now pleasure consists first and foremost in the absence of trouble, and trouble can be identified with perturbation. The Epicurean happiness is this *ataraxia*, or the absence of trouble, and the fundamental virtue is prudence, which wards off risks and excesses, for trouble comes from excesses and risks. Epicurus's attention is thus focused on the suffering of failure, not the joy of success. He turns men away from everything they regard as noble, for there is no nobility without trouble. He is at the opposite pole from the hero.

Epicurus pushed pessimism and negative ethics as far as a Greek could. It is in China, as I see it, that this negative ethics is best systematized, in the doctrine of Lao-tse. The teaching of Epicurus is a middle-class Taoism.

It is true that Lao-tse will not admit he is a pessimist. His is a smiling detachment, but his ethics is a real ethics of emptiness. It may not necessarily involve an ascecis characterized by the usual forms of physical and social renunciation, but it

184

goes as far as is possible in its indifference to every human value. Yet this detachment is not the counterpart of an attachment to anything at all.

## 2. *The wise men's ethics and altruism*

I am using the word 'altruism' this time in preference to the word 'social' to indicate relations between individuals, no matter whether they depend on a social organization or not. But the word 'altruism' also is full of ambiguities.

Altruism exists, in the most general sense, as soon as a man takes others into account. But in contemporary parlance, altruism also implies assistance given to others. Now we can take others into account simply by respecting them. We must thus distinguish two degrees in altruism, respect-altruism and assistance-altruism. Respect-altruism is negative; it confines itself to forbidding a man to treat another as an instrument. Assistance-altruism is positive : it implies activity in the service of others.

Respect-altruism may be a duty without assistance-altruism being so. But in addition, altruism raises a third question, that of knowing whether others constitute an element in my personal development, to what degree and how. This last question I shall examine in the next chapter, which is devoted to personal morality.

For the moment, following the method which has inspired us up to now, we should begin by noting that there is no ethics that does not take others into account. We have already observed the peculiar spirit of apostleship common to all wise men. They try to spread their ideas and to form a school. Then again, we have seen the prominence of kindness and justice in social ethics. This forms part of every social ethics and wise men more or less integrate it into their system.

All of them consider at least that we should respect our fellowmen. Nietzsche, who believes in an ethics of masters and slaves, calls on the masters to respect each other. They should be honest and kind to their equals, and they should practise mutual aid. It is the same with the ethics of the good man, wherever we come across it, and with the hero-ethics. Even Lao-tse regards it as obligatory.

Lao-tse enjoins men to return good for evil. This, as we have seen, is an element common to almost all ethical theories, or to be more accurate, this notion crops up everywhere, even though there are often other contradictory elements there as well. Lao-tse teaches that we must practise disinterested kindness, because other men share like us in the *Tao*, and that in a certain sense, to lose ourselves in the *Tao* is also to lose ourselves in humanity, or to lose ourselves in humanity is to lose ourselves in the *Tao*. We find much the same idea in Epictetus, and generally speaking it is more or less discernible in every doctrine in which there is a pantheist element. I say 'a pantheist element', because pantheism is more of a trend than a doctrine, and is nowhere to be met with in a pure state. Regarded in itself it is, moreover, a doctrine which it is impossible to formulate. We find in these doctrines as it were a prefiguration or a rough draft of the Christian doctrine of the divine life which is diffused among all the faithful and is the source of a community that goes deeper than any human community. Since Christianity was preached, moreover, no new prescriptions for the unity of men in God have been put forward.

\*    \*    \*

Let us now run through some descriptions of altruism.

First of all, altruism is depicted as resulting from human sociability. This is the most widespread explanation.

We know the importance of friendship in the Greek conception of life. Aristotle makes it something like the supreme good. He devotes two books of the *Nicomachaean Ethics* to it, books eight and nine, while book ten concludes the work with a portrait of the wise man who lives through his mind, like the gods. In Aristotle's view, the perfect friendship is not that of young people, which is founded on pleasure, nor that of old men, which is founded on interest: perfect friendship is founded on virtue. The friend finds such happiness in the good of his friend that he is ready to sacrifice his own to make him happy.

Epicurus, again, finds the supreme happiness in friendship, which is all the more interesting because friendship seems to have no place in the logic of his system. But then Epicurus seems to have had a particularly attractive personality. He lived surrounded by disciples who worshipped him.

Throughout history we meet with the idea that a man can only be happy if he is surrounded by friends. In the eighteenth century, Adam Smith built a system on it in his *Theory of Moral Sentiments*. For him, man's first need is to be loved. He therefore needs to live among other men and to enjoy their sympathy. Good is merely what makes a man sympathetic.

In short, the whole moral experience of the human race seems to show that it is good for man to concern himself with others. On the one hand, he is loved for it, but on the other, he himself needs to love and to do good.

The Thomist tradition took over from Aristotle the metaphysical notion that the good tends to spread: *bonum est diffusivum sui*. And Nietzsche, talking of his superman, who lives only for himself, declared: 'In the foreground (of his consciousness) is the sentiment of plenitude, of power that has to overflow, the happiness of high tension, the consciousness of a richness that has to give and spread. The noble man, too, comes to the aid of the unhappy, not out of compassion, or barely so, but rather out of an impulse that comes from the superabundance of strength.' (*Beyond Good and Evil*).

In all these theories, altruism is always traced back to the self. Hobbes gave a more systematic expression to this than some others, when he reduced altruism to egoism in a way which some people find cynical, though it is at least frank. For him, altruism derives from the need for domination: when we do good to somebody, we feel superior to him. Psychologically, there is a good deal of truth in this. Altruism does often correspond to thoughts of this kind: to give flatters the pride, to receive humiliates. But that is not the question. The question is whether altruism *ought* to be practised for these reasons; whether altruism deriving from over-flowing vitality, from the desire for domination or from the pleasure of asserting our superiority is a *moral* value. Ostensible explanations of altruism as a source of sociability are psychological analyses but shed no light on the moral question.

This is equally true of the phenomenological analyses of the present century, which show that man is not self-sufficient from any point of view, but needs others, just as much to attain knowledge as to attain moral development. These analyses stress the idea that man knows himself only as a one-in-a-whole and cannot realize himself except in communion with others. But it is still a question of *self*-realization, a question of the self. It cannot be a question of others *qua* others.

*　*　*

We now come to altruism born of detachment, which is less widespread but more important from the moral standpoint.

In this view, altruism is a means to and also a sign of detachment and self-mastery. It is therefore strongly emphasized in primitive Buddhism and in Taoism. From one point of view, it is still centred on the self, though it contains a completely pure element of genuine altruism. I say 'a pure element', because it is real altruism, but is only an incomplete element of it.

When Jesus says: 'If a man strikes thee on the cheek, offer him the other cheek too,' he is obviously thinking of detachment rather than charity. But the phrase should not be taken on its own, and all the teaching of Jesus is dominated by charity and unified in it. When altruism out of detachment is isolated, what it yields is a wise man holding himself aloof from the mob, mixing with friends as refined as himself, kind to the obscure, the weak and the unhappy people he meets, even letting men take advantage of him, quick to show compassion when confronted with the destitute, but in no sense devoting his life to sacrificing himself for others. On this level, the Sister of Charity is inconceivable.

This altruism of detachment may not be Christian charity, but we should note all the same that most Christians are aware of no other, except for the altruism of egoism which we have just discussed.

*　*　*

Thirdly, there comes religious altruism, which we have seen in Lao-tse and Epictetus and which Christianity has systematized more perfectly than has any other doctrine. Men are all my fellow-beings, creatures of God, brothers in Christ, called

188

to the same glory, and we should love all men because God loves them and because we ourselves are associated in the divine love through the supernatural life. This love of men thus proceeds in the last resort from the love of God. It is associated with it and it cannot be divorced from it.

\* \* \*

All the forms of altruism we have just examined are individual. They are addressed to the individual as such and are expressed between individuals. But social altruism too plays a considerable role in theory and in practice.

Social altruism bears on the community of which we form part, particularly on the 'city' or the country. It bears on individuals in so far as they are fellow-citizens, but its direct and principal object is the community.

It is in Greek thinking that this conception bulks largest: the Greek thinking of the great Classical age was dominated by it. It was the century of democracy; the Greek city-states were communities of citizens. Later on, the philosophers of the Roman Empire focused their thinking in a quite different direction, because they were living in a world in which the citizen was not called on to concern himself with public affairs.

But for Plato and Aristotle, the fundamental objective of thinking was the organization of the city. For Aristotle, good citizenship was fundamentally the same thing as friendship, but was the highest form of it. It was the final end of all morality, and Aristotle coined phrases which became household words: the whole is nobler than the part, the part is for the whole, the citizen is to the city what the arm is to the body, society is more divine than the individual.

These ideas were revived in the Middle Ages. St Thomas, among others, reproduces them without discussion, and his remarks were then in their turn taken over by his commentators. Starting with the twentieth century, thinkers of the sociological trend set the primacy of the community against liberal individualism. Under one formula or another, these thinkers depicted society as the supreme manifestation of what is human. The individual must thus devote himself

189

completely to the social good, for this is his own supreme good. Man only finds his supreme good by losing himself in the community, in so far as he can be regarded as something distinct from it.

The most complete systematization of this doctrine today is to be found in Communism. But we meet it almost everywhere in more or less clear forms, and it has always been present in patriotic theories. I have tried to clarify these ideas in other works, and I shall confine myself here to recalling a few fundamental ideas.

Man is naturally attached to his environment, because it forms part of himself. For that matter, he is attached to the landscapes and the house that are tied up with his life, as well as to people. This is a mere psychological fact which has no moral bearing. Man is also attached to his people, as to every group which gives him the impression of increasing his stature. Everyone feels that his country is superior to others and is proud to belong to it. Does any duty result from this? Yes, to the extent to which membership of a group forms part of the conditions through which a man fulfils his mission as a man. The duty of attachment to our country and to all the groups in which we may find ourselves is one of the expressions of man's duty to achieve his task in the conditions in which destiny has placed him. It comes down in the end to the duty of accepting himself, with the body, intelligence and all the qualities and failings with which nature has endowed him. It is a duty of acceptance, which is a logical one if we believe in a Creator, but impossible to justify logically without God. Without the idea of God, it ends either in the rebellion of the atheistic Existentialists, or in the illusion of a greater being than ourselves other than God, which we locate, for instance, in society.

Social altruism is thus not in itself the basis of altruism, unless society is credited with an unreal permanence. If we assign its true place to it, social altruism is no more than one element of altruism.

Of all the systems which justify altruism, the religious systems are the only ones which provide it with a completely satisfactory basis. All the others give the impression that the moral philosopher has decided in advance to find a basis and that he is straining reality as he conceives it in this sense. Whether it is a question of the pleasure of friendship, or of renunciation, or indeed of love of our country, it is clear that in such explanations self-seeking is mingled with altruism properly so-called, and psychological observation with consideration of the moral rule.

### III. THE DUTY OF ALTRUISM

To conclude this chapter, we must try to clarify the notion of the duty of altruism, altruism on behalf of others and not of ourselves. I shall inquire in the next chapter how altruism assumes a place in the exigencies of my personal development. But altruism is not really itself, it is not really altruism, unless it really has others as its object, and it has not if I practise it for my own sake.

The question therefore is why regard for others *qua* others is incumbent on me. That refers to any others, whoever they may be; the question is why I must see my brother in every man, and why my brother compels my respect for him. This question goes far beyond that of the human community; those who are determined at any price to link it up with social life must engage in veritable intellectual acrobatics to see a virtual, implicit or possible society implied in every man they meet. It is clear that the notion of society, in the sense of organized society which it bears in sociological literature, is much narrower than that of humanity.

It seems easy to resolve this question of mutual aid through the intermediacy of God. We have just seen that the religious basis is the only one that appears sound. Even so, there is some clarification to be done, for since God is the basis of everything, he is in one way the basis of nothing, that is to say that in order to know whether God is the basis of any particular value, we must know whether this value is binding on the mind. God is the basis of everything that is binding on the mind, because a value is only binding on the mind because God has made it so. But how are we to know that God has made it so except by discovering that it is binding on the mind?

Fourier used to say: 'Passions come from God; we must

therefore abandon ourselves to them.' It is true that if I pursue my good, it is because God has put it in me; but that gives me no indication of the nature of my good. We must therefore examine the question of altruism closely so as to determine what is its place in human condition as a whole, what arguments can provide it with a valid justification, and what are its limits.

Respect-altruism is in a different position from assistance-altruism, particularly when assistance-altruism goes to the extent of sacrificing the self. Respect-altruism is based on equality: Nietzsche allows it between equals. But equality cannot provide a basis for mutual aid. The fact that somebody is my equal cannot oblige me to jump into the water to rescue him.

## 1. *Respect-altruism and equality*

It seems that it is a self-evident fact for human beings that equals should respect each other. When Kant makes the primary expression of the categorical imperative: 'Always act on a principle such that you would be willing to see it become a universal rule', he was only translating into what he thought was philosophical language the universal formula: 'Do unto others as you would they should do unto you.'

For it is a universal maxim. We meet with it everywhere, constantly repeated, constantly violated and constantly recalled. The justifications advanced for it are as often as not unconvincing, because the rule can only be fully justified if we go beyond the human. As long as man remains centred on himself, others can only be thought of as instruments. Kant was impregnated with the Christian tradition. Since he had lost his faith, he believed he was thinking independently, with no *a priori* assumptions, but the things he accepted as self-evident were those that came to him from his environment. If a thinker deliberately throws over the idea of an Absolute existing outside of man, he lapses into incoherence, as we have seen.

The precept for respect-altruism is to be found in commutative justice. Since men have all the same rights, we should respect those of others for the same reason that we expect ours to be respected. The precept for commutative justice is 'Give and take'.

At first sight this appears simple. Respect for the life and property of others, the duty of telling the truth, respect for marital rights (moral philosophers class adultery as theft) can all be justified in this way.

It is all simple, indeed, as long as we are dealing with the usual type of case, where two equal rights are in conflict: I should pay the just price for an article. But this very equality leads to a breach of material equality when a man defies law and order and when two unequal rights are in conflict.

The first case is not too difficult; it is the case of legitimate defence. Another man defies law and order. He treats me as an inferior by, for example, molesting my life or property for his personal advantage, and I have then the right to defend my position as an equal. The case of legitimate defence which is most often cited is that of the defence of one's life. It is also the simplest case, because the two values confronted in it are the same; on both sides alike, the right to life is at stake.

A more difficult case is that of conflict between two un-equal rights. There is a hierarchy of goods; one man's right to an inferior good cannot prevail over another man's right to a superior good. In virtue of this principle, Catholic moral philosophers teach that a man can violate the right to property in order to save his life, because the right to life is a right superior to the right to property. They also teach that a man can conceal the truth in certain cases, when higher interests are involved. They justify this last rule in more than one way, but they are all agreed on the fundamental idea.

Nevertheless, the cases we have just cited are almost the only ones theologians allow. At first sight, this seems surprising, for there are many other cases of conflicts of rights, particularly where property is concerned. On one hand it is laid down that property as a whole is put at the disposal of men as a whole, that property is thus designed to be common, and that its owners are caretakers for the community. But on the other hand, when an owner fails in his duty of stewardship and does not help others as he ought to, these others are not allowed the right to restore order in the use of the property by taking what ought to have been given them.

Let us imagine the case of a poor man with a talented son, who is capable of making the best of a good education and of occupying an important place in society. The social order is such that this child cannot become the man he might because his parents are poor. Their neighbour is a rich man who makes a bad use of his property, and who could help the poor man, but does not do so. Why cannot the poor man appropriate some of the resources of his rich neighbour, if he can do so without being noticed and so avoid social conflict? The moral philosophers oblige the poor man to submit to the 'established disorder'.

The argument they put forward is, moreover, as often as not an indirect argument. They appeal to the need for social order. If everyone could right his own wrongs, there would be bound to be abuses, because most people have strong feelings and are not intelligent enough to be able to pass an equitable judgment on their own case. The philosophers therefore call on men to respect the established order, even if this order is a disorder.

It will be seen that the considerations which prompt these solutions are by no means those of the rights which are in conflict. Casuistry is anyway a not very logical science. Cases are resolved in accordance with an overall view into which there enter the most varied practical considerations, such as the social order or the fear of abuses. What is more, philosophers are subject without realizing it to the influence of their environment. The ethics of the good man, which is inspired by current ways of thinking, often comes into their thinking, justified by remarks which look like general principles, such as 'We mustn't make morality too hard for ordinary people', or 'We must make allowances for use and custom'.

Inspired as they thus are by varied considerations, casuistical systems are not usually intellectually satisfactory. They raise a certain number of questions in which we shall have to try and clarify the principles involved. One which concerns the object of this chapter is how far ethics should make allowances for the customs of the community and the conditions of life in common. Another, which we shall examine in the next chapter, is how far a man should make up his mind in accord-

194

ance with his personal judgment and, should occasion arise, assume the right to be an exception to the rule.

But all these questions raise that of the unity of ethics. In order to clear the ground, we will start by trying to clear up the question of ethics for an elite and ethics for the majority.

## 2. *Elite-ethics and majority-ethics*

We have seen that wise men are non-conformists, individualists, and in a manner of speaking, aristocrats : they tend everywhere to shy away from the masses. The wise men's ethics thus stands in contrast to that of the masses.

The thinker who expresses this in the plainest terms is Nietzsche, and he did a service to thought by raising the problem in such an outspoken way that it is now impossible to evade it. At first sight, his conception seems to be in contradiction with the traditional conception, and with the Christian conception in particular, and he puts it forward as such. The traditional conception is that of an ethics which is the same for everyone. Duty is duty and sin is sin. What is a duty or a sin for one man is so for all.

All the same, certain passages in the Gospels strike a more relativist note. An example is the parable of the talents, which declares expressly that duty is not the same for all and that he who has received more must give back more. We meet this idea in varying forms in every ethical theory. It appears in such proverbs as *'Noblesse oblige',* and wherever ethics assumes a social aspect, we find a popular ethics and an ethics for the elite, obligations for the masses and obligations for the elite.

This double ethics emerges as soon as an attempt is made at a social organization of ethics. In his Republic, Plato pictures an ethics for the ruling class of philosophers and another for the warrior class, while he exempts the working class from a moral rule, since they should not think but should confine themselves to doing what they are told.

We talked earlier of dualist ethics and of the double ethics that the Cathari prescribed for the perfect and for believers respectively. In Buddhism we find a not dissimilar arrangement, an ethics for the pious devotee, the *upasaka,* who pledges himself to avoid the five fundamental sins, and an ethics for the monk, who commits himself to a higher degree of perfection.

It is true that these freely accepted rules are not accepted as moral rules by those who link ethics and duty, in accordance with the outlook that has prevailed since Kant. But if they do not form part of ethics, what are they? What is more, duty and moral aspirations are inextricably interwoven.

The most thorough examination of the question is to be found in Catholic moral theology, whose finely shaded system makes it possible to understand the problem's delicacy.

Moral philosophers have distinguished sin from imperfection. Sin is a transgression of the moral rule, which is the same for all. The impression given is that of an absolute uniformity. When the sinful character of theft is determined, an attempt is made to specify what a theft consists in and how big it must be to be gravely or slightly sinful. Imperfection is not contrary to the law, but it is better to do what is perfect.

So far, every obligation is common to everyone. But a man may commit himself to the way of perfection, and undertake obligations which are not applicable to everyone. The question has been systematically discussed in connection with religious vows, but it applies to all Christians. A man who engages in a profession contracts obligations which are not those of the common man. When a man accepts a post as minister or president of a republic, he is accepting responsibilities which it would be sinful to try and evade later. The head of a business has responsibilities which go beyond those of his employees or workmen, and a man who is at the top of the social scale has duties, in particular that of setting a good example, which do not concern those at the bottom of the scale. We find here, in a much more finely shaded form, the conceptions of Plato in the Republic.

When we read the lives of saints, we see that they regard themselves as sinners on account of acts which are not considered sins according to the general rule. It is the same with many of the people who hold positions of authority, though they do not always formulate their feeling, for lack of the appropriate training. All this results in an ethics of many levels, very different from the undifferentiated ethics that seems to emerge from the manuals.

196

What is more, in the Gospels, there is a manifest difference in the Saviour's attitude according to those he is talking to. To the crowd, his attitude is one of mercifulness; he knows that men are weak, and he grants forgiveness at the least sign of good will. But at the same time he preaches an uncompromising ideal of purity, renunciation and love, an ideal which he may be said to launch at the crowd, with a 'he that has ears to hear, let him hear . . .' He calls for an unreserved generosity from those who present themselves to him as disciples. All these elements make Christian ethics an extremely finely shaded and varied one, which allows for every situation in a manner suited to its real importance.

But this being so, can we say that ethics is the same for everyone? Here we are once more confronted with the twofold idea of code morality and wisdom morality.

\*     \*     \*

Code morality is an ethics inspired by social considerations and wisdom morality one inspired by individual considerations.

The man who teaches code morality is not concerned with himself, but with the people, and he is not concerned with perfection, but with the virtues to be required of the masses.

The most advanced of code moralities is that which developed, first among the Jews and then in the Catholic Church, and we have seen why. In the Catholic Church, it was elaborated with the idea of mercifulness, so as to try and make the conditions of salvation as little of a burden as possible. Hence certain attitudes which I noted earlier, that of not putting forward an inapplicable ethics, for instance, and that of allowing for human weakness. The problem of code morality is to raise the masses to the highest moral level accessible to them. That is a social consideration.

How it works out can be seen as soon as a community is formed and a rule has to be adopted for a body of men. In the Catholic Church, the religious orders constitute an unrivalled criterion in this domain. Their sole objective is perfection. Nevertheless, they demand no more than a perfection which has been carefully calculated on the basis of what can

197

be expected from ordinary men. When an order is launched, its founders concern themselves to make it 'viable', that is to discover a rule of life applicable to a certain number of people.

In contrast, wisdom morality is little concerned whether those who will follow it are many or few. Jesus seemed convinced that his disciples would always be a minority—'the harvest is plentiful enough, but the labourers are few'—and we have seen the individualist character of those who teach wisdom morality. The moral teacher is concerned with the good, the One and reduction to the One, with perfection or renunciation. He does not ask himself whether many people will follow in his footsteps. That does not interest him, and if the question is put to him, he will readily agree that 'the labourers will be few'. That is not an objection for him. So much the worse for men if they do not understand.

The conflict between the two kinds of ethics is eternal. The parish priest who has a logically perfect ethics put up to him will reply: 'It's useless to preach that to my people.' He needs an ethics he can teach with some chance of success, and it is the same with everyone who has a social responsibility to shoulder. But that is of no interest to those who are concerned with wisdom morality. The question about the Sermon on the Mount or Kipling's If is not whether many people will put them into practice, but whether they are true or whether they are beautiful.

\*　　\*　　\*

When men organize an ethics for a people, social sense, that is to say concern for men in a body, causes them to concentrate on what is visible. Now what is visible is outward phenomena. When we adopt a collective standpoint, intentions and individual conditions fall into the background. What is common is physical attitudes.

People actuated by social considerations find it tedious and embarrassing when questions of intention are brought up. In the army, soldiers are expected to be in line and in a factory, workers are expected to clock in punctually. Those who put forward individual excuses for exemption from the rule are a nuisance. The ideal that comes naturally to every man with social responsibilities is the ideal of the anthill: perfect conformity, working for the common good. When moral teachers have social interests, they want a virtuous anthill, but it is an anthill all the same. They apply themselves to working out prescriptions for virtue. What matters most is the form of prayer and the act of devotion which they try to persuade the community to use, not spontaneous, free and personal prayer, which can only be the act of a minority. They lay down acts of charity and forms of alms or of mutual aid to be recommended to everyone, and they attach more importance to these than to developing a feeling of love for one's neighbour, the manifestations of which have a personal character. The man actuated by social considerations has the impression that everything that is inward, that is feeling or that is intention, is of its nature vague. He seeks to draw up a code to which the whole community can be subjected, with rules of sobriety, decorum, godliness and kindness which will ensure a common life conforming to the moral rule.

This code morality, which tallies in its main lines with the ethics of the good man, often becomes a crushing burden for some people and extremely easy for others. If, for example, a moral rule is laid down on the subject of theft which takes into consideration solely the value of the object stolen, the rule will be far less severe for a rich man, who has no temptation to steal, than it will be for a poor man. The gravity of theft depends also on the mutual positions of the thief and his victim, the motives of the theft, the means of the victim and those of the thief, and the use the thief plans to make of what he has stolen. Discerning casuists try to take all this into account, but the spontaneous tendency of the man who is concerned with the good moral order of the community is simply to try and make sure that people do not steal. The man who does not steal will pass for upright, and nobody will worry whether he has any merit.

Christ set himself against this way of looking at things in the story of the widow's mite. He praised the poor woman more than all the rich for her alms-giving, though it was far more modest than theirs, for 'the others all made an offering to God out of what they had to spare; she, with so little to give,

199

put in her whole livelihood'. This remark of Jesus is characteristic of wisdom morality, but it always seems more or less paradoxical, because for most people there is no other morality
than code morality, and this is essentially quantitative.

The good man of code morality can thus easily be a conventional egoist, devoid of generosity, but observing the rules of
good breeding, leading an orderly life, displaying few passions, but giving no more evidence of a passion for good than
many other people. The man who gives his goods to the poor
is not the good man of code morality. Such a man inquires
what he *ought* to give to be right with the moral law. On the
other hand, if the man who has given all his goods to the
poor should display occasional ill-humour, the good man of
code morality will upbraid him. If a rich man says that he
hardly sees he has any merit for giving what he has been told
he *ought* to give, because he can do so without depriving himself of anything, the partisans of code morality will tell him
he is over-scrupulous; once a man has done his duty, they will
say, there is no further problem . . . But the implication of this
statement is that duty is the same for everyone. . . . The man
of wisdom morality will tell the rich man : 'Perhaps your duty
goes further' . . .

Code morality is thus often easy for the mediocre and stifling for strong personalities. The result is a sharp reaction
against it by all those who have a feeling for moral purity. The
attitude of Christ is very characteristic. He never talks of social
rules of ethics except to say that we must transcend them.

\*      \*      \*

In contrast to code morality, wisdom morality is an ethics
for the elite, for those who have a concern for the moral. Concern for the moral, as we have seen, is concern for the good,
the absolute, the individual and the One.

Wisdom morality looks on life as a whole. It is not out for a
recipe which will ensure that a man is 'in order' and specify
the conditions on which he can be certain of having a good
conscience, leaving him free thereafter to pursue his own interests. Wisdom morality is out for unity in life, and since
man is manifold, unity in life means order and harmony. The

important thing in these circumstances is not the value of each part considered in itself, but the harmony of the whole. Life is a concert, and all its notes must contribute to the total effect.

Individual acts thus assume a very different aspect according to the place they occupy in the whole, according to the spotlight on them. To give a pound, a hundred pounds or ten thousand pounds to the poor can never have the same value for two men. One must be congratulated, while the other must be told: 'That's not enough': the widow's mite again.

But in this case, duty assumes an extremely subjective aspect. My duty is to do what fits in with the harmony of my life. Now the harmony of my life is my perfection. My duty is thus to achieve my perfection, or to do what I can to attain to it, and in practice, my perfection consists in doing what I can to attain to my perfection.

The word perfection has thus two senses here. In the first sense, perfection is what I should be able to achieve in theory, that is to say, it consists in the complete development of everything I have in me. But in practice, this perfection is beyond my reach, because I am the victim of a series of pernicious tendencies which I also have in me, and which are the result, either of my character or of my past life. The perfection I can attain today is thus inferior to the perfection which is deduced from taking account of my qualities alone. And my perfection today is to achieve the perfection of which I am capable now, with the collection of qualities and defects that are in me.

What is the position of this ethics in relation to code morality?

To start with, perfection can be a source of obligations. Here we have the principle 'noblesse oblige', and this manifests itself on the psychological plane by the diversity of vocations. A man's vocation corresponds to the lines along which he must realize his own perfection, and the man with a moral sense sees in his vocation a source of obligations. It is a source of obligations, because he is anxious to pursue the reduction to the One which is the prime objective of his life. Whereas on the level of code morality, the problem of vocation arises only in the form of a call to which a man is free not to respond, since duty is merely to do what everyone ought to do.

On the level of wisdom morality, everything which allows me to realize the objective of my life is a source of obligations. This is a strictly personal point of view. I do not have to worry about what others do. As in the parable of the talents, I only have to worry about what I have received.

But though perfection may be a source of obligations, it is also a source of freedom from them. In proportion as a man accedes to a higher level of life, he is freed from obligations which are necessary on a lower level. In workshops and offices, the men who are at the top of the hierarchy are freed from the obligation to clock in on time; the man who devotes himself completely to the service of his neighbour or who uses his property only to make his fellow-man happy need not worry about what he is bound to do. Duty disappears, as it were, in the superabundance of good.

It is possible, all the same, that a man may have to submit to a rule out of social discipline, though it has no more object as far as he is concerned. A man who does his job conscientiously, and whom there would be no reason to hold to fixed hours of work if only he were concerned, must sometimes consent to put up with the general rule, because if he were dispensed from it, others, who do not deserve it, would demand the same concession. Cases of this kind are common : they explain why, even in monasteries, fixed hours for prayer or common rules for mortification are laid down. Whatever the degree of perfection the wise man has attained, he must still accept social discipline as long as he is living with his fellow-man.

This is what Nietzsche did not see. His superman was supposed to shake himself free from all obligations because he acknowledged nothing above himself. But if man is a creature, he must take into consideration the social order of which his fellow-men form part; he must accept the common life which forms part of the law of man, and the discipline which is a consequence of it.

\* \* \*

This allows us to clarify the position of social ethics. There are elements of truth to be found even in the ethics of honour and even in the confusion between ethics and morals.

It is true that every state of life makes its own demands, and that these accord a particular importance to certain virtues; it is true that physical courage is particularly important for the soldier and respect for his word for a tradesman. A properly interpreted ethics of honour, which confines itself to emphasizing the virtues specially necessary in a given environment, without prejudice to the body of rules which govern life, results in a professional or class morality which takes differences into account, but produces conflict. There are legitimate differences between different social circles, and one question for practical ethics is, which are legitimate differences which should be taken into account, and which constitute abuses which we should not tolerate.

In the same way, to a lesser degree, morals can affect ethics, in the sense that acts and words sometimes bear the meaning that men attribute to them, for example when it is a question of rules of good manners or commercial practices.

But ethics would go astray if it had no other rule than normal practice, because this reflects an average morality which keeps man at a somewhat low moral level. For example, it is normal practice to mislead men to some extent, but not to exceed certain limits, and to pursue our own interests to some extent, but not to go too far but to avoid injuring others beyond a certain point. As we have seen, when a man confines himself to code morality, he can easily lapse into a condescending attitude towards normal practice which kills moral fervour.

And yet it is true that certain acts draw their meaning from normal practice. We should take this into account, but we cannot do it without danger unless casuistry is inspired by a concern for wisdom morality which orientates life.

Again, a man who has adopted an attitude of wisdom morality should refrain from following certain practices, because the very fact of his drawing his inspiration from wisdom morality is contrary to them. The first sign of wisdom morality in a man is that when he is confronted with a particular practice he asks what is its value. The man who has committed himself to code morality never raises this question; he confines himself to asking exactly what he ought to do according to

203

the established rules. Now custom assumes that men are mediocre, and the social environment reacts against anyone who adopts a personal attitude. The man who pursues wisdom morality is thus departing from custom; he is a non-conformist. We find this phrase cropping up on every page.

Customs correspond to normal virtue. The man who seeks wisdom seeks something quite different from virtue which is normal. He seeks virtue in itself and for itself. Other men vaguely realize that he is not like them and look for an attitude on his part that will cut across the normal. They look for a certain disinterestedness, for example, and they will be more than a little shocked if they see that he values money and creature comforts as much as they do, though they do not feel they are doing any wrong.

On the other hand, if the wise man interferes with their habits or their prejudices, they regard him as unmannerly or tactless. It is customary in fashionable society to say only pleasant things. The wise man, for his part, is seeking the truth, and if he is surrounded by people like himself, friends or disciples, they practise brotherly admonition, because they all desire wisdom. If he leaves this circle and practices brotherly admonition, he is not understood, because those to whom he is speaking are satisfied with themselves, want a pleasant life and have no desire to be admonished out of their failings. They will not even allow anyone to accuse them of failings. On the other hand, people attach particular importance to the wise man's judgment, because they count on him to tell the truth. Thus they will not agree either to the wise man telling them unpleasant truths, nor to his paying empty compliments. He is often reduced to holding his tongue. If, in order to conform to custom, he pays the compliments everyone does, people are astonished as if it were a weakness. They do not regard the paying of compliments as a weakness in others. On the contrary, it is a virtue to be amiable; but there are certain virtues that become weaknesses for the wise man.

Thus, as soon as we go into the question of relations between men, we come up against problems which we cannot solve if they are considered in isolation. Only wisdom morality, the morality of the orientation of life, can provide the solution.

## 3. *The basis of the three forms of altruism.*

We are now in a position to determine the extent to which concern for others modifies individual morality, whether it is a question of human contacts in the broadest sense or of social collaboration in the more restricted sense. There are three aspects to the question: respect-altruism, assistance-altruism, and social sense-altruism.

\* \* \*

First for *respect-altruism.*

It is based, as we have seen, on the fundamental equality of men. Men apprehend this fundamental equality as a self-evident truth, though they apprehend it somewhat vaguely, because it is contradicted by innumerable inequalities of every kind, and because it only manifests itself decisively in terms of the future life. A clear idea of commutative justice seems to call for synthesis of our ideas, linked with the notion of God as a sovereign master. Before him, human inequalities lose their importance, and men rediscover their fundamental equality in reduction to the One or possession of God, which is their common end.

The problem of respect-altruism is thus that of allowing every man to fulfil his destiny. Any infraction of commutative justice thus amounts to depriving another man of a means of action to which he is entitled.

But this identical right of men to fulfil their destiny is expressed through varying vocations. Everyone has the same right to achieve his perfection, but this right assumes different forms.

Aristotle believed certain men to be slaves by nature, and Nietzsche revived this idea in connection with the herd-man. But though slavery may be contrary to the rights of man, because it puts one man at the service of another without taking his own aspirations into account, it is also true that some men have a vocation to be masters and others to be subordinates. Ford notes in his autobiography that it is difficult to find workmen who will agree to shoulder responsibility, even if they are offered extra pay. Many people fear responsibilities more than they want powers of initiative. If one set of men is cut out

205

to be masters and the other to be subordinates, one set of men is also cut out to be teachers and the other to be disciples. There are some men who like to propound ideas, and others who are afraid to do so, and who are only interested in reporting what the first class have said. The second class is far the most numerous.

Consequently, real reciprocity between men in material things is rarely possible. The example that comes naturally to the mind when commutative justice is discussed is the commercial example of the exchange of goods, for there it is a question of material values. But as soon as it is a question of human relations, we come across moral values with no material equivalence. The love of a woman for a man is never the same as the love of a man for a woman, and the relationship of the employer to a workman has no equivalence in material terms to the relationship of the workman with the employer. It is the same with the relationships between parents and children, masters and servants, rulers and ruled. Their duties are different, though the fundamental duty remains the same, that of respecting the personality of others.

If one man must take orders from another, it is still in order to achieve his destiny. He from whom the other takes orders must allow him to achieve his destiny, his personal destiny. The inferior must only subordinate his destiny to that of his superior in so far as the achievement of his own destiny lies in this subordination. We are thus back at the principle of an equal right for men to achieve destinies which differ among themselves according to their situation in the world.

\*     \*     \*

We now come to *assistance altruism*.

This also corresponds, as we have seen, to something that is self-evident to men. This self-evidence has always been unmistakable on the level of patriotism, whether the object of the sentiment was the clan or the tribe of primitive peoples, the city-state of antiquity, the modern nation, or any other form of human community. But in the past, it was impossible for the sense of human solidarity to extend beyond the limited communities in which men became aware of their common

206

destiny. Only a few wise men extended their thinking to the whole human race, generally in connection with the pantheistic conception of a spark of the divine existing in every human being.

The development of the idea of civilization has led modern western thought to see human collaboration in a completely new light. For the idea of civilization makes the basis of human life the duty of collaborating in a collective task, which can only be achieved by the co-ordination of activities.

On one hand, men can improve their living conditions through this organized mutual aid, and if they can, they should. This is a self-evident truth which is not disputed.

On the other hand, human living conditions can be improved indefinitely, not only on the level of particular societies, but on that of the entire human race. The human race is seen as a single whole. The work of progress is a collective task of a universal character. When a scientist makes a discovery, he does not make it for his country, but for humanity; when a cure for a disease is found, it would seem cruel to reserve it to the country to which its discoverer belongs.

Men should thus devote themselves to the collective work of the progress of the human race. All ethics is dominated by this prospect, and the duty of mutual aid is first and foremost this duty of collective mutual aid, which is social in the sense that it is concerned with the entire human community, and not in the sense that it is concerned with a particular society. Whether humanity as a whole forms or does not form an organized community, man's life is dominated by the necessity of this mutual aid.

On the other hand, this collective mutual aid does not stand in the way of individual mutual aid. The notion that the whole human race is engaged in a collective task only accentuates the idea that men are all brothers and that they must feel about one another as brothers. This trend of thinking is producing a growing reaction, whose development can be followed for two or three centuries past, against differences and inequalities between classes, races, colours and nations, and even between sexes and ages.

As we have already seen, the arguments advanced to justify

207

altruism are a farrago. When we try and sort these ideas out, it becomes apparent that this duty of mutual aid can only be accounted for by making it dependent on a mission which man has received, and that man cannot receive a mission unless there is someone to entrust him with it.

We are still up against the same dilemma. In the first place, man's end may lie within himself; in this case he cannot be obliged to subordinate himself to anything whatever, he need not accept any discipline and can have no other objective than to assert himself. Under these conditions, he will only take others into consideration in so far as he thinks it in his own interest. Or secondly, man may himself be subordinate. In this case, he must agree to identify himself with an order of which he is not the author and to perform the task which falls to him in this order.

If there is an order which compels man's recognition, he cannot attain his complete fulfilment if he fights against this order. Kant's line of argument comes to mind at once: this fulfilment of man is not always achieved on earth, and we must therefore admit the existence of another world where justice is done. Kant's only mistake was to advance this argument as apodeictic, whereas it entails no more than a presumption, and it remains to be seen whether we can reach the conclusion that things are so by other means.

If the existence of a creator God is admitted, the human situation appears to be as follows; man has been put on earth to give glory to God and to serve him, which is the same thing, or to perform the task to which God has called him. This task is to subjugate the world to his reason and to achieve a collective life where all men are perfectly developed and devote their lives to the divine praise. This divine praise can be thought of on the lines of a work of art and of certain mass demonstrations where poetry, music and dancing blend to express man's highest sentiments in a completely harmonious way.

We are here on the level of a prophetic vision picturing a perfect age from which the human race is so far away that we cannot even visualize the contingency of attaining it. Nevertheless, this end where we do not expect to arrive is the goal towards which we must strive. But if he is to organize his action, man must assign himself other and nearer goals.

The starting-point of humanity is that man finds himself on earth with an intelligence capable of progressively coming to understand the world and turning this to account. But at the moment when he appeared on the earth, man understood almost nothing and was almost incapable of using his intelligence. Hundreds of centuries had to pass before he could even begin to harness nature to his service. Then the development accelerated, one discovery leading to another till finally the idea emerged that the mission of man was to transform the natural conditions of the world so as to be able to live more and more by his reason.

Primitive man is subject to nature. Civilization frees man from nature or, to be more accurate, subjects nature to man and makes it an instrument in his hands. Civilization frees man successively from all the servitudes of nature, from hunger, dark, cold, distance and gravity, and it postpones the moment of death. It allows man to develop training and education, and permits him to stamp out moral infirmities such as drunkenness and debauchery, laziness and instability. But though civilization can do all this, it does it only in the course of a turbulent evolution, with trends in every direction, advances and relapses, progress in one direction being often neutralized by a new obstacle to progress. We develop hygiene and discover cures for a hundred and one diseases, but there is a parallel increase in nervous disorders ... We fight alcoholism, and the use of drugs spreads ... Nevertheless, man *can* progress; he therefore must. Is he doing so? That is a question of fact that is outside our present scope.

But we should realize the profound transformation of thought brought about by this discovery of the possibility of progress.

The ancients argued in terms of a static humanity. When Plato or Aristotle, or St Thomas in the Middle Ages, considered human problems and social organization, they never anticipated that the conditions of man's life might change. They took the state which civilization had then reached and sought the formula for optimum communal organization, taking into account existing conditions. From time to time a discovery would change certain conditions. It was then integrated into life, and the philosophers resumed their speculations taking into account the new position. But they did not anticipate the possibility of further changes, still less propose that men should actually seek change. The utopian novels, which put forward the picture of an ideal humanity, all picture it in the form of a return to a primitive life on the simplest possible lines.

A reversal of that trend of thought has occurred in the last two centuries, under the influence of technological progress. This reversal did not happen all at once, but little by little, and it is still far from being at an end. Even in our days, we still find champions of the old-time 'sheepfolds', who rail against progress. But their number is diminishing as it grows clearer that the whole progress of man is bound up with the progress of his knowledge, and that this is dependent on the forms of material and moral progress, moral progress governing all the others because it points the way for action.

The progress of civilization is necessary, were it only to allow men to eat their fill. Up to now, the men who have eaten their fill have never been more than a minority of the human race. Providing an adequate diet for the whole of mankind is even today an objective which has still to be realized. Now in our days, the achievement of this objective depends solely on moral conditions, that is to say on the spirit of mutual aid, of disinterested mutual aid, among men, for technological civilization has reached a point where it would present no physical problem to feeding the whole human race. Not only is it easy to produce the necessary foodstuffs; it is just as easy to transport them. What is not easy is to make men accept the necessary conditions; to get the underfed people, for example, to change certain habits of life to which they are accustomed, and to get the rich people to sacrifice a part, even though it were an infinitesimal part, of their well-being.

When we compare a point like this with the ideal picture of a happy humanity which we outlined earlier, we realize that prophetic visions of the end before us are utopian, that is to say they portray an ideal we know we shall never attain. But if we start to think about it, we shall see that the chief obstacle is a moral one; it lies above all in the pride and egoism through which men evade their duty of mutual aid.

In any case, the concrete objective we must pursue lies along the lines of a threefold material, intellectual and moral progress, one stimulating the other or the others, with a view to achieving ever improved living conditions.

Here is an example which will bring out the interdependence of all the forms of progress. Progress in medicine is bound up with progress in the specialized industries which permits the manufacture of ever more perfected instruments, and with progress in chemistry, which is itself bound up with industrial progress. These various forms of progress enable doctors to remedy physical deficiencies which themselves lead to disturbances formerly attributed to moral causes. It is thus possible, through scientific progress, to make men more balanced, calmer, more stable in character, and consequently more efficient workers. This improved balance then provides the individual with a new starting point for his personal progress. It has always been true that certain privileged circles have a higher average moral standard than those outside them. Scientific progress provides a means of extending to the masses what was once reserved for a privileged few.

These implications of collective progress are commanding more and more attention as the effects make themselves felt. The whole of Western social thinking is now focused in this direction; so is that of the Communist world, and the Far East is offering no resistance to the doctrine. Inadequate moral dispositions are now the only obstacles to its achievement. But the problem I am concerned with here is that of the basis we must attribute to this duty in order to embody it in a tenable synthesis.

The question is why man *should* devote himself to a progress of the human race from which he is unlikely to profit himself; why, that is to say, he should exert himself in order that the men of the future should enjoy better living conditions. The old conception was only concerned with organizing a happy community for the men living then. Nobody worried about working towards progress down the centuries. Today humanity is moving forward in a sort of apocalyptic dream, shot with nightmares, no doubt, but focused on the prospects held out by realization of the possibility of continuous progress. The question is therefore not merely why men now

211

living should combine to organize the best possible communal life, but why they should subordinate their action to a progress of which generations still unborn will be the beneficiaries.

The question is different too from that of old-style patriotism. The starting point of this was the consciousness of a security which could not be assured without the protection of the community. It is enough to read Homer, and see how Troy was treated after its defeat, to understand that, under those conditions, only the city-state could guarantee a truly human life. It is therefore easy to see why the permanence and prosperity of the city should be looked on as the supreme blessing, to which citizens must be ready to sacrifice everything. It was against this primitive background that there developed the tradition of patriotism, in whose name men are still repeating the same slogans, without bothering whether they still hold good. *Pro aris et focis,* we read on some war memorials: 'They fell for their altars and their homes' . . . In reality, in modern wars, neither altars nor homes were concerned.

In any case, the contemporary idea of civilization is very different. All humanity is engaged in a common task, which will go on indefinitely down the years. Everyone must take his place in this endless chain, and he must not ask whether he will benefit himself from the progress towards which he is lending a hand.

Men thus have the mission of bringing into being a more and more humane humanity or of bringing out more and more the specifically human character of man. But—we must repeat the question—how can man have such a mission if no one has entrusted it to him? If there exists no higher being having power over man, logic lies in the Nietzschean conception of the superman, or in eudaimonism.

When we talked earlier of the 'moral shock', we noted its individual character, and indeed this moral shock results from the intuition of the nobility of the individual person. The moral philosopher, as we have seen, is sensible of this value; that is why he is a non-conformist, and his spontaneous tendency does not go along with the modern conception of the primacy of civilization or collective life. On the other hand, there are a certain number of elements in Christianity which look like a prefiguration of contemporary thinking.

All the same, at first sight the trend of modern thinking does not seem to have developed in sympathy with Christianity, still less under the inspiration of it. The development of technological civilization and the trend of thinking linked with it originated in great part, and may even be said to have originated as a whole, apart from the Christian tradition, and even in opposition to it. Nevertheless, this development occurred in a part of the world which had been subject to Christian influence. Could that be an accident? It is true that, at first sight also, this trend of thought seems to grow stronger as the Christian tradition grows weaker. We may ask ourselves how far this appearance corresponds to reality, and also how far it corresponds to transitory historical circumstances and how far to the nature of Christianity.

The second question is the only one that concerns us here. There is much that we could say about the question of facts. What concerns us here, however, is man's duty, not what he does. Our interest is in the conception of duty which emerges from Christianity; we do not need to inquire whether Christians are faithful to their calling.

Now the starting point of the 'good news' that Christ came to preach is that God loves men, that he loves them all alike, that he wants them to be happy, and they must all work together, animated by his spirit, to establish on earth conditions of virtue which will give them happiness beyond compare. The instrument of this happiness is love between men, and this love, as we know, is the love of God himself, which lives in his disciples.

The Church of Christ is the community of the faithful in whose souls Christ lives through grace, and this community is destined to spread to the whole world. All men are summoned to enter it, and Christ enjoins his disciples to preach to every nation. The universal character of Christianity goes back to its beginnings. We find nothing like it in any other religion. Here, it is the founder himself who, right back at the foundation of his Church, manifested his will that it should spread throughout the earth. This universal character did not emerge later on, under the influence of circumstances and success. It was deliberately willed at a moment when the Church did not yet even exist; it forms an integral part of the basic conception of Christianity. We have seen earlier that certain thinkers, almost everywhere, have hit on this idea of a human brotherhood in an incidental way. But no other doctrine identifies itself with this idea in anything like the same fashion.

This does not mean that Christ expects that all men will be converted. Whether they are in fact converted is one thing, whether they are called is another. All are called, and that is what is important doctrinally.

The Church forms a body, the body of Christ. That is to say that, since Christ lives and acts in Christians, these form together the body through which he acts in the world. This life of Christ in them, the same life of the same Christ in all the millions of Christians, gives the Church a real unity incomparably more solid than that of human societies. Society has often been compared to a body, and the sociological thinkers of our time have revived the expressions of antiquity and tried to justify them. But the social reality of the Church is of quite another kind, and not even the strictest definition will deprive the unity of the Church's body of its solidity.

Christians must thus carry out a common task, which is the building of the Kingdom of God. The building of the Kingdom of God is the growth of Christ in the world. It is beyond the individual; the Christian must dedicate himself completely to this work. It matters little whether this growth of Christ comes to pass in his time or in the course of centuries. It matters little whether this or that individual will benefit perceptibly from the conditions of life it will establish among men. The fulfilment of the Christian vocation lies in action in the service of the Kingdom.

This is quite different from the principle of mutual aid which is roughed out in more or less pantheistic doctrines, in Lao-tse, in Epictetus and in Hinduism. According to this, man has in him a spark of divinity, which he meets with in other men, in every man, so that for every man, other men are other selves. This conception has nothing to do with the idea of the Kingdom of God and of a duty to work together

214

at a common task which is God's task, and even less with the idea that this task of the Kingdom should be the central object of the care or of the duty of man.

We need not inquire here through what tragic misunderstandings the idea arose in certain circles that Christianity was opposed to material satisfactions and even to earthly satisfactions in the most general sense. No doubt, like every religion, Christianity calls on men not to set their hearts on material goods, but to seek spiritual values first, and the Christian is told to be wary of comfort. But when Christ wants to express the signs by which his disciples will be recognized, the examples that come to his lips are that they will feed the hungry, take in the homeless and clothe the naked. When this is linked with the universal vocation of Christianity and the conditions of our times, it leads straight to aid to under-developed countries and the universal solidarity of the human race.

It is true that in one way the object of Christianity is confined to Christians. Its primary aim is to summon men to the Christian life, and the human community which is the result is a community of Christians. The modern conception of human solidarity, which covers all men irrespective of their faith, might be described as a de-Christianized Christian conception. But though Christ may not speak of a task of civilization to be undertaken over and above the propagation of the faith, which is the direct and primary object of his message, he does teach his disciples that they are 'the salt of the earth' and 'the light of the world', and this means that the Kingdom of God, in so far as it unites all the Christians on earth, should extend its activities to all humanity. In the present position of the human race, this conception summons Christians to make themselves the agents of any mutual aid calculated to improve the living conditions of the human race.

\*　　\*　　\*

It remains for us to clarify the idea of *social sense-altruism*. The question is an easy one after what we have just seen. By society is here meant organized life in common. It is organization which characterizes society in the strict sense, whereas the duty of respect-altruism like that of assistance-altruism extends to all men, organized or not, to each man in particular and to all in general, to the whole and to the individual members of it.

The duty of taking into account the demands of social life fits into this general obligation, and becomes of secondary importance for the man who has grasped his duty to humanity as a whole. But common membership of a society, like common membership of a family, gives birth to a collection of sentiments which convince members of either that they are confronted with a sacred reality, superior to the individual. Hence the extravagances of every form of patriotism.

These extravagances do not mean that it is not true that man must accept the fact of living in society and accept the conditions of social life. These imply a certain discipline, that is to say they imply that the members of a society must be ready to forgo certain elements of their personal fulfilment for the good of the whole. This discipline ranges from the most commonplace acts, such as the observance of polite usages and sartorial conventions, to the gravest acts, such as the devotion of a man's life to the service of the community, the surrender of his worldly possessions and even, in certain extreme cases, the sacrifice of his life.

The sacrifices a man must accept out of a spirit of social collaboration can be reduced to two types, those which are inspired by the needs of co-ordination and those which are a consequence of human weakness.

The needs of co-ordination oblige men to comply with rules of life in common without which collective action would be impossible. A business cannot function unless its staff complies with a time-table which may not perhaps suit everyone in terms of his personal tastes, but which is necessitated by work in common. In the same way, in a modern town, street traffic cannot be easy and safe unless drivers comply with regulations.

Other forms of rules are dictated by human weakness. In so far as men are unreliable, they must not be trusted. Hence the forms of supervision and the regulations whose object is to validate legal instruments. A man who is getting married must comply with formalities, as must a man who is entering

216

into an important commercial contract, and these formalities would be unnecessary if men were all really trustworthy. Those for whom these formalities are unnecessary must submit to them all the same, because the common good requires that they should be applied without any discrimination between persons.

Social life is thus continually prescribing attitudes which ethics requires man to respect. Ethics calls on a man to be a good citizen, and it is at this point that organized social life comes into ethics.

Reduction to the One, the final object of moral life, thus entails acceptance of the human situation, which is to be engaged in a common task expressing the will of God for man. The genuine completely developed wise man is thus eminently social, non-conformist as he is. He is social because he realizes that he will only achieve the reduction to the One which is the object of his aspirations if he accepts the human order. All the same, he remains a non-conformist, for he passes judgment on this human order and appraises it in terms of the reduction to the One which he is pursuing and which he would like other men to be following with him. This position makes him extremely different from the instinctive and impersonal masses, who conform without any constraint to the usages of their environment.

The perfect wise man is thus at once social and a non-conformist; he collaborates in the common task of men and remains independent. And it is in so far as his whole life is unified in the One, that the collaboration he brings his fellowmen is really efficacious.

217

# Chapter Six

## *Moral Values*

WE SHALL conclude this book with a survey of the principal notions which come together at the basis of moral life. We could find a number of labels for this group of questions: 'constants of moral life,' 'moral values' or 'the balance of morality'. These are the elements which must be taken into consideration when it is desired to work out a theory of ethics. In the opening chapters, we sought to determine the central point, and if we confine ourselves to that, the moral problem appears simple. But when we try to set that single central point in its context in life, a number of other factors immediately occur to us which pertain to human nature, in which nothing is simple. The chapter *Ethics and Society* has already shown the complexity of this question. We shall meet with it again here. Almost all moral values come up in pairs or as alternatives, not to say as opposites. Man is perpetually being torn asunder. But he must put up with this process of striking a balance. What is simple is almost always wrong. Perfection lies in equilibrium.

## I. THE LAW OF UNITY AND MULTIPLICITY

All moral life is reduction to unity. But the reason life must be reduced to unity is that man is manifold and subject to the law of multiplicity, and that his action is always manifold. He has a body and a mind: the body itself is manifold, and the mind is too. A man may have an astonishing memory and be an idiot, or a marvellous imagination and lack judgment, or an unerring judgment and a defective memory.

Even reduction to the One is not a simple idea. There is

218

the reduction to the One, in so far as the One is the primary Being. But there is also a reduction to one, which is reduction of multiplicity to unity. We have seen that a distinction should be drawn between reduction to the One and the unification of life.

What is more, reduction to the One and unification can only take place in the manifold and without abolishing the manifold, because man's life is subject to the law of multiplicity and there is no means of getting rid of this. The unity lies in the mind : it is a unity of order, a co-ordination.

But this unity which lies in the mind is also objective. It is part of reality, but only the mind apprehends it. When books are ranged on shelves in a library, it is the mind which conceives of the appropriate order and carries it into effect (thanks to the body, of course), but this order is a reality which exists in itself, independent of the mind which conceived of it and carried it into effect. If the author of this order dies and another mind turns up, he will be able to rediscover the order worked out by the first if he in his turn applies his capacity for unity to the job. It is in this way that men succeed in deciphering hieroglyphs, by rediscovering the principle of unity which inspired their authors.

Man therefore seeks for unity, and a high proportion of the failures of life result from his seeking for unity where it does not exist. The most frequent case is the pursuit of unity in human love and sometimes, almost exclusively in physical love, the pursuit of the thrill or the ecstasy of love. Anyone who wants evidence on this point will find a copious literature, of every period and in every language, and its tone is one more of disappointment than of joy. Those who describe love as a state of uninterrupted enjoyment seem on the whole to be dreamers; as soon as we are confronted with concrete human experiences, we come up against the limits that hem man in on every side.

The moral problem is thus at once a problem of order and balance, and a problem of unity. This unity is a unity in multiplicity which assumes that we are looking for unity where unity is and that we also accept multiplicity where multiplicity is. The mistake of sectarianism lies in attributing multiplicity to the One; the mistake of positivist sociology in

219

attributing complete unity, in the sense of the absolute, to society, whereas this forms part of multiplicity.

Man must thus achieve unity by making use of the manifold. But the manifold comprises good things which are mutually exclusive, because each individually embodies an aspect of the absolute, and at the same time they rule each other out. We must thus choose and pursue the Absolute by way of the contingent, and the One by way of the manifold, and assert unity in an ever-changing multiplicity. Now this choice is renunciation, selection of one value, but renunciation of all the others. We do not accomplish a task unless we drop everything else that we could in theory do.

I have discussed this idea in other books; what is more, it follows from everything that has gone before. But it should be stated at the outset of this chapter, because it is the starting point of the moral task.

## II. The Law of the Creature

To say that man is a creature is to say that he did not make himself. He is consequently subject to nature, and is master only of what nature subjects to him. To begin with, he must accept himself, with his potentialities and his limitations.

But man has within him the sense of the absolute. The sense of the absolute is the sense of what a being who was not a creature, was not subject to a law and was thus a creator, would be. Now man is incapable of understanding what it means to be a creator, and at the same time he has in him a series of creator-reflexes which derive from his sense of the absolute. He *is* a creator in so far as, thanks to him, there appear in the world things that would not exist without him, works of art or works of speculation. But creation by man is never more than a relative or partial creation, for it is confined to introducing an element of creation or an element of thinking into something that was there to start with.

The moral law requires man to accept himself. He must accept both his capacities and his limitations. He must accept that he has come into the world without having asked for it and indeed without his own awareness, in conditions which he did not choose. The world does not depend on us and our presence does not change very much in it.

In the order of knowledge, we understand something of everything and everything of nothing. We are always between two limits. What is true of life is true of all knowledge: man enters and leaves the world without his own awareness and without deciding the conditions. He always starts from a given situation beyond which he cannot go back.

The order of action tallies with the order of knowledge. We must accept the essential physical, intellectual and social conditions of life. The problem of life is to turn a given situation to the best account.

The moral virtue which corresponds to the acceptance of the human situation is humility, which is a virtue of truth. The man endowed with perfect humility accepts himself and the conditions of his existence; humility is a virtue of lucidity.

People generally have a mistaken idea of it; they believe that a humble man must debit himself with failings he has not got and refuse to recognize his own qualities. But if he deviates from the truth, he will not be able to place himself at the service of God by using all that he is and all that he has.

The opposite of humility is pride, the essence of which is untruth. The proud man takes himself for the absolute: truth is what he thinks, good is what he does. He is the measure of everything. What he does not know does not exist, what he cannot do cannot be good. The proud man makes himself God, for a man who makes himself the measure of everything makes himself God.

But just because man has the sense of the absolute within him, he has within him an undercurrent of pride. He has a natural tendency to make himself God, that is to say to make an absolute of himself. That is why the pursuit of humility, which means the pursuit of truth, is the primary condition of the moral order. It is a sort of atrium. We can enter the moral order only through the doors of humility.

Pride leads a man either not to accept his limitations or not to accept his duties.

Some men do not accept their limitations. We encounter this both in action and in thought. In thought, the man who does not accept his limitations is the 'man in revolt' to whom

I referred earlier. In our days, a whole school of writers follow this line. In the field of action, he wants to do something other than what he is capable of; he refuses to admit that he is incapable of what he wants to do. This ends in failure and revolt. The 'man in revolt' of philosophy is nothing but the intellectual echo of the proud man we meet with everywhere.

On the other hand, pride also leads a man not to accept his duties; he cannot accept them, since he does not acknowledge his limitations. Now it is these that show us the way. We are walking between fences, capable of walking but obliged to do so in one direction. The proud man refuses, and if he cannot go in the direction he wants to, he sits down on the ground till he dies of hunger.

We have just said that those who do not accept their duties are to be met with in the field of thought as well as in the field of action. In the field of thought they accept nothing that transcends them. Thus they do not accept God, because they want to turn themselves into God, and they do not accept any system that subordinates them. They refuse the human situations of research and of work. To begin with, they refuse to subordinate their life to reduction to the One and to be bound to seek the conditions of it.

One of the forms of this pride wears a mask of modesty. It is the contemporary positivist attitude, which deprecates even a consideration of the existence of the One, on the pretext that it is inaccessible to man and that acceptance of the human situation implies our limiting ourselves to what man can master. To a large extent this attitude permeates the scientific sociological trend. This refuses to consider the philosophical problem of the search for causes transcending experience, and declares that such questions as these, and especially those concerned with God, lie beyond the reach of the human mind. This attitude, which is very common nowadays, is a perennial one: we meet with it as far back as Epicurus.

Now it is not true that the One is inaccessible to man. What is true is that it is only accessible in a certain way and to a certain degree. Man cannot order his life except in terms of the One, and to do that he must know the One as well as he can and steep his life in it as far as he can, too. He must accept the law of man, which is to know, but to know incompletely;

he must seek to know all he can know and submit to the incapability of going beyond certain limits. If he purely and simply strikes the One out of his life, because he cannot know it in the same way as he knows a tangible object, he is condemning his life either to incoherence, or to the fundamental confusion of a semblance of intelligibility based on a false first principle. That is the case of those who take the human community or the Socialist society as their basic principle.

All the same, humility could hardly fill its role of guidance and balance unless it were founded on the idea of the God of love, which is peculiar to Christianity. When man considers himself without illusions, his limitations impress him more than his capacities, since at the start he thought he was capable of anything. When he discovers that he cannot do everything, he soon comes to the conclusion that he can do nothing. If he does not know that God loves him, that God wants his good, and that God is ready to help him providing he is ready to submit himself, he may well find humility depressing. That is why the Stoics' humility is cheerless, as is that which we find in the East. Humility is only healthy when it is the counterpart of confidence in God.

But pride is always folly. Error can do nothing but harm, and pride is error. It is impossible to introduce genuine order into life apart from the truth. Error is confusion, and no order can be founded on confusion. Apart from the truth, the question is insoluble.

In spite of everything, man seeks for an order, that is to say he seeks to unify his knowledge and his action. Nothing is more suggestive in this connection than the contemporary philosophy of absurdity. For its partisans, after asserting and insistently repeating that everything loses itself in the manifold like water in the sand, and that everything is incoherent, end up by putting forward a rule, that is to say a principle of action.

Since humility is depressing for a man who does not trust in God, those who are not aware of the divine fatherhood often extol self-exaltation as a source of strength. Pride is indeed a stimulant, but it is a dangerous stimulant because it is founded on error. In history, the best example of sheer unlimited pride is that of Hitler, and everyone knows what that led to. But the temptation of pride inevitably appears the moment men ignore the God of love.

Is the balance of humility, then, impossible outside the Christian framework? Even within Christianity, those who become fully conscious of the presence of the divine love in man are few. That is why many Christians are almost as susceptible as non-Christians to the idea that pride is a necessary stimulant, and that man loses the impetus essential for action and the joy of living if he does not clothe himself in pride. Men may all have more or less of a sense of the One, as we have seen. But to become fully conscious of the unification of life in the One, or even to attain, not the realization of this unification, but merely the understanding that it is the objective to be pursued, seems a difficult thing, to judge by the number of people who succeed in it.

But here we must return to the attitude of the wise men's ethics. The question is not whether there are many or few, but whether it is in this direction that man's vocation lies.

Once again we find ourselves up against interdependent terms. Humility can only develop sanely in terms of an unlimited trust in a One who is ineffable and who is love. But this very trust assumes the existence of humility, for the proud man, with a big idea of himself, considers that if God loves him, God is merely giving him his due, and he puts God at his service instead of putting himself at the service of God.

Nietzsche, in the last century, was an impassioned champion of pride, and he has been followed by a large number of those who declare themselves atheists. This trend of thinking can only end in a confrontation of forces and an attitude of mutual destruction. Since pride leads everyone to turn himself into God, it peoples the world with gods the struggle between whom knows no limits. But we have only three hypotheses to choose from: the pride I have just been discussing, the annihilation which we met in the ethics of emptiness, and absorption in the One which assumes that the One is love, for if the One did not come to man of its own accord, how could man ever raise himself up to it?

# III. The Threshold of Morality

The question of the threshold of morality consists in clarifying just when act begins to be moral, that is to say begins to display a moral character. For man performs many acts devoid of moral character, though from another point of view, every act has a moral character.

Now that is a very confused paragraph, but it expresses the confusion that in fact reigns in men's minds. We shall try to clear it up, and we could set about this in a number of ways. I am going to follow the classical line of the distinction between the objective or ontological character of the act—ontological or real—and its subjective or intentional character.

A definition which has progressively taken shape and which has today become traditional lays down that the morally good act is the good act performed with a good intention. On the other hand, for the act to be morally wrong, it is sufficient either for it to be materially wrong or for the intention to be wrong. But the current attitude diverges from this rule. Most people regard it as of little importance for a man to have a good intention when he is doing good. A man who does good because he likes it will say: So much the better; if I like it, it's a sign I am virtuous. On the other hand, the man who commits a sin with a good intention will ask to be excused: I didn't think about it, he will say. That is to say that in analogous circumstances he will claim the merit of the good action performed without a morally good intention and refuse to admit the guilt of the wrong action.

Only a minority of humble people deny the merit men impute to them for good actions without a specifically moral intention. We have encountered this case already. There is no merit in that, such people will say, for I like doing good; or: I did it without thinking. On the other hand, public opinion judges by the objectivity of the act. Comedies have been written in which the audience is set laughing at the spectacle of a man who instinctively performs an act which circumstances turn into an outstanding feat. In any case, it is clear that there are two elements in morality, and that general

\*    \*    \*

Primitive peoples concentrate almost entirely on the objective value of an action. Primitive man is not much of a psychologist: for him, facts are facts. Ceremonial impurity is incurred just as much by good as by evil acts. It is the substance of the act that results in impurity, and the legends of antiquity represent heroes such as Oedipus being punished for crimes they committed without knowing it.

The horror of acts which constitute a crime if they are committed intentionally persists among ordinary folk even if they act without any intention, and on this point most men are still ordinary folk. There are men who will go mad, or go through a long depression, should they kill anyone by accident or in self-defence, even though the victim was entirely in the wrong. They do not tell themselves: I acted like a physical cause; I have no more responsibility than a tile which the wind blows off the roof. Or even if they do think that, it does not prevent them from being distracted.

What is more, in the most cultivated circles, moral judgments continue to be inspired by the objective value of acts. People are classified on the basis of this. Those who belong to a social group where a high objective morality obtains despise outsiders. They regard themselves as better, and morally better, than thieves, prostitutes and tramps.

It is particularly interesting to discover this phenomenon in Christian societies, for no attitude could be more flatly opposed to the morality of the Gospels. Christ is constantly denouncing this attitude, and yet it continues to be the habitual attitude of many Christians. Nothing could show better the degree to which this outlook is rooted in human nature.

The point of view of the Gospels is not exactly what we are discussing here, but it leads up to it, because the first element of Christ's teaching is that every man should acknowledge himself to be guilty in face of God. That is the meaning of the parable of the Pharisee and the publican: a humble sinner is better than a righteous man inflated with pride.

Then, according to the Gospels, virtue assumes that we abandon ourselves to the divine will; it assumes detachment from worldly goods, and the gift of ourselves to God. Once Again the fundamental vice is pride, which revolts against this course.

Yet those who call themselves good men and believe they are such are frequently proud, and are sometimes the proudest of all. Christ's moral judgment is concerned first of all with pride; that of most of us is concerned with virtues which Christ regarded as secondary. Pride is widespread among those who believe themselves to be good Christians, and training in humility takes a very small place in moral training, particularly in modern times. But humility is a virtue which attaches importance first of all to what is within a man, that is to say intention.

* * *

As thinking progresses, men come to pay increasing attention to the subjective value of acts. They note that an act has no specifically moral value unless it is performed with a moral intention.

What is moral intention? It is the intention to perform the act on account of its moral value. But what determines moral value? This value is not to be distinguished from objective value. It is merely objective value in so far as it is willed, and objective value depends on the relationship of the act to absolute good. Moral intention is therefore the intention out of which we perform an act because it is an application of absolute good or, in the case of a morally wrong act, despite the fact that it diverts us from absolute good.

Once our attention is directed to this point, we see that moral intention depends solely on reason, that it is thus purely intellectual, and that there is no moral character in sentiment. The man who does good out of sentiment is thus devoid of morality, and we are all the more moral the more we act out of moral intention, that is to say out of rational will. If we are to progress in morality, we must thus steer clear even of good sentiments, because sentiments are alien to morality. We end with the Kantian definitions, which the Stoics had already

227

roughed out: 'It is not enough to do our duty; we must do it out of duty too.' Good done from a motive other than duty is not moral, but licit. We must mistrust sentiment: if I like doing good, it is to be feared that I have not done it for its own sake. And this brings us to the good men whom Nietzsche jeered at, whose goodness lay in doing good with aversion, the paragons with long faces.

*     *     *

How are we to resolve this antinomy?

First of all, it is clear that the purely instinctive act has no moral value. A man is drowning and I jump into the water to save him: a dog can do as much.

But I begin to wonder if I see that a dog jumps into the water in just the same way to retrieve a stick. We teach dogs life-saving by getting them into the habit of jumping into the water after a stick. Man does not work that way; when he jumps into the water to save a drowning man, he is obeying some impulse other than instinct.

We find in the moral tradition of the Catholic Church an effort to define the moral character of the act which probably, as I noted earlier, is without parallel in history. Kant's analyses are elementary stuff in comparison with this tradition, which is unfortunately little known outside theological circles, for a number of reasons. First of all it is buried in Latin works which are inaccessible to the modern intellectual public, and secondly this effort of reflection was prompted almost exclusively by the wish to determine what was a sin.

This tradition distinguishes three fundamental notions: that of virtual and habitual intention, and that of the multiplicity of intentions, these two notions being concerned with minimum morality; and that of the actualization of intention, which is encountered principally in ascetic literature.

First for the notion of virtual intention, which is bound up with a whole range of degrees of attention.

*Actual* intention is that which is deliberately brought to bear on the action. *Virtual* intention is the continuation in acts of a previous actual intention, without this intention having been forgotten. Virtual intention becomes *habitual* intention when the original intention has been forgotten, but its effects continue, because it has not been repudiated. In habitual intention, the original actual intention has become more or less unconscious and has led to the formation of a more or less automatic habit.

From this analysis it emerges that there are several layers of attention in consciousness, and moral value is attributed to every act which corresponds to one of these forms of attention.

Moral value thus extends far further than the deliberate act. The act retains moral value as long as the original intention has not been disavowed; as long as we *can* disavow this intention, there is still something rational and voluntary about the act. This doctrine, which is a traditional one, tallies with contemporary discoveries about the role of the subconscious and the unconscious, but it approaches the question from the other end. Twentieth century research tries to discover how far man is determined by the unconscious. The traditional Catholic line of thinking leads us to inquire how far man can act on what is sub-conscious.

Now for the multiplicity of intentions.

Catholic casuists have long noted that man can have several intentions at once in the same act. He can, for example, want to serve God, but at the same time want to satisfy a desire of his own. If he is not strong enough, he will be happy at being able to please God while satisfying a desire of his own, but the very fact that he is happy at it proves that he wants to please God.

We find a similar shade of meaning in the theory of permissive will. This consists in a man's submitting to a consequence of the act, of which he is aware, while directing his voluntary intention towards another consequence. This applies to acts with a twofold effect. A classical example is that of the thieves who force someone, under the threat of death, to hold the ladder with which they are climbing over a wall. The victim remains permissive with regard to the theft and directs his intention towards his desire to save his life. The same case occurs when I am told to do something pleasant. I can act out of obedience: I am ready to do anything if I am ordered to, and I remain permissive with regard to the pleasure. All this admits of a wide variety of shades of meaning.

229

There is thus a danger of these distinctions resulting in a lower kind of ethics, and those who are concerned with moral purity are not satisfied with them; but it is a question of the threshold of morality. All these acts possess a moral character or moral value, and consequently the fact of acting with enthusiasm or with pleasure does not deprive an act of its morality.

It follows from these distinctions that morality is compatible with a partial eudaimonism. Partial eudaimonism consists in wanting to be happy and being glad that good coincides with what we believe to be happiness. But complete eudaimonism seeks happiness alone, and is prepared to reject the moral rule if it does not appear to be of a nature to make men happy. This complete eudaimonism is therefore incompatible with moral value.

Finally comes the rule of *the actualization of moral intention*. We are no longer dealing here with the threshold of morality or with the ethical minimum, but with the maximum, the pursuit of perfection, and the rule is to seek as pure an actual intention as possible. It is one of the fundamental rules of spirituality.

Its follower sets out to cultivate virtual and habitual intention in the lower forms of action—to develop what are known as 'good habits'—so as to free the mind and allow it to bring all the weight of its deliberate will to bear on the purest forms of action.

Perfection would be to do everything with an actual intention of reduction to the One or of love of God, the rest being relegated to the domain of the virtual and the habitual. When I eat, my deliberate, actual intention should be to serve and to praise God. Any thoughts of feeding myself, preserving my health or enjoying the good cooking should be relegated to the obscurer domain of the virtual and the habitual, or of what moderns call the sub-conscious. The more the divine praise stands out, the more every other intention will fall into the background, and the better it will be. Sanctity is nothing else but this.

Here, in a way, we are back at Kant again. It is true that the intensity of moral value depends on the intensity of the intention directed towards moral good. But Kant's teaching is a mere skeleton. The doctrine of the actualization of intention and of the levels of morality has the richness and suppleness of the body, where the skeleton is covered with flesh and threaded with veins and nerves.

## IV. The Momentary and the Continuous

We have seen that the wise men's ethics is one of tendencies and code morality one of the act. The wise man says: You must tend towards this. Code morality says: Do that. One is thinking of the development of life; the other is thinking of the act in isolation, of each act in itself.

These two attitudes have always existed; indeed they are sometimes combined, when wisdom expresses itself by giving advice on practical conduct. But their point of view is different.

In our times, wisdom morality has found an unexpected confirmation from psychology and sociology, the two sciences which now tend to dominate man's existence, for both of them emphasize the continuity of life. The present depends on the past and paves the way to the future. What matters in the act is less the act in itself than all it involves. Some deep-lying instincts take form from the moment of conception. Parents should attend to the future of their child as soon as he is conceived; then, when he comes into the world, they should attend to his education. When he begins to gain control of himself, the essential problem is that of the moulding of his habits and his attitudes. The human being has to make himself, and what distinguishes him from other creatures is that his will comes into it. The others are purely receptive towards their inner tendencies and their environment. The fact that reason comes in gives the human being a capacity for intervention and personal action of an entirely different kind.

Most people make very little use of it. They live at random. And those who do use their reason, the wise men, do not begin to use it till they are adult, that is when they are already overgrown by a jungle of attitudes that have become instinctive, intellectual habits, ready-made opinions and automatic actions. The problem of wisdom is thus a collective problem, since any preparation for wisdom must begin before even a child is born, with the wisdom of its parents. Wise men such as have been known up to now represent no more than rough drafts of the wisdom man could theoretically attain. A transformation of the social environment which would make it a 'wisdom environment' should be one of the objectives of sociology. If it were possible to eliminate the obstacles to wisdom, the number and quality of wise men would increase.

It is true that human problems are so complex that unexpected difficulties crop up every time a bit of progress is made. But that does not mean that there is no genuine progress at all.

The literature of 'commitment' falls into the same line of thinking. The growing mental clarity which is a consequence of reflection on life and of the scientific developments of which we have just spoken, results in a fear of life which makes some no longer dare to commit themselves in life. They shy away from definitive commitments: this is clearly seen with regard to marriage, and in the political and social field in the movements characteristic of our time, the Nazism of yesterday and the Communism that is still with us today. The partisans of these movements do not admit that an institution, or a commitment, can have a definitive character. Institutions and commitments remain valid only as long as conditions stay the same. We are thus living in a perpetual state of the provisional: only the tendency does not change. The ideal of the Socialist society in Communism remains what it was, but the means to attain it are subject to an absolute opportunism.

Nevertheless, man must commit himself, for life is one and we cannot complete a work unless we devote ourselves to it continuously. A home and a family can only be built up through the permanence of the link involved. Hence the literature of 'commitment', which is a reaction against the fear of the definitive. Man can only fulfil himself by accepting his limitations, and one of these is that of determining himself progressively as he goes forward. To determine ourselves is also to limit ourselves. The architect who is building a house can only build it in one way, and he must abandon other possible plans. He must choose between them, and once he has chosen, he must stick to his choice till the job is finished. Now man's job is life; but whereas the architect can build a number of houses, man has only one life . . .

He must therefore take his life in hand and run it; but how can he run it if he does not have an idea, an idea that has unity, if he has no plan of life? All this assumes commitment, and since life is one and continuous, the commitment must be determined progressively, from the outset of existence. At each stage, a man must define his commitments, that is, his limitations. The time when men generally make their big choices, the time for conversions, vocations, marriage and the decision on a professional and social career, is the period of adolescence and youth, between the ages of fifteen and thirty. We must be ready to choose without having completely examined any single question.

\*　　\*　　\*

Set against the continuous is the momentary.

*Carpe diem* is the perennial motto of the crude pleasure seeker, and thinkers have turned it into a philosophical theme. 'Sufficient to the day is the evil thereof', say the Gospels, putting quite a different complexion on a similar idea. We shall see presently how the Gospel idea should be understood. But whichever way we take it, it plainly represents an attitude of welcome towards the moment which contrasts completely with that of planning and concern for the future.

A strong trend of thinking in the Christian tradition sets out from faith in Providence to extol a life that takes no thought for the morrow. A well-known anecdote of St Louis of Gonzaga relates that when the saint was asked one day at recreation what he would do if he was told he was going to die in an hour, he replied: 'I should go on with recreation.' That implies that we should do at every moment what we ought to do and not worry about the future; that there should be no balancing of advantages. We have a Father in heaven. He is watching over us; to provide for the future is to show lack of confidence to him, this attitude would maintain, and there is a 'virtue of improvidence'. At the same time, casuistry has developed a piecemeal moral conception, which considers each act in itself. A certain way of representing the sacrament of penance plays its part in this. The penitent confesses his sins and receives absolution: the past is wiped out, and he starts off again on a new life; nothing of the past remains. On the other hand, as we have seen, every act is big with eternity. The act is an absolute.

In our times, the absolute of the moment, which comes to the absolute of the act or of the present, has taken on a new form and a new vigour in Existentialism.

For the Existentialist, there is no reality but what exists. Now only the present exists. The past has ceased to exist; the future does not yet exist and may never exist, for if tomorrow I am no longer existing, nothing will exist. The words 'for me' should be added, but they are not.

There is nothing for us to do, then, but concentrate on the moment where we are. The ideal is to pack into a moment the whole value of life. One of the favourite themes of Existentialism is the novel portraying a character who knows he is going to die, in two days or immediately, and who calmly sets about concentrating all the intensity of life in this niggardly stretch of time or in the crowning act which is his death. That is the case with Hemingway's hero in *For Whom the Bell Tolls*, and with Cordelier's hero in *Les yeux de la tête*.

The Existentialists like to relate this paroxysm of life to death, because if a man dies immediately afterwards, the moment becomes an absolute. That assumes that there is no future life, but they do not even raise this question.

Using a method which may be an easy way out, they often end, through a sort of necessity, in locating this paroxysm of life in carnal love. Since the novel lends itself to everything, this carnal love is always completely happy and involves no disappointment. But the basic idea, the one that matters to us here, is that of concentrating the whole of life in the moment. Sartre, Camus and others transpose this idea to a more abstract level, but it remains the same: time matters little, we do not have to remember or anticipate, the only thing we have to do is to live the moment as intensely as possible. Will there be other moments afterwards? That is not what matters: for the moment, only the present exists. If other moments emerge from nothingness afterwards, we will treat them in the same way, each of them being a thing unique, an absolute involving no sequel.

It is an outlook that suggests an internal combustion engine, or the hand of a clock moving forward in jerks. Each explosion in the cylinders, each jerk of the hand, is a thing in itself between two immobilities.

This Existentialist conception comes down, in different terms, to the old eudaimonism. What we are seeking in the moment is self-exaltation; that is to say that we are seeking ourselves, and seeking only ourselves. We are seeking the absolute in ourselves. The cult of the moment is the pursuit of the absolute in the moment. Nothing exists but ourselves. There is no more question of foresight; no more question of the methodical development suggested by psychology and sociology, with a view to attaining a perfection which lies in the future or which can even benefit others. There is no question of taking our place in a whole; no question of a mission of man, nor of a co-operation in a common task. The moment becomes a thing unique and the self becomes an absolute. Since it is impossible to attain to happiness on these lines outside novels, those who think thus end up in the hopeless pessimism of the 'tormented philosophers', for if the moment does not achieve this absolute, there is no more good.

This conception is also a young man's conception and ignores the development of man. Its heroes are grown men, who are detached from their past and who will never grow old, because they are going to die soon. It is impossible to fit marriage, the family, the rearing of children and the fulfiment of a role in society into this conception. It leads to Camus's *The Stranger*, a neutral character, indifferent to everything, useless, amoral, living and dying without making up his mind about good and without finality, in short, approximating to an animal as far as it is possible for a man to do.

\*     \*     \*

The Gospel morality successively tackles the two aspects of the question. Christ dwells on providence and trust in God in texts that are often cited. He reacts against man's tendency to trust in himself, and that is the chief thing people remember in his teaching. But the implications of this teaching are entirely different from those of Existentialism, which we have just been discussing, or of classical eudaimonism. The fundamental idea is that of surrender to God, though from the human point of view, the emphasis is laid on the present. On the other hand, other texts tally with the notion of the continuity of life advanced by the scientific movement of our times.

'If one of you has a mind to build a tower, does he not first sit down and count the cost that must be paid, if he is to have enough to finish it? . . . Or if a king is setting out to join battle with another king, does he not first sit down and deliberate, whether with his army of ten thousand he can meet the onset of one who has twenty thousand? . . .' We often encounter the idea of the duty of a continuous and planned action, in the parable of the talents, for instance, and in the saying that a good tree bears good fruits . . . The value of the tree depends on everything that happens to it from the moment its seed is dug into the ground, and therefore we should turn our attention to the conditions of the tree's development, since its fruits grow spontaneously.

The Christian's outlook thus involves a certain balance. On one hand, Christ lays stress on trust in God. The prime object of his revelation, as we have seen, is the divine fatherhood: God is a father, he loves us, he cares for us, he protects us and guides us. The Christian attitude is above all an attitude of trust in God, and the Gospel utterances against forethought are designed to stimulate trust in God, as well as to curb the confidence men put in themselves. When Christ reminds us that death comes like a thief in the night, or tells the parable of the rich man who built great barns to store his crops and died the day he should have started to enjoy them, the moral he wants to point is that man is a creature and cannot trust in himself. And this mistrust of ourselves, as we saw in connection with humility, is a counterpart of trust in God.

But though the consciousness of being a creature may lead a man to mistrust himself, it also impels him to accept the conditions in which God has placed him. To accept God is to accept being what he has made us, and that leads straight to contemporary psychology and sociology, which confine themselves to detailing the conditions of our nature. Now it is our nature to have a continuous life, we are beings who grow, develop progressively, and develop together, beings whose task is a collective one. Surrender to Providence thus implies an unreserved acceptance of the human situation. There is no contradiction between the Christian surrender to Providence and foresight, because both depend on faith in the divine love.

It is true that in practice, Christian wisdom seems to have laid more stress on improvidence, in a reaction against the sort of shrewdness that is prompted by human considerations and by confidence in ourselves, without regard to the will of God. But this is a question of practical application, which may vary from one generation to another and from one country to another. The key point is to grasp the way in which Christianity weds the momentary to the continuous, taking both into account.

If we try to fit contemporary Existentialist thought into this Christian synthesis, we may get a clearer idea of the importance of the moment or of the absolute value of every act. It is true that only the present exists, that the past is finished with, that we can do nothing to change it, that it is therefore an established fact and that, from the point of view of the present, I have only to turn it to the best advantage. It is also true that the future does not yet exist, that I do not know what it will be and that the present is the only means I have of acting on it. But that does not mean that I need not be concerned with the future, my own future, which I am moulding through my present, and the future of those I can help, or that I need not take my place in the great collective task to which God has assigned me. The perfect Christian takes into account everything that the human situation implies, including the fact that death 'comes like a thief in the night'. Above all he knows that the human situation is dominated by the God of love.

## V. Absolute Good and the Contingence of the Means to It

The absoluteness of the moral imperative is one of the ideas which emerge most clearly from all our investigations.

Kant's analysis of it is a classical one and remains valid provided it is corrected by substituting for the absoluteness of duty the absoluteness of good. I have already referred to this and there is no need to bring it up again. What concerns us now is to see how this absoluteness of good fits into practical action.

The first consequence of the absoluteness of good is that an act or a refusal to act which is necessarily bound up with good is an imperative of an absolute character, an unconditional imperative, whatever its intrinsic significance. Everything assumes the value of an absolute in so far as it is a necessary application of the absolute.

The Second Book of Machabees tells the story of the old man Eleazer. King Antiochus, who was persecuting the Jews, had ordered that they should all be made to eat pork. The Jewish law forbade it, but it was obviously a thing without importance in itself. Eleazer was one of the most respected scribes of the Jewish community. He refused to eat pork. The meat was forced into his mouth, but he spat it out. His friends begged him to pretend to have eaten it, though he had in fact eaten permitted food. He refused once more, because he could not allow it to be said that he had broken the Law. Finally he obliged the officials who should have made him eat the pork to lead him away to his execution. Cases of this kind are encountered in every religious persecution.

Christianity has developed this sense of the absoluteness of good most powerfully in developing the sense of God. But since this absolute attitude is never more than a minority affair, and since an attempt has been made to put forward an ethics accessible to the masses on the level of code morality, casuists have devoted themselves to an analytical operation with a view to cutting down duty to a minimum. Once men commit themselves to this course, they reach an intermediate

238

zone where it is impossible to determine where good begins and ends.

During the persecution of Decius, an attempt was made to force Christians to abjure their faith by obliging all citizens to offer a sacrifice to the gods. Those who did so received a sacrifice certificate. Alongside the Christians who flatly refused and those who did sacrifice, there were a certain number who tried to dodge the issue. One way of doing this was to pay money for a certificate without sacrificing. The Church condemned such people, but in every period we find hairsplitting of the same kind in the casuistry of lying.

We have seen that words and gestures always have a more or less conventional sense. That is why the only way of settling delicate questions once for all is to have a love of the good. The problem of the exact delimitation of good for the benefit of those who do not love it is insoluble. The man with a strong moral sense makes no mistake about it. He does not inquire whether this or that act is permissible, that is, whether it is possible to produce an argument justifying it. He reacts spontaneously to the good.

When we have a sense of the good, moral value becomes the only value that matters. The rest does not count any more, and values are graded according to the place they occupy in the moral scale.

It is the same with all wise men. One of their commonest characteristics is their contempt for wealth; another is their contempt for social values. Generally speaking, they impress people by their austerity and their scorn for physical comfort and for what flatters their vanity. These traits make them stand out unmistakably from ordinary folk. The very impression they produce shows that there are not many of them; a delicate moral sense is an exceptional phenomenon. In the eyes of most men, the aim of life is pleasure or the respect of those around them, and morality comes to seem a hindrance to this. Hence the fairly general view of morality as a millstone, and the reaction of antimoralism: we have discussed this.

On the other hand, the man who has a pure moral sense is in danger of 'moralism' if his metaphysical training is inadequate. I have used the word 'metaphysical' here, but it is a question of something very simple, which we find in people

239

who do not even know what 'metaphysical' means. 'Moralism' is the term for a realism which leads a man to think that moral good is nothing more than real good, every good, any good whatsoever, in so far as it is offered to a free will, and that good is to be found in truth and beauty and cannot be found elsewhere.

*　　*　　*

Nevertheless, though moral good may be an absolute, it is attained only in contingent objects. Now the contingent object displays only one aspect of reality. Man has the sense of the absolute within him, and he only meets with limited, particular and relative things. We must resign ourselves to this, cultivate the sense of the absolute, be constantly guided in our lives by the thought of the absolute and the sense of the reality of the absolute, and at the same time put up with expressing this sense of the absolute in the relative, with the help of 'worn-out' tools, as Kipling puts it.

This results in a general disappointment among those who have not pondered over the matter. And who has pondered over it, except for a few old professors? The convert asks: 'Now that I've made up my mind to seek perfection, what ought I to do?' He is told: 'Do a good job of work, be a good citizen, a good husband, a good father ...' He replies: 'But I've always done that ...' Conversion assumes that a man does it in another spirit; if the spirit changes, the substance of the acts will undergo sometimes imperceptible modifications; certain attitudes will assume more prominence, others will fall into the background. But we cannot think of any specific act to do which will constitute a face-about and whose importance will be proportionate to the absolute the man wants to embrace.

In this respect, the sinner who is converted may be said to be in an easier position. He knows there is something essential to change in his life. He can signify his adhesion to the absolute by an unmistakable move. All the same, that can only happen once. Once the sinner has renounced his sin and restored the balance of his life on another plane, that life goes on in the same way without any abrupt modification. The

240

temptation of all those who aspire to perfection is to want to express their ideal by means of acts of as intransigent a kind as their ambition.

That explains ascetic exaggerations and the tendency to the ascesis of emptiness. The only absolute that seems within our reach is the absolute of destruction. Even in the Christian tradition, which is so temperate in itself, we find a certain number of saints with a sort of fury of self-destruction. They do not erect it into a rule, pleading that they are unusually depraved, and that their flesh will never be broken in unless they employ these violent means. But the real starting point of their attitude is the impression that their ego is an obstacle to the absolute.

It is the same in the field of mysticism: the absolute is to be found by a man losing himself in the One. Here again, the ego is eliminated in the One. Besides, ascesis and mysticism generally go together, for we do not lose ourselves in the One unless we are first lost to ourselves.

Nevertheless, though the ego may stand in the way of the absolute, and though the relativity of means may prevent us from reaching the absolute, we can only attain to it through our ego. We represent to ourselves the only means we have of attaining or achieving the absolute in our life, and we must thus accept our human situation, of which in any case the sense of the absolute forms part. We noted earlier that man is a being who is torn apart. To accept the human situation is to accept this tearing.

'The measure of love is to love without measure,' a classical saying tells us. Yes, but we never succeed in loving without measure, because we are limited. We are limited by our body which gets tired, by time which hems us in, by space. When we study the greatest contemplatives, we realize that the states of supreme contemplation of which their lives talk were no more than fleeting moments. Others seek the absolute in the world and in the flesh, and we have seen that this quest is expressed in the form of legends and of fiction. Some seek the absolute in human love. But it all ends in disappointment. The only way we can really embody the absolute in our life is by accepting the contingency of means.

A very symptomatic doctrine about mystical union has

241

developed in the Catholic tradition. These states of union are regarded by theologians as supernatural states, that is to say that the union the soul experiences in such moments is one which is inaccessible to man and can only come from God, who brings it about when and how he pleases. It is a divine caress, a free grace, that is to say that man has no part in it. Since it is ineffable, no human phraseology can express it, and consequently it is impossible by a description to distinguish genuine mystical states from human states in which some people believe they are experiencing divine action.

The way they can be distinguished is that the genuine mystical state promotes humility and charity. For since the genuine mystical state is the presence in us of God, it gives us the sense of truth while giving us the sense of God: when we have a clearer vision of God, we apprehend every truth in a clearer light as a result. Purifying the sense of God in us purifies the sense of the scale of values. It follows from this that the genuine mystic is better able to apprehend the absolute in the relative, and in proportion to his mystical life assigns everything its place.

That does not happen to those who seek the absolute elsewhere. The only way to the absolute is progressively to cultivate the sense of the absolute in the relative.

\*       \*       \*

This search for the absolute in the relative involves the danger of aberrations in more than one direction. The balance which is the aim there is a very delicate one.

A first form of aberration is to attach little importance to the relative, on the pretext that only the absolute counts. If I am concerned with a particular aspect of the relative, if I practise a profession, for example, it will be solely because it seems the means for me to introduce the absolute into my life. The relative only matters in so far as it is a means of achieving the absolute, and if another means were better, I should choose it. Thus I do not apply myself to the means for itself.

The result is an attitude of detachment which is unhealthy, for though it may be true that the relative only possesses value in so far as it permits me to attain the absolute, it is also true

242

that there is no other means of attaining the absolute, and I shall not attain it unless I apply myself to the relative in itself. I must apply myself to it for the absolute, but apply myself to it in itself at the same time, for it is in it that I find the absolute.

In every religious community, we find certain of the 'perfect' displaying an attitude of disdain for human values, for example, personal cleanliness—they will be dirty and slovenly in their dress—or of neglect for their social duties. In the West, we encounter this in certain Christian circles, but we also meet with it in the Moslem and the Indian world. In the philosophical field, this attitude finds expression in idealism and moral subjectivism.

When the Kantian tradition stresses the exclusive value of the intention in morality, it ends by disregarding objective value and preaching an ethics of sincerity. It matters little what we believe to be good, its partisans assert; we are on the right road as soon as we are sincere. They show the same regard for all those who are sincere, even if they are following opposite courses. They do not ask who is right any more. Everyone must work out his own ethics.

Outside the Christian world, the strongest contemporary reaction against this subjectivism comes from Marxism. Marxism comes out against idealism, calling for submission to reality. What matters is not the idea, the idea in my head: what matters is the external reality, and I must submit to it.

If Marxism were confined to this, it would be in agreement with the tradition which Christian thinkers have always defended. The notion of creation implies that God and the world are realities which compel recognition from the outside. But in its reaction against idealism, Marxism believes it must react against any acceptance of a spiritual reality. There its realism shows itself short-sighted.

It is none of our business here to inquire into the causes and the origins of Marxist materialism, nor to investigate its nature. Since it had no links with the great philosophical tradition which goes back to the Greeks, it was unable to take an overall view of the question. Fascinated as it was by the social and political issues which were at the origin of its conception, it contented itself with partial views which leave

243

room for considerable modification by the generations to come.

But as things stand, it is this notion of 'objectivity' as opposed to idealist subjectivism that is responsible for Marxist intolerance. Claiming that their solutions are dictated by the facts, the Marxists conclude that they are the sole custodians of the truth, for truth is what is—and we are in agreement with them over this principle. Applying this to the political, social and economic order, they end with authoritarian systems on the social level. It is none of our business to discuss these systems here. But we should note that, so far as general principles are concerned, Marxist realism or objectivity is a return to tradition, despite its glaring over-simplification.

\*     \*     \*

An aberration of an opposite kind to that we have just been discussing consists in placing the absolute in the relative while treating the relative as if it were the absolute.

Here we shall encounter the sanctimonious devotees who are to be found in every age and every community, the people who take themselves for 'pocket Gods' because they are in the service of God. We shall meet the self-styled wise men who attribute an absolute importance to the least of their acts, on the pretext that they do nothing that is not in the service of wisdom. We shall find that such wise men and devotees are the most susceptible of men because they feel that anything that reflects on them personally reflects on the absolute with which they believe themselves to be impregnated.

An argument we often hear from these pseudo-saints is: If it were only a question of me, it wouldn't matter, but to reflect on me is to reflect on Value—or God, or whatever other value they regard as supreme. We even meet this over patriotism, in the form of the Englishman, the Frenchman or the German who happens to be abroad and takes it as a reflection on his country when people do not treat him with the consideration he expects.

We must therefore be able to treat the relative as relative

and the absolute as absolute, but accept the fact that the absolute is only attainable in our human life through the means of the relative. We must further treat this relative with the respect that the absolute demands, in so far as this relative enshrines the absolute, but nevertheless maintain a detachment from the relative except in so far as it expresses the absolute. This is such a delicate form of balance that, from one point of view, our whole life's work is to achieve it, and nobody achieves it perfectly. It is none too easy even to express it without ambiguity.

It can thus be said that we must take everything seriously in so far as it is a means of reduction to the One, and take nothing seriously in itself or as an instrument for us. If we apply this attitude to the great synthesis of the Kingdom of God to be built in the world, there emerges from it a soul-stirring vision of life which rules out any pettiness and any self-regard.

## VI. Inner Life and Action

The key role played by intention in moral life results in ethics concentrating on the life within; hence the primacy of contemplation which we have encountered in every school of wisdom. Nevertheless we have seen that in Christianity, this inner life, however important it may be, still remains no more than a means, the end lying in charitable action which unifies man in the service of the Kingdom.

All the same, inner life constitutes an indispensable and essential means. In order to unify our life in God, we must direct our thinking, and realize what God is and just how all value in general and every value in particular is related to him. We shall never set our life in order unless we have a clear and habitual consciousness, as actual as possible, of the way in which each of our acts is related to the general task of reduction to the One which we must achieve.

The moral significance of acts derives first and foremost from their intentionality; our acts have value as acts of ours in so far as they embody an element of us, and this is intention. The moral value depends on love and on the intensity of love.

That is the meaning of the Gospel incident of the widow's mite, to which we referred earlier.

In so far as there is little intentionality in the act, it approximates to a natural phenomenon, the growth of a plant or the fall of a stone, and it loses its human character. It is from the inner life that moral value draws its source.

Thus we can only set our life in order if we are constantly alive to the relationship of the act to the One. This awareness assumes a lively consciousness of the One, and this consciousness of the One is not directly developed through action.

Action puts us in contact with limited goods, and when we are concerned with one of them, we must concentrate attention on it. I can only write this book if I concentrate on what I have to say, and the human situation makes it impossible to concentrate on several things at once. That is why action distracts us from the One. It has a bewildering effect, and action can only be well-ordered if we fix our mind on the One to start with. This is achieved in recollection, only if our consciousness of the One has become sufficiently deep for us to be able to refer to it spontaneously whenever we are called on to act. This being so, we can understand why all the wise men attach such importance to the meditative retreat.

Here again, however, we are confronted with the antinomy which is peculiar to everything human.

First of all, there is a danger of illusion. The man who holds aloof from action is in danger of crediting himself with the virtues about which he thinks. This is a form of pride. Many contemplatives suffer from pride, for often it is active life and contact with the outside world, nature and other men which makes us conscious of our weakness. The workman becomes aware of his incompetence when he starts to use his tools. It is easy to dream up masterpieces in our imagination, and it is also easy to love and desire virtue shut up in a cell. It is only when we come up against the obstacle of our own weakness and of the opposition or the misunderstanding of others, amid the sacrifices, the renunciations and the humiliations of action that we become conscious of our limitations.

Human experience shows that it is easier to have an idea of good than to do it. A man who sees a mountain from a distance gets the impression it is easy to climb; it is only when

246

he starts to climb it that he becomes aware of the limitations of his strength and the obstacles with which reality confronts him.

Next, there comes a danger of weakness. We may believe we have attained perfection because we like the thought of it, and we do not realize that we are deviating from it because our will is becoming anaemic for lack of exercise.

It is here that the essential role of sacrifice in moral life comes in. This role is so obvious that it is fundamentally sacrifice which gives the 'moral shock' which we discussed earlier. We met it in connection with Kipling's *If,* and with the Sermon on the Mount, and we shall be returning to it. The aspect of the question which concerns us here is that the man who does not sacrifice anything loses his strength. Sports champions must go without a lot of pleasures if they are to keep in trim.

That is also why, when men organize a contemplative way of life, it is always a life of mortification. Everyone knows about the Catholic contemplative monasteries, but the same rule is to be found everywhere the contemplative life appears. All the same, this form of sacrifice is less efficacious than that which is a consequence of action. For an indispensable element of sacrifice is that of not being chosen, and action demands constant sacrifices of every kind, without a man's own will coming into it. It is true that few men of action profit from it, because they do not base their action on the inner life. But the inner life also lacks an essential element if it is not put to the test in action.

The contemplative monasteries may be said to live retired within themselves, applying themselves to the creation among the religious of a miniature kingdom of God, where all the virtues shall reign. But they also apply themselves to combining elements of active life with the contemplative life, for most of the religious have a job to do in the house, some of them being very material, such as cooking or laundry work.

Finally, the inner life involves a danger of becoming self-centred. Through too much thinking about the relations of our soul with God or the pursuit of perfection, we come to think of nothing but ourselves. Whereas the object of the inner life should be to forget ourselves so as to lose ourselves in the

One, we end up by thinking more about ourselves than ordinary men who lose themselves in action.

The man of action loses himself in action because he cannot achieve his task unless he lets himself be absorbed in it. The artist cannot do his job, nor the craftsman, nor the workman either, unless he is entirely absorbed in it at the moment he is doing it. The self-centredness of the contemplative is one more form of illusion. There are no delusions about the external object: if I make a pair of shoes, I must follow the rules of the craft. To discover God in ourselves is a much more delicate affair, and even more delicate is it to discover the good, which is an abstract idea. It is only at the cost of extreme purification that we succeed in distinguishing how to do it. Hence the need for putting contemplation to the test in action.

It may be asked why, despite this, wise men are all agreed in praising the inner or the contemplative life almost exclusively—witness the remark: 'Every time I have mixed with men, I have come back from it less of a man.' The reason is that the mass of men are so exclusively swayed by material and social ambitions, and so completely ignorant of the inner life; they do not even realize that such a thing can exist. The wise man therefore feels so far removed from the human herd that all he can think of is extolling the inner life. It is a phenomenon of reaction.

A book which had its moment of success bore the title *The Soul of the Apostolate*. Nobody has yet written one entitled *The Body of Contemplation*. Yet contemplation runs the risk of declining into a morbid dream if it holds aloof from all action, just as action becomes incoherent unless it is based on the inner life.

\* \* \*

We are living in a century in which the problem of the inner life and of action forces itself on us with peculiar insistence. The technological civilization characteristic of our times lays enormous stress on action—we are going to discuss this—but subjects it to an ever-increasing tempo which makes thinking difficult. Human life is more and more dominated by excitement and noise. As a reaction, a desire for silence, reflection, calm and deliberation is spreading among an elite. In the United States, which passes for the typical country of the strenuous life and the cult of action, contemplative monasteries are springing up on every hand in the Catholic community, while in non-Christian circles, schools of wisdom are appearing, on lines adapted from that of Epictetus or of Confucius. Even in the world of technology, there is a rash of research departments where research workers pursue their investigations at leisure, while research institutes have been set up where men can work in peace. The very exaggeration of action has thus provoked contemplation.

At the same time, there is an unparalleled vogue for Oriental contemplative literature. This Oriental literature, particularly the Hindu literature, is purely contemplative. It is a mystical literature devoted solely to the emptiness of the soul and the pursuit of the One. It is exclusively contemplative in a way we never find in the New Testament, because the Christian message is the news that God is with us, that God is in man's life and that the whole of man's life is divinized, with no necessity to get rid of the human situation. Moreover, Christianity is linked, in one way, with the development of the civilization of action which originated in the West. Thus certain minds who want a purely contemplative spiritual good are drawn to the great Hindu contemplative books, and those who do not believe in the Christian faith find in this literature a religious value which leads them towards the sense of God.


## VII. CREATIVE ACTIVITY

We now come to the aspect of moral life which is most characteristic of our times. The notion of creative activity undoubtedly forms the essential contribution of our age to ethical thinking.

To understand this, we must recall the transformation of man's outlook brought about by modern civilization.

For the ancients, as we saw, man came into the world in conditions of stability that ruled out any possibility of a transformation either of the nature in which he was immersed, or of his own living conditions. Consequently the problem of wisdom was essentially an individual and an inner one. It was how to live through the mind and hold aloof from the world.

Certain thinkers attained to the conception of collective action. For the Greeks of the Classical age, the fundamental problem was, from one point of view, that of the best organization of the city. All the same, this was itself focused on the personal search for wisdom, for the perfect city is the one which disposes its citizens to be wise men. In the same way, Chinese thinking, particularly in its Confucian form, was largely centred on the collective good: virtue will reign if the State is well-organized. But these thinkers took man in the state in which they found him, with the mental and material resources he then possessed. God had placed man in the world and endowed him with an assortment of blessings, but there was no question of man transforming the world in his image.

On the contrary, the thinkers of antiquity are in general strictly conservative, respecters of the old-time traditions. There is a presumption in favour of everything that comes down from their forebears. From time to time, a discovery is made by chance, and changes certain conditions of life. It is then integrated into the existing civilization, and men go on much as before, never dreaming that yet further discoveries lie ahead, still less trying to make them.

The sixteenth and seventeenth centuries are generally regarded as the age of the great discoveries which set the Western mind on the track of a new conception, one that laid down the transformation of the world as the goal for man. We discussed this in the last chapter in connection with assistance altruism. Our business here is to go back to these ideas, looking at things from the point of view of the individual.

The human situation then appears as follows:

Man is a being compounded of acts and potentialities, that is to say capable of changing. Indeed, he changes of necessity; he either develops or decays. The object of life is to develop. This links up with our whole synthesis: God has put man into the world with a capacity for progressive perfection, and this is indeed the object of his life. The body develops, the mind develops, and this twofold development must be put at the service of a moral development which will ensure an increas-

250

ing mastery of himself, an increasing capacity to utilize all his faculties and an increasing reduction to the One. Life should thus follow a constantly mounting curve, and the physical and mental decrepitude which overtake men at a certain age should not prevent a continuation of the moral progress which eventually issues in perfect absorption in the One through death.

Man is thus a compound of acts and potentialities. The potentialities are active or passive: the passive potentiality is a capacity for absorbing and the active potentiality a capacity for action. When man comes into the world, his passive potentiality is at a maximum. There is nothing he cannot become; his passive potentialities only dwindle from then on. On the other hand, his active potentiality is at a minimum to start with, and constantly increases.

When his active potentialities yield fruit, that is to say when they become means of action, man becomes capable of acting, but he limits himself when he determines himself. The baby who cannot talk is equally capable of learning any language. The day he has learned to talk, he has of necessity learned to talk *a* language, for we do not learn to talk in the abstract. When he knows a language, this knowledge constitutes an active potentiality, but he has no longer the same passive potentiality for learning any language.

Man develops his personality by actualizing his passive potentialities by their transformation into active potentialities. We have an active potentiality when we 'can do something'. Man's active potentialities permit him to select from the outside world what is necessary to develop his personality. When I eat a dish or read a book I am developing my personality by selecting something from the outside world. This selection is virtuous when it does in fact develop me, as does wholesome food or a good book. It is vicious when its aim is dissolute pleasure.

But this development of potentialities is only an initial stage. Man should not develop for the sake of developing; he should develop in order to act, to fulfil his task. Active potentiality tends towards the act.

St Thomas took over from Aristotle the saying: *bonum est diffusivum sui,* the good tends to spread, and this saying

251

explains creation. For the two philosophers, the statement was a self-evident one, which they asserted without dreaming of proving it. But analysis of man, psychological and phenomenological alike, confirms that the fact of a completely balanced well-being manifests itself in him through a desire to produce, that is to say to extend his personality beyond its own limits, to put the stamp of his personality on something other than himself, or so to act that there shall exist other beings in whom the stamp of his own personality will reappear.

Plato had observed earlier, in an *obiter dictum,* that the two crowning forms of human activity are the work of art and procreation. We can take over this idea by assimilating to the work of art any sort of intellectual achievement, philosophical system or political constitution, and to procreation any activity that directly tends to transform man. In the Christian vocabulary, men are constantly using terms connected with procreation to talk of the apostolate. St Paul writes to his disciples that he has 'begotten' them in Christ, and there is frequent talk of spiritual childbirth, spiritual fatherhood and spiritual children.

Between *selection,* whose aim is self-development, and *production,* through which man fulfils his task in the world, comes *conquest,* through which man seeks simply to display his value, in order to increase his stature in his own eyes or in the eyes of others. It is a sign of health in a young man to want to make himself master of everything in order to affirm his value to himself. If he sees a ditch, he wants to jump over it; if he sees a mountain, he wants to climb it; if he sees a country, he wants to explore it or to conquer it. Children who have no temptation to climb trees, rob nests or steal apples are children with something missing in them. In the same way, the normal man cannot see an unknown object without wanting to know about it: lack of curiosity is, moreover, a sign of being at a sub-human stage. It is the same again with the taste for risk, for danger, or for adventure, all of them means of affirming ourselves.

The foregoing is a phenomenological analysis. It is replaced in philosophical synthesis by the principle that the earthly expression of reduction to the One is to produce the work which we are capable of producing to the greater glory of

God. Through my work, I affirm my will to express God in my life and in the world. Certain saints have made the symbolic gesture of branding the name of Jesus on their chest with a red hot iron. It is a means for a man to express his self-dedication; but this act displays no more than a desire. Man's fulfilment lies in expressing the One in his life, expressing it through his work in the world, because the sign of human maturity is the work through which we display our personality.

\* \* \*

It is thus a question of work, of any work through which man expresses his personality.

The sign that denotes man is the manifestation of thought. In our times, many people have been led astray over this notion, because they were hypnotized by technological progress. They have believed that the sign of intelligence is to be found in the machine, or before that in the tool, and that the whole evolution of man can be explained by economic values. Hence Marxist historical materialism, and capitalist materialism which sets man the goal of getting rich. Hence also, on a more general plane, the Bergsonian concept of *homo faber.*

Bergson sets his conception of *homo faber* against the traditional conception of *homo sapiens* : according to him, the sign that indicates man's appearance on earth is not intelligence, but the tool. In prehistoric diggings, the sign which shows that man was there is the presence of tools, that is, objects which have been transformed with a view to acting on nature.

It is true that the sign of man is the manifestation of intelligence, but it is not true that the tool is the chief way intelligence displays itself. It can display itself by way of the tool, but it can also display itself in other ways, for material achievements are not the only thing the mind has to cope with. Nobody knows the motivation of the paintings that have been found in prehistoric caves. They may have had a religious significance, they may also have had an aesthetic one; in any case, they are not tools. In the same way, among the most primitive peoples who have been met with in our times, ornamentation sometimes comes before clothing. It is thus true to say that the sign of man is the intellectual achievement; it is not true to say that it is the tool.

\* \* \*

The virtue peculiar to creative activity is what the tradition of antiquity knew as the virtue of fortitude. It is a many-sided virtue, which includes energy, the sense of responsibility, readiness to take the initiative or to take risks, exhilaration over the consciousness of developing and acting, and pleasure in work. It is the virtue of zest and enthusiasm, the flat contrary of every form of weakness. Components of weakness are the fear of responsibility, the desire for security and melancholy.

The virtue of fortitude is characteristic of primitive Christianity. Later on, however, under the influence of bad Christians who saw nothing in Christ's message but an obstacle to the satisfaction of their desires, Christianity altered its course in a negative direction, and though Christian enthusiasm remained alive among the saints, ordinary people regarded it as puzzling and paradoxical. This led to the position Nietzsche jeered at when he wrote: 'They will have to sing me better hymns if they are to make me believe in their Saviour; his disciples will have to look more saved.' In reality, Nietzsche, like most of the enemies of Christianity, did not know good Christians; but it must be admitted that the superficial look of the millions who call themselves Christians supports him.

Contemporary literature shows that the virtue of fortitude is being more and more looked up to as the pre-eminent virtue. The typical hero of fiction is the man who displays this virtue: the explorer, the flyer, the inventor, and so on. Books that tell this sort of story become best-sellers. But, like the return to contemplation, this trend indicates a reaction against the contemporary habits of thinking which exacerbate every form of anxiety. These take the shape of an exclusive concern for security of which Neo-Malthusianism is a good example. The Neo-Malthusian is afraid of children because he is afraid of risks, and this fear of risks stifles creative enthusiasm. The same outlook is to be found everywhere in so far as society is stricken by a spirit of decrepit old age.

The rarer the man who takes a risk, the greater his prestige. The virtue of fortitude has always been responsible for the kudos of the hero. But today, through the doctrine of creative activity, we are in a position to formulate the theory of it, in terms which bring it within the framework of the ethical synthesis.

## VIII. INDIVIDUAL GOOD AND SOCIAL GOOD

The fundamental rule of the integration of the individual into the community and of individual good into social good is easy to work out if we take into account what has been said about assistance-altruism and creative activity. All the same, we should clarify it from the point of view of the perfection of man, for the community is there for the service of man and cannot, in the long run, result in interfering with his development.

Man achieves his perfection in work: we have just seen this. Strictly speaking, he *manifests* it in his work, for the work depends on the perfection of the workman. Theoretically, this should thus come before the work. Before I begin to write, I must learn to write. But we have also seen, in connection with the inner life and action, that a man trains himself in virtue by practising it. An apprentice's work is no more than a rough draft. We shall never guess at all the problems of a job of work as long as we envisage it in the abstract. A workman is judged by his work, and a man does not become a good workman unless he sets to work.

The influence of the worker on his work and of the work on the workman is thus mutual. Man manifests his value through work, but he increases it too. From every point of view, then, man fulfils himself in his work.

On the other hand, this work is social, that is to say that the activity which constitutes it forms part of the general activity of the human race and of all the particular communities to which the workman may belong. Activities which seem most individual are profoundly influenced by a man's environment, for example that of the artist or the philosopher. All of them bear the stamp of their time and reflect the techniques, the sentiments, the tastes and the general outlook of their environment. Rubens and Raphael would not have painted as they did had they grown up in a different world, and Plato and Descartes would not have thought as they did had they been contemporaries of Bergson. Man is a reflection of his environment and he is at the service of his environment, even when he least believes he is. It is thus essential for a man to co-ordinate his action with his environment. A work that laid claim not to take its environment into account would be an abortive work.

This dependence on the social environment explains why, even from the individual point of view, man does not attain to his full stature unless he is in harmony with his environment, though in other respects the wise man is master of his environment. The vast majority of men, as we have seen, are passive towards their environment, and the wise man stands out through his independence; but that independence is a relative one. The wise man uses his environment to perfect himself and to accomplish his work. The human ideal is thus not an ideal of withdrawal, but an ideal of conscious and rational collaboration.

Chinese ethics furnishes an excellent example of this good use of the environment in its doctrine of the *li*, which may be translated as social rites. The *li* correspond to the rules of politeness or good breeding and no people has carried the refinement of courtesy so far.

But the *li*, as the Chinese see it, have a metaphysical implication. They are no mere conventional rules of good manners. Through the *li*, man shapes his life to the universal order. They therefore complete this. They turn man into an element wholly co-ordinated with the universe. The *li* make man a participant in the eternal order. There is nothing arbitrary about them.

What concerns us here is the moral aspect of the question. The Chinese are, I believe, the only people who have included manners in ethics. Everywhere else wise men like to effect a certain churlishness which is due to the fact that what they see in politeness is chiefly hypocrisy and vanity. The wise man is concerned with simplicity and frankness. What the Chinese see in politeness on the other hand is a mastery of the self. It shows a lack of manners and of tact to feel we have to say what we think to all and sundry. The man who contains himself is master of his words and his gestures. Moreover social life is so much easier if everyone conforms to the rules of courtesy. These provide a complete set of prescriptions for behaviour which we assimilate the more readily in proportion as we are schooling ourselves in virtue. Besides, reflection on virtue is never over. The practice of the *li* furnishes a harmonious body of ready-made attitudes, laid down by tradition and providing a frame for rational development.

When the Western world came into contact with China, Westerners accused the Chinese of being hypocrites because they practised a courtesy which did not correspond with their inward feelings. For their part the Chinese were shocked by Western coarseness. It is true that politeness does not automatically make a man virtuous, but the Chinese were right in thinking that it may help him to be so. On the other hand sincerity turns to coarseness when the sincere speaker *is* coarse.

The Chinese are thus alone in having deliberately made politeness a part of morality. All the same, we find a certain respect for forms in every civilization, because life in common is not possibile without conventions. These forms are already there among primitive peoples; we find them in all the great civilizations, and especially in the aristocracies. In religious life, just as much in the Buddhist monasteries and lamaseries of the Far East as in Christian monasteries, we always find a collection of attitudes and ritual formulas which regulate relations between religious.

The contrast with China is that the link that connects these rules of good breeding with morality is a rather loose one. Nevertheless, the rules of good breeding followed by the English gentleman recall the Chinese doctrine of the *li*. The difference is that Western moral philosophers do not generally express much respect for this good breeding, and tend to question its honesty rather than to praise its refinement.

\*      \*      \*

257

We have discussed man's duty to participate in the common task of the human race. He must be ready to consent to certain sacrifices for that; and sometimes big sacrifices. Nevertheless he will not achieve his own task unless he accepts his created state. This is what has never been grasped by the 'men in revolt' of whom we hear such complacent talk today, but it also explains their perpetual defeat.

Another reason why man must accept social discipline is mistrust of himself. When he comes into the world, he is incapable of looking after himself, and it is only little by little that he becomes capable of doing so. He has got to put up with being taught, and this necessity continues to some extent right through his life.

Nevertheless, man is responsible for himself. The proper proportion of humility and self-assertion is another of the delicate problems of every life. We must decide for ourselves and at the same time take our pattern from the precepts of the wise men.

Many people hunt around for an authority into whose hands they can unreservedly commit themselves, but such an authority does not exist. Men can all make mistakes; there is no absolute wise man. Ultimately, we must all shoulder our own responsibilities.

All the same, generally speaking, the community tries to exact an absolute acquiescence from man. Whether it is a question of mere polite usages or of opinions on vital questions, the community imposes a conformity to which most people defer without resistance. Here again we find the wise man a non-conformist.

This social conformity is accentuated by the tendency of all those in authority to lay down the law, with any discussion ruled out. The most extreme example of this social authoritarianism is to be found today in the Communist regime, but the tendency is common to all those who exercise authority. They demand intellectual assent as well as compliance in action. Fascism used to teach that 'The Duce is always right' and Nazism that 'The Führer is always right'.

Nevertheless, man has an irreducible minimum of autonomy. When he obeys, he is still responsible for his obedience, and in the long run, he only obeys because he thinks he ought to, because he himself thinks so. This irreducible character of independence is what constitutes the nobility of man. In the last resort, the only thing he has to lose is his life; but there have always been men who have been ready to die rather than go against their conscience.

The most outstanding attempt to organize an absolute form of obedience is that of the Catholic Church, and it shows clearly the limits beyond which it is impossible to go. Under Catholic doctrine, the Church is infallible in matters of faith and morals, that is to say in the interpretation of Revelation. What is more, the Church has been entrusted by Christ himself with the mission of guiding the faithful, who must therefore obey her as they would God himself. This rule appears to leave no loophole whatever for any check on the part of the faithful.

No other doctrine has founded obedience on such an absolute basis. There is a lot of talk nowadays of Communist obedience, for the Communist must follow the party line. But Marxism contains no doctrinal formula laying down that the truth emanates from this or that source, from Moscow, for example. If the Chinese or Italian Communists declare one day that they interpret Marxism differently from the Russians, and that their interpretation is the right one, there is no doctrine which will allow the discussion to be stopped. On the other hand, the statements that Christ entrusted the deposit of Revelation to Peter and the Apostles, that the Pope is the successor of Peter and has inherited his powers, and that he is, in the last analysis, the organ of the Church's infallibility, all form part of Catholic *doctrine*. The Catholic ceases to be a Catholic if he does not accept it.

But this very formula shows a certain limitation on the power of the Church: her authority rests on the firm belief of the faithful. In a word, it is for the faithful to decide on their own authority whether or not they adhere to the Church.

Again, when the Church defines a doctrine or issues an order, the faithful only accept it if they see they ought to accept it. In the last resort, it all boils down to this: I do not believe myself obliged to obey unless *I* believe this; it is always I who must make the decision in the last analysis. If men sometimes accept a doctrine or a watchword with their eyes shut, this merely means that they have directed their attention and their critical faculty, not towards the particular object of this doctrine or this watchword, but towards the confidence inspired by whoever put it up to them. We always come back to the same point: if I trust in the Church—or if the Communist trusts in Moscow or the Chinese in Confucius—it is in the last analysis because *I* myself have reached the conviction that *I should* trust in her.

Every man thus possesses an irreducible share of responsibility for himself. But in contradistinction to conformity, a certain number of people also profess an irrational and incoherent independence, based on the arrogance of self-assertion. We have said enough about the 'man in revolt'. There is every sort of such men: sometimes they revolt in one field, sometimes in another. There is a classic age of incoherent revolt, that of adolescence, the age when the young being becomes conscious of his personality, wants to assert himself and does so no matter how, as often as not in a ridiculous way. This sort of revolt is not that of a wise man. The wise man is not a man in revolt; he is independent.

This independence always leads to a certain conflict with the community. We have seen that the community does not like those who break loose from conformity; the community is a tyrant which does not tolerate independence. Even if a man conforms to its canons, it also expects him to do so because it is the rule of the community, and not because he considers he should behave in this way out of personal choice. This is a close parody of Kant's maxim: 'it is not enough for a man to do his duty, he must do it out of duty;' the community's rule is that it is not enough for a man to conform to convention, he must do it because it is the convention.

This explains why there is always a latent conflict between the wise man and the community. This conflict generally remains latent, but it sometimes takes an acute form. Certain historical cases are classical, such as those of Socrates and of Jesus, who paid for their independence with their lives. We are considering Jesus here as a type of wise man, leaving out of account what Christian doctrine teaches about his person. These wise men are the most normal of men. All the same, they come into irreconcilable conflict with the community, because they will only conform to its rules when these agree with what their conscience tells them.


## IX. SUFFERING AND SIN

When we take into account all that has just been said, we shall understand why suffering occupies a considerable place in moral life from more than one point of view.

Suffering is not unhappiness. Unhappiness is an absolute and stable state, the state of a man who is conscious of not fulfilling himself, of not achieving his task. The conception of moral life which emerges from everything we have said identifies happiness with perfection. In so far as a man attains his perfection and achieves his task, he is 'satisfied'. The etymological sense of the word speaks for itself. We are satisfied when we have 'enough'. What satisfies is reduction to the One. The task through which man at once affirms and attains his perfection, through which, in short, he attains and manifests reduction to the One in whatever way suits, is one that satisfies him. Happiness is the resulting inner satisfaction, and joy is the mental exaltation which follows from this apprehension. The term 'exaltation' is, it must be added, ambiguous, for the word conveys an idea of excitement which is characteristic of a transitory state. Whereas happiness is essentially calm, because it is stable and because it is an absolute, a consciousness of fulfilment, and true fulfilment brings peace.

Suffering is thus not unhappiness, any more than pleasure is happiness. Suffering and pleasure correspond to particular goods and partial states of consciousness. A man may suffer from hunger, ignorance or solitude and still be happy, if his life is dominated by a consciousness of fulfilment. In the same way, a man who is reading an interesting book, drinking a good wine or having an interesting chat with a friend enjoys this particular good; but this pleasure, which is particular and transitory, is not happiness.

Complete happiness and unhappiness do not exist on earth. Man is more or less happy, more or less unhappy. Perfect happiness would be a happiness without suffering, complete unhappiness an unhappiness without pleasure. Since man is

261

CMC 10

a divided being, these complete states are inaccessible to him. We are always more or less happy—or more or less unhappy. In everyday life, we call a man happy when pleasureable things preponderate in his life and unhappy when painful ones do.

Suffering is thus not unhappiness, and in the situation in which man finds himself on earth, suffering is actually necessary to his happiness. It is necessary from a number of points of view. Let us start by going through them.

\*  \*  \*

We have seen that the perfection of man lies in a task in which all his potentialities for action display themselves completely, and in which he thus shows what he is capable of. But this task implies a risk. We do not show what we are capable of unless we undertake a task that will try our capacities to the full, and we do not know just what these capacities are. Now the very risk entails suffering as well as pleasure, and there is no real risk unless there is a possibility of failure. Failure causes suffering.

Then again, if we are fully to employ all our potentialities for action, we have to strain ourselves to the limit. Effort also entails suffering. Success brings joy or pleasure, but effort in itself is difficult.

Moreover, the joy of success is all the greater the more we have toiled to achieve it, because it is in toiling that man becomes conscious of showing what he is capable of. But looked at in itself, toil is difficulty, that is to say it is difficult, and difficulty and difficult imply suffering.

This shows clearly the mixed character of human states. For toil is suffering in so far as it calls for the sacrifice of a pleasure, but toil is also pleasure in the consciousness of our value or in the consciousness of having shown what we are capable of. When we climb a mountain, the joy is in proportion to the difficulty, because a difficulty overcome gives us a sense of our value.

We thus arrive at the formula that man only attains complete joy, that is to say complete consciousness of perfection, when he has suffered to achieve it.

Then again suffering makes man conscious of his limitations. Suffering comes from obstacles, and it is obstacles that make a man conscious of his limitations. Now this consciousness is at the basis of any moral life.

Reduction to the One assumes knowledge of the self and of God, and there is no knowledge of God without knowledge of the self. We know God in antithesis to ourselves, and we cannot be conscious of the divine transcendence unless we are conscious of our own limitations. The man who believes himself to be more than he is necessarily believes God to be less than he is.

Now man only knows himself when he has suffered, that is to say when he has encountered obstacles and has become aware at once of his capacities and his limitations. Obstacles, and the suffering which comes from encountering obstacles, enable man to know through experience that he is limited, a creature and dependent. They teach him that he must submit to what exists, and that what exists does not await his permission to exist, that is to say that the good is independent of him, and therefore outside him, and that he must seek it where it is to be found. Finally they make him realize that it is not for him to decide what is good, that he must accept it and use it, and that he is not a creator.

The man who has not suffered, that is to say the man who has not met with failure is almost inevitably infatuated with himself. He thus cannot find the Good and the One; he is incapable of seeking them, for to a certain extent he confuses himself with the Good. Inevitably, because he cannot completely understand that he is not the Good and the One unless he knows from experience his limitations.

That is why a man who has not suffered remains a child, for the characteristic of the child, or at least one of his characteristics, is not to be conscious of his limitations. It explains the role of suffering in the life of most strong personalities, particularly among the saints. We do meet exceptions from time to time, but the man who has become aware of himself and of God without having suffered is the most astonishing of men, the most astonishing and the most exceptional. We can take it as a general rule that when we meet a man in whom we discern some profundity of character, that is to say a strong personality, we almost always find when we come to know him well that he has been scarred by suffering. That is why those who aspire to perfection and who belong to what is known as the privileged class, because they have 'all they need to be happy'—good health, a good character, a pleasant background, plenty of money, a ready understanding and so on—often feel at a certain moment that one type of human value is inaccessible to them because they have not suffered.

Besides, there is every kind of suffering: physical suffering and moral suffering, sufferings that come from within and from outside. This also explains the role that mortification plays in the life of those who aspire to perfection: mortification is a suffering that a man imposes on himself. All the same, it is no more than a makeshift, for the fact that a man imposes it on himself and has therefore chosen it deprives it of its purity as suffering. Pure and genuine suffering is the suffering that comes without our having chosen it or wished for it, for it is this suffering that goes completely counter to our inclinations and that makes us completely conscious of our limitations.

Finally, suffering is the supreme testimony of love. Christ said: 'This is the greatest love a man can show, that he should lay down his life for his friends,' and in saying this, he was not revealing a new truth, he was recalling a truth that was already familiar to his listeners. The new truth that Christ did announce was that God loves us to this degree, and that he, Christ, had come to manifest this love. But the statement that suffering is the supreme testimony of love is a point on which everyone is agreed.

Nevertheless, it was to Christianity that it fell to place suffering at the centre of moral life in so far as it is the supreme proof of love. For though the wise men may all be agreed on the key role of suffering, in systems like those of the Cynics or of Nietzsche, or in Kipling's *If*, suffering is regarded exclusively as a means of self-development. The Buddhists, the Stoics and some others also see it as bringing about awareness of our limitations. There are only hints at suffering for love. Thus there is no other doctrine that makes suffering, as does the Christian doctrine, the supreme expression of love and that at the same time makes love the whole of morality.

The idea which is the basis of suffering as a testimony of love is that a pleasurable act done out of love is ambiguous, because it is impossible to know whether it has really been done out of love. The painful act is a proof of love, because we should not have done it otherwise. Suffering is thus a proof of love.

Nevertheless, love is in itself independent of suffering. The perfect being displays his love in all his acts, and according to the Christian doctrine, the blessed in heaven love perfectly without suffering. But Christ's suffering relates to man on earth. Since the starting point of human action lies in man's natural egoism, which is so deeply rooted in our being that we are seeking our own advantage even when we do not believe we are doing so, the only way of displaying a love that shall ring true, an unambiguous love, is to do out of love acts which we should not do if we did not love. That is why we often encounter among the saints a desire for suffering which may seem morbid to some, but which is explained by the desire for a love without ambiguity. The desire to lay down life in order to prove love, in particular, is one that arises spontaneously: in the Christian tradition, it takes the form of a desire for martyrdom. It is undoubtedly most prominent in Christianity, but it is to be found elsewhere too. In popular Buddhism, certain stories portray the Buddha giving himself up to be eaten to a wild beast in order to feed it . . . In the same way, in the medieval romances of chivalry, it is usual for the hero who wants to show his lady his love to undertake in her honour feats which all involve courage, dangers, risks and suffering. A very general human experience shows that a man does not really feel he has proved his love till he has suffered for it.

\* .\* \*

The principles we have just been considering allow us to determine the way in which suffering fits into life. We might talk at this point of a *regimen of suffering*.

To begin with, suffering which is good is first of all involuntary suffering, for the reason we have just seen. It is suffering

265

which is accepted because it is the counterpart of a good which we are seeking, or because it is a consequence of the human situation. It may take the form either of the weariness which follows a great effort or continuous work, or of the suffering which comes on us unexpectedly, the trial—the loss of someone we love, the failure of a business, sickness or ruin. As soon as the will comes in, as soon as we have chosen it ourselves, suffering entails an element which pleases us, and it ceases to be pure; there is a danger of it flattering our pride. The suffering we have not chosen is pure, that is to say there is nothing in it that pleases us.

Danger is an essential element of suffering, for we do not know whether we shall stand up to it. We run the risk of being broken; our limitations are thus brought right home to us. From one point of view we ought to be broken, indeed crushed; the love of ourselves must be rooted out if God is to be able to live in us.

This results in a tragic conception of existence, a conception which is already present in Nietzsche, in Kipling and in the heroes of antiquity. Reduction to the One cannot be brought about without resistance, violence and tragedy. But what is no more than self-exaltation in the figures we have just cited assumes quite another nobility when the climax of the suffering is that we are invaded by the One, that is to say, in Christian language, by God.

This union with God is thus not achieved without a thorough destruction of the ego, in so far as the ego is attachment to the self. This is no milk-and-water virtue; it is virtue which is forged in blood and tears.

In practice, all men have to suffer; suffering almost always enters into life at one time or another. The stages of life are normally punctuated by the loss of people we love, usually our parents first. Then, if we live long enough, we begin to see our contemporaries disappearing around us, here husband or wife, there friends. Everyone who has a full life, who is seeking perfection and who is trying to fulfil his life's work meets with failures. When we read the lives of great men and of saints, we see that their failures generally outnumber their successes. No doubt posterity remembers only their successes, but they saw the failures. In the same way, speaking more generally, it is almost impossible to undertake any personal work without arousing opposition. And opposition brings suffering, all the more so since under this neutral word there lies a reality which is more often than not an impassioned one, bringing in jealousy, insult and misunderstanding.

Suffering is the instrument God uses to school us. The sufferings God sends us are almost always those which we would not have chosen. That is indeed the sign that they come from him. He is more intelligent than we; he has an art which is beyond us, that of choosing the suffering we do not want so as to break the shell of our ego. In this sense, suffering really makes life a dialogue between man and God. It is the experience through which we become most unequivocally aware that God is speaking. Thanks to it, life in its deepest recesses, underneath all external events, becomes the echo of the soul to the divine action, the reply of man to God.

But we cannot see this until we have transcended the plane of sensible events, their human character, war and peace, social questions, our emotional life and human affections, everything that goes to make up life, that really has no meaning except as a path to God.

All the same, life should not be focused on suffering. The object of life is reduction to the One, and the task through which this is expressed. Now reduction to the One is the same as happiness. The ethics that is a consequence of this conception is a profoundly optimistic one.

There is thus a danger in identifying suffering with moral value. However important its role, suffering is none the less incidental. It is the instrument of our training. It is a means; it is not an end. There is only one end: reduction to the One. In Christ's life, the passion only lasted a matter of hours.

When we consider the role of suffering in moral life, there is a danger of seeing nothing else, and of picturing moral life in a light which excludes joy. A certain sort of Christian spirituality has succumbed to this danger. These are the Christians Nietzsche talks of, who are incapable of mentioning life or virtue without remarking how difficult they are. 'Yes, you've got to give up a lot of things and suffer a lot too, if you want to be good,' we hear them say. But we never hear

267

them say: 'Virtue does call for certain sacrifices but it ends in a joy the wicked have no idea of.' Some of them lay stress on the use of little vexations; there is a spirituality of 'little crosses', and it sometimes results in people only paying attention to what is troublesome in life, seeking for what is troublesome, instead of abandoning themselves to the great joy of the task. The Kantian trend in ethics, which carries on from the Calvinist trend, tends in this direction, because it refuses any moral value to joy, and because duty is more easily apprehended, and we are more certain of acting purely out of duty, if duty is not pleasant.

There is, however, an apparent antinomy between suffering and joy, because absolute suffering, a suffering which took hold of the entire being for good and all, would be unhappiness. But suffering is never absolute, as long as man is conscious of pursuing his end. Though we may sometimes feel we are submerged in absolute suffering, and go through moments which might be described as a spiritual death agony, these moments can be no more than fleeting. They cannot continue without danger.

We sometimes see men go under, men who give the impression of having been tried beyond their strength. We do not know the final explanation, for we know little about the depths of the soul. What will always be the core of thinking from this point of view is that those who do attain to the nobility possible to man are scarred by suffering; that sometimes they themselves, from time to time, have felt they were going under completely; but that most often, at this very moment, those who saw them got the impression on the contrary of a resplendent nobility; and that the only men who attain to human perfection are those who build suffering into their life.

\*　　\*　　\*

Suffering is thus a permanent element in life; so is sin.

From one point of view, we may say that man is dominated by suffering. In the same way we may say that man bears the stamp of sin. And suffering comes from sin.

But on the subject of sin, we shall have to discard the outlook of modern moral theorists. The search for the essence

of morals of which Kant was the most outstanding representative among philosophers, but which impregnates the whole
of modern ethics, as we have seen, links sin with the independent will, with intentionality and with the act, and thus ends
up in a theory which separates moral value from the other
forms of value.

There is another conception, which goes much deeper but
which is more difficult to clarify, which links sin with evil and
regards evil from the ontological, that is to say the objective
point of view. When I discussed the threshold of ethics, I
talked of the sense of the objective value of the act, ethics
being linked with the subjective value, though it cannot however be separated from the objective. We are now entering
on what might be called the mystery of moral value. And
the mystery of sin is undoubtedly one of its essential manifestations.

Man bears the stamp of sin because there is evil in him,
and suffering comes from sin.

When we try to imagine what a humanity without sin
would be like, we realize that it would be a humanity without
suffering. That was what the earthly paradise amounted to.

Whether it is a question of diseases or of mental troubles or
of all the various forms of human strife, everything comes
from sin. Perfect men would have a perfect mastery of themselves. They would be perfect in their forethought and their
temperance, their justice and their charity, their courage and
their prudence, and all human sufferings stem from failings in
these. What is more, civilization as we know it today represents no more than a hang-over of barbarism compared with
what the human race could realize, if history had not been
packed with human clashes and excesses and cruelties un-
worthy of a being endowed with reason. In point of fact, man
has used his reason very little. It is the characteristic that
distinguishes him from the animals, but he has made very
little use of it.

When we say here that man bears the stamp of sin and that
suffering comes from sin, we are adopting an outlook very
different from that of modern theorists. When we say that
suffering comes from sin, that does not mean that every
individual man suffers on acount of his personal sins, and that

269

his suffering is proportionate to these. It means that man's suffering comes from the fact that there is sin in the world. We suffer from ill-health because our ancestors sinned, because they lacked prudence and sobriety, did not behave reasonably, and so on. We realize today the determining influence of the social environment on crime and the various forms of immorality, and this influence sometimes derives from causes that go back several centuries.

I suffer from defects that come from the environment in which I was brought up and the people to whom I belong— defects and virtues too, for the matter of that—but the point that concerns us at the moment is sin. One day when Jesus and his disciples passed a blind man, whom Jesus later cured, the disciples asked him: 'Master, was this man guilty of sin, or was it his parents, that he should have been born blind?' It was a natural question for a man to ask: evil, including disease, comes from sin. It is true, too; a particular evil does not always come from a particular sin, or not necessarily, but if there is evil in the world, it is because there is sin, and if there is suffering, it is because there is evil.

In the sense in which we are speaking of it here, sin may thus be identified with evil. This is a non-moral sense. After all the analyses of modern moral philosophies it may seem absurd to talk of non-moral sin. Yet a whole section of contemporary thinking is still impregnated with the notion of an evil which it regards as acting in the world, fighting against good and sometimes defeating and destroying it.

People no longer speak of the devil, or of the spirit of evil, nor do they locate evil in matter, as the Cathari did. But when we read Sartre's *Nausea*, we recognize again the evil spirit of the dualist mysticisms of antiquity and the medieval idea of the devil hiding in tangible forms. It is true that this idea is decked out in completely new trappings and employed in the service of a very different philosophy. But we cannot help feeling that it is still the old conception of the Greek tragedies, that of a blind and malevolent fate hounding down its victim. And that victim is man.

Now it looks as if contemporary psychological work can help us to put into plain language such things as are obscure in this tradition. I have said more than once, and the importance of this point of view cannot be exaggerated, that what will probably always remain the most essential thesis of contemporary psychology is its emphasis on the continuity and thus the unity of psychic life, on the inter-dependence of acts and on the dependence of conscious acts on the subconscious and the unconscious.

Quite a number of consequences follow from this. First, the free act is not a single act which stands out in contrast to others; freedom is a trend which operates in the whole of life. Next, acts are more or less free; there are perhaps completely free acts, but there are very few acts which are completely divorced from free activity. Finally, the problem of the responsibility for a particular act is more often than not insoluble for us—not insoluble in itself: it is clear to God—and responsibility is bound up more with the trend of life than with acts considered in themselves.

Here we are at one with St Paul, when he wrote: 'My conscience does not reproach me; but that is not where my justification lies ... it is the Lord's scrutiny I must undergo.' We might almost think St Paul had anticipated twentieth-century psychology. This is the very essence of man. Man is a divided being. He has lofty aspirations, generous impulses, and a swarming mass of unhealthy appetites. Nobody can sort them out with certainty. God alone judges us. But we know that anything that impedes the onward march of mankind towards purity and towards good is a sin.

\*    \*    \*

The ideal of a happy humanity has always aroused men's enthusiasm. This dream is eternal and universal; it has been expressed in a hundred and one ways. Some people locate this ideal in the past: in the golden age. There are some who abandon it: such is Hindu wisdom, which believes life is sorrow and limits the wise man's task to avoiding sorrow. Finally, some place it in the future, and it was above all Christianity that gave birth to this dream of a happy humanity, where all would toil together at the setting up of a kingdom of happiness in divine charity.

In genuine Christianity, that of Christ, we find no more

271

than a summons to a personal life which will kindle the divine life in the disciple. But if this life were kindled in every man, we should indeed reach a perfection and a happiness of which nothing that has happened in history can give any idea. No wonder the first disciples, when they contemplated this prospect, had the impression that the Kingdom of God was going to transform the whole condition of the world. We find this outlook in St Paul: from time to time, carried away by enthusiasm, he declared that in Christ all will be transformed —there will be a new heaven and a new earth.

Later on, this dream gave rise to what has been called *millenarianism*, the vision of a time when Christ would reign without contest, and when the human race would know the glory of the Kingdom of God on earth. In our times, millenarianism has become divorced from Christianity, and has been perpetuated in a field alien to religious values, in the ideal of a machine civilization which will make life easy for everyone, and in that preached by Communism, the ideal of a brotherly society where all men will help each other.

If we take a closer look at things, we shall see that this happy society would have to be a society without sin. When we tell Marxists that in their egalitarian society, men will still be what they are today, egoists, arrogant and so forth, their final retort is always a retreat into millenarianism. In the Socialist society, they say, everything will be different from what we know. If men are depraved, it is because of capitalism, but once the Socialist society is here, bad character will disappear.

In a word, there will be a new heaven, a new earth, and a new humanity.

But mankind can only be happy if it is without sin, for it is sin that is the cause of all injustice and all suffering. It is true that man longs for a life without suffering, a life that will be all joy. But the only way to attain it is through good, through perfection and reduction to the One.

\*     \*     \*

Another trend which has something in common with millenarianism consists in the denial of sin. This has always existed, in the form of glorification of passion, but the passion in

272

question is solely sexual passion. In the nineteenth century Fourier said: 'The passions are good, for it was God who put them in us.' That is true enough, but it does not alter the fact that they have got to be disciplined, for if they were left to themselves, there would be chaos. Moreover, Fourier did not justify a passion for lying or for theft.

Nowadays, this trend of thinking, which might be described as modern millenarianism, has taken a scientific form in psychoanalysis. We have already said a little about it. Basing itself on the psychology of the unconscious, psychoanalysis attributes all disorders of the character to sexual repression. Man has only to be freed from this to achieve balance and virtue without any effort.

We have seen that psychoanalysis ends up in a sort of pansexualism, and that it makes much play with the deepest levels of the soul, which are generally regarded as unwholesome. It claims that there is nothing unwholesome about them, but that if they are set free, they are exorcized.

Psychoanalysis reacts against the obsession with sin, believing that morality can be indentified with this. In reality, psychoanalysts know nothing of the moral rule. They do not know that morality conduces to the glorification of our natural propensities, simply by setting them in their proper context in the order of things. It would seem that the moral rule as it applies to the sexual propensity is specially difficult for many people to understand, because it is linked with social values, such as the family and marriage. All the trends which glorify free love are trends which see no more in love than its individual aspect. There is a whole division of literature which might lead a reader to believe that marriage is a source of depravity and unhappiness. Probably the ethics of chastity is often not explained too well. Too little effort is made to present chastity as the guardian virtue of the family, and the family as the guardian institution of chastity. I do not need to set forth this doctrine here, for I have done it elsewhere. All the same, it is interesting to note that the very countries where psychoanalysis is most fashionable are those where there is most uproar about the spread of juvenile delinquency.

\*      \*      \*

273

All the same, it will be asked whether there is not, despite everything, a contradiction between the attitude of the moral philosophers, who glorify suffering or, when they come down to simpler language, extol hard living, effort, renunciation, sacrifice and mortification, and the impetus which is sweeping our technological civilization towards the elimination of suffering.

For what was merely a nebulous dream with the millenarians of bygone days has become a plan that looks as if it could be carried out. Civilization is eliminating the causes of suffering one by one. Here a city and there a whole country have eliminated the sufferings of hunger and of cold, of ignorance and of poverty. We are discovering cures or preventatives for one disease after another; we are doing away with bodily infirmities; we are using machinery to replace heavy physical labour. The benefits of this civilization could easily be extended to the whole human race, were it not for the moral infirmities of egoism and pride and laziness.

This trend is giving rise to a realistic millenarianism. Besides, whereas moral theorists attach such importance to hard living, the human race has always aspired to an easy life.

Nevertheless, we cannot assert that the progress of our civilization has made men happier, for in contrast to the grounds for optimism of which we have just been speaking, mankind is trembling under the threat of a cataclysm. A good part of modern thinking and literature is impregnated with a pessimism as profound as is the optimism in the other direction. We eliminate physical maladies and mental disturbances become more frequent; we eliminate physical effort and nervous tension gets worse.

It is not our business here to inquire whether men are in fact becoming happier. The aim of this book is to discover the rule, not analyse the facts. From the point of view of the rule, the position is clear. It is a good thing to work for the elimination of suffering, for in itself, suffering is an evil. It is linked with evil and sin; it forms part of a whole which is the essence of evil.

What is more, many forms of suffering hamper man's progress. Poverty is a bad counsellor, and it is useless to talk of virtue or to try and arouse a desire for perfection in a man who is hungry. We must start by feeding him, and we must teach the ignorant and care for the sick.

But the effort to lessen suffering only leads, in reality, to shifting its incidence, for suffering, as we have seen, is a concomitant of any generous and active life. Suffering is bound to appear as soon as a man sets out to achieve his task. The elimination of collective forms of suffering is thus confined to limiting the sufferings that diminish man.

We know that under-nourished peoples are incapable of steady work. They are not masters of their nerves, and switch from indolence to ill-temper. For quiet, sustained and steady work, a man must be well-fed, properly housed and decently clothed. He must also be in good health. Does this mean that work then entails no effort and no pains? Quite the contrary, there is more of it than there is in the idleness of primitive man, interrupted by fits of agitation.

As long as man is a sinner, there will still be suffering in the world, and it will be in proportion to sin. Millenarianism assumes a man who is no longer a sinner: such a man should not suffer any more. Ethics teaches that man must seek perfection, which implies the elimination of sin. A form of technological progress which seeks to do away with material suffering while neglecting moral progress or relegating it to the background may lead to regression just as easily as to progress. The reason why pessimism is nowadays contending with optimism, amid the utmost incoherence on either side, is that the greater part of those who are the architects of civilization, as well as of those who think about it, have no clear ideas on the relationships between suffering and sin, or on the role of ethics.


## X. Death

It is death that confers its full significance on everything that has been said above, for death is the decisive fact that imposes humility, the incontrovertible sign that marks the limitation of man.

It is death that gives life its final meaning, according to what is going to follow death, and it raises on the plane of life the problem of rational knowledge. For these three reasons, death dominates life.

First of all, death is the irreducible limitation that compels man to become aware that he is not the absolute and that he must submit.

But man has within him the sense of the absolute, which is a sense of the eternal. Now we are limited, above all, because we die. That is why man tries to cheat death, and he tries in a hundred and one ways.

The most common is to avoid thinking of it. Man talks of his life as if it were going to go on for ever. In his flight from the idea of death, he treats it as if it were an unexpected, irregular and shocking accident. Men of eighty make plans as if they were going to live for ever, and children greet the death of their parents, however old these may be, as if it were an unforeseen blow.

Christianity has tried to react with its doctrine of eternal life, but nowadays the flight from death has intensified, under the influence of the spread of non-Christian ideas. The thought of death is treated as a demoralizing thought and men exalt evasions of it to a system: sick people, even those their doctor has given up, must be told they are getting better, because it put them in good heart and because morale plays a part in keeping life going.

One of the effects of technological civilization has been to prolong life. In the most developed countries, the average expectation of life has more than doubled. Death is receding, and as it recedes, it becomes easier to avoid thinking of it. The sick and the disabled have more and more grounds for believing that a remedy for their trouble will be found. For the young man, the prospect of death is so distant that he feels he is immortal. A whole aspect of our civilization conduces to our rejecting death by our practical attitude. We know theoretically that man must die, but for ourselves, the prospect is so distant that we need not take it into account.

Nevertheless, though death may recede, it does not disappear. The same science that has postponed death has pin-

276

pointed the signs of ageing. It has been noted that the first signs of ageing appear between the ages of thirty and forty, the period when sporting champions retire. And to age is to begin to die, for the essence of ageing is that a department of life atrophies. When we begin to discover we can no longer run or jump, it means that something in us has died. That is why, in order to reject death, we try to reject old age. Our civilization has made old age something to be ashamed of; we take a pride in not growing old and we hide the fact that we are ageing. Once upon a time, young folk used to wear grey or white wigs in order that people should take them seriously; today, old women dye their hair so that nobody shall see they are growing grey.

All the same, death compels recognition from anyone who thinks. Postponing it does not do away with it, and it matters little whether it comes soon or late. It is an absolute; the fact that we have got to die changes everything.

Among those who do not believe in God, one reaction consists in resignation. It is to be found in the Buddha and in Marcus Aurelius, in Epicurus and in the modern positivists. We have got to accept facts as they are and ask no questions. It is a resignation that leaves an after-taste of melancholy, with an incontestable but cold nobility. Typical of it is the wise man who kills himself when he considers he has come to the end of what the good life has to offer him. He stands out against the masses with their passion for living; his lucidity towers above the crowd which shuts its eyes because it is afraid. He masters the instinct to live through reason. But this nobility is a cold one, because it harbours no love.

Other unbelievers react passionately and in more than one way. There is Heidegger who considers that because we know we have to die, we have a sort of taste of nothingness in our mind, for to know we are going to die is to be dead already: life is worth nothing if it ends. This theory is one of the most expressive testimonies to the sense of the absolute that exists in man. Or again there is Camus in the opening passage of his *The Myth of Sisyphus*: 'There is only one really serious philosophical problem,' he writes 'that of suicide. To decide whether life is or is not worth living is to reply to the fundamental question of philosophy.'

On a less speculative plane, men have always tried to link death with life by making death the supreme act through which the nobility of the soul manifests itself. Greek and Roman literature is full of heroes who gave their lives for a good cause. 'To die for one's country is the sweetest fate,' it used to be said. When men talk of death on this plane, they try to identify it with life through imaginative touches, such as the memory men will preserve of the hero and the way in which his fame will live on in the traditions of his people. Looking at things objectively, if he dies once for all, it matters little to him whether the living still think of him, and anyway there is no certainty this will happen, for men often forget. But these notions serve as a smoke screen.

We have already noted in Existentialism a similar attempt to concentrate all the zest of life in death or in the act through which a man dies. It is death which gives the moment its decisive character. All this is no more than an attempt to identify death with life. But it all remains more or less unconvincing.

It is only if man is a creature that death assumes its full signficance. If life is a journey towards God, if life was given us by God to achieve reduction to the One and if it opens on to what is beyond, then death becomes the hinge on which life turns and incontestably the decisive act of life, because it is the last act which fixes man's destiny for eternity. We die as we have lived: the final meaning of life is to prepare for death. Growing old, which is the beginning of death, becomes the road along which man gets his training for the beyond.

\* \* \*

Finally, death gives life its meaning, that is to say it is death which raises in an unequivocal form the problem of the beyond.

Death forces the problem of the beyond upon us. If man did not have to, he might not worry about it. But he has to die, and life is quite different according to what the beyond is.

We saw above how Camus put the problem; the question whether life is worth living arises because life does have an end and man can put an end to his life. Now according to what the beyond is, life assumes a different meaning. It is not merely a question of whether there is a beyond, but of just what it is. From this point of view, Christianity has played a decisive role in the evolution of thought, because it alone gives a clear picture of the future life, which makes of it the complete fulfilment of the need for the absolute in man.

Outside Christianity, we find popular religions presenting a picture of paradise inspired by earthly life: it consists of a happiness which corresponds to the complete material happiness that most men want on earth. Such are the 'happy land' of Amidism, the paradise of Mahomet and the popular Christian conception which pictures a paradise of feasting entirely alien to the beatific union of the theologians; such again is the Greek conception of Elysium, the abode of the blessed shades, where souls separated from their bodies console themselves for no longer being alive by recalling the joys of the present life on earth. For many Christians, the biggest question that arises when they think of the future life is whether the joys of this life will go on, whether for example they will still know and love the people they have loved on earth, and whether they will meet their parents again. The thought of the beatific union or of union with God remains for them an abstraction without objective reality simply because it is, on earth, no more than an abstraction.

Now the genuine Christian conception is entirely different. The future life, as Christianity conceives it, is a life incomparably more beautiful and happier than the present life. I say *incomparably,* because in fact no comparison holds. But since for most Christians the life of faith is only intermittently known, what is incomparable with the present life has no meaning.

For the Christian who lives his faith, that is to say for the Christian in whose thinking the truths of the faith become existential values, the future life may be said to eat up our life below. All the values of the present life derive their coherence from the future life to which they all lead; death becomes, as it was for the primitive Church, the *dies natalis,* the day of our real birth. It is on earth that we live in the kingdom of shades; it is on earth that we are ghosts. Entry into eternal life is entry into light and peace, complete balance

279

and complete fulfilment. Plato already had a presentiment of this conception, and we find it in other thinkers too. But, as we have seen over other questions, these were no more than presentiments, bearing witness to the aspiration of humanity as it reveals itself in the greatest thinkers. It fell to Christianity to provide a complete and coherent answer to it as a whole.

Death may raise the problem of the value of life as a reality, but it also finally raises the problem of rational knowledge, because the beyond linked with God is, like God, an object of pure rational knowledge.

The senses give us no information about God; he is a pure object of rational knowledge. If rational evidence yields contact with a reality, life in God becomes a reality and the prospect of a future life becomes a prospect of reality.

We have seen that, here on earth, the idea of God fascinates the mind in its own right, quite apart from the question of the existence of God. The reason for this is that we have no intuitive knowledge of God. But the beyond depends on the existence of a spiritual world, and especially of God, that is to say on their being ontological and not merely logical realities. That is why, when a metaphysician acknowledges the existence of God, his attitude towards death shows whether his metaphysics represents a mere piece of intellectual acrobatics or whether his life is committed to them.

It is thus to death that philosophy owes its seriousness. Philosophy, as we know, has a two fold starting point : reflection on the origin of the world, the cosmos, and reflection on the origin and destiny of man. In itself, the problem of the world is not a distressing one. It is a speculative problem, interesting for those who like thinking, but it does not commit life. Metaphysical anguish results from the problem of the destiny of man. This anguish is brought out by the philosophies of our time, which raise the question of destiny while rejecting any future life. These philosophies may be said to constitute a test. The problem of the beyond, which comes down to the problem of God, may thus be regarded as the essential spur to thought.

\* \* \*

Everything is dominated by God, the One, ineffable and transcendent, and yet the key to all knowledge and all orientation of life as of thought.

Back in the sixteenth century, St Thomas More was already remarking that 'some of the most famous philosophers of antiquity told those who asked them what was the object of philosophy that it was meditation on death or preparation for death'. Since then, preparation for death has become one of the standard exercises of Christian life, and preparation for death is preparation to appear before God.

It is thus to death that life owes its seriousness. A life which ended in nothingness would have nothing serious about it; it would be a game, because there would be no accounting for it to anyone. It would be delivered over to caprice and to chance, because there would be no goal at the end of it.

Even a life which was continued in another life, as in the doctrine of transmigration, would be a game. Only what is final is serious and that is a form of absolute. Life draws its nobility from the fact that it opens into eternity.

That is why we should lay hold on life with both hands. Man has one life at his disposal, only one, to fulfil his task and to show what he is made of. Everything depends on this life, and it is according as man has worked in this one life to fulfil the task he was destined for, it is according to this alone that everything will be fulfilled.

# INDEX

Absolute, 89, 93, 127, 234, 277
in the act, 73, 116, 234, 237, 240
good, 238-45
of destruction, 241
by way of the contingent, 220
in ethics, 71, 116, 156-7
in the relative, 242-5
man's sense of, 221
Abraham, 125, 126
Achilles, 181, 182
Act, absolute nature of, 73, 75, 234, 237, 238
concentration on, 81
moral character of, 225-31, 245-9
expresses personality, 252-3
Action, philosophy of, 16-8
ethics of, 42, 120
human conditions of, 84, 221-2
Adam and Eve, 140
Ahriman, 140
Albert the Great (Saint), 30
Alcibiades, 179
Alexandria, 146
Altruism, 34, 122, 145, 185-91
respect-a., 185, 192-5, 205-6
assistance-a., 185, 206, 255
duty of, 191-217
of friendship, 186-7
of detachment, 188
religious, 188-9
social, 189-90, 215-7
in Christianity, 213-5
America, 9, 115
American Indians, 130
Amida, (Amitabha), 175-6
Amidism, 175-6, 279
Anselm (Saint), 102
Anthropocentrism, 18ff

Antiochus, 231
Antimoralism, 85-9
Antiquity, philosophy of, 18, 39, 78, 80, 94, 139, 209, 249, 250
*Apatheia*, 182
Aristotle, 9, 50, 52, 54, 78, 112, 118, 142, 146, 164, 168, 187, 189, 205, 209, 251-2
Ascesis, 72
of emptiness, 153-8
dualist, 138-41
of balance, 142-9
Ascetic, 180, 184-5
Avalokiteshvara, 175

Babylon, 139
Benedict (Saint), 51, 180
Bentham, 105, 116
Bergson, 13, 37, 46, 253, 256
Bernanos, 43
Blondel, 13-4, 16
Bonaventure (Saint), 102
Brahma, 87, 88, 91, 128, 130, 133, 135
Buddha, 7, 116 (Sakya-Mouni), 134, 139, 175, 265, 277
Buddhism, 10, 136, 175-6, 188, 195-6, 264

Calvin, 81, 141
Camus, 42, 75, 105, 106, 109, 234, 235, 277, 278
Cathari, 139-41, 195
Catholic Church, 24, 43, 63, 101, 114-5
ethical practitioners in, 9, 18, 51, 121, 173
code morality of, 54-5, 65-6, 75, 172-3, 197
jansenism in, 81, 141

283

instinct of, 142-3
and natural ethics, 164-5
doctrine of salvation in, 177-8
moral theology of, 193, 195, 228, 229
limits of authority of, 259-60
Chastity, 156, 167, 173, 273
China, 5, 50, 53, 54, 71, 126, 136-7, 143, 160, 184
Chinese, ethical thinking, 53-4, 69, 71, 88, 155, 160, 256-7
philosophy, 111, 112, 117, 130, 136-8
Cicero, 9, 168
Christianity,
and ethical problem, 9, 163
and other ethical systems, 10, 29-30, 36-7, 48-54, 74-6, 100-1, 111, 145, 159-60
historical development of ethical teaching in, 24-38, 78-9, 166
rational aspect of, 60
twofold aspect of ethics in, 62-8, 124, 161
and the moral imperative, 72-7, 104-9, 213
and moralism, 78-83
pessimism in, 80-1
and intentionalism, 81-3
attitude to God of, 98, 100-1, 124, 130-3
dualist asceses in, 138-9
and Zoroastrianism, 139
and Western thought, 142, 212-3
asceses of balance in, 142-3
penitence in, 143-5
and Greek thought, 146
and ethics of good man, 158-63
and natural ethics, 163-9
objective of, 165-6, 213-5
universality of, 213-5
and sense of absolute, 238-45
and death, 279
Civilization, 18, 114-5, 137, 206-15, 248-9, 258

Classical philosophy, 11-12, 14, 37, 130
Class moralities, 169-71
'Cloud of unknowing', the, 129
Commitment, 232-3
Common sense, ethics of, 119-20
Communism, 127-8, 190, 232
Confucianism, 10, 54, 142
Confucius, 3, 7, 52-4, 55, 58, 70, 88, 111-2, 116, 117, 139, 143, 145, 156, 249, 260
Contemplatives, *see* Mystics
Contingent objects, 240-5
Continuity, of life, 231-3
Creation, idea of, 130-3
law of, 220-4
Creative activity, 249-55
Cynics, the, 86-7

Death, 23, 175, 236, 275-81
Descartes, 11, 16, 26, 37, 74, 102, 125, 256
Desirable, the, 128
Detachment, 188
Devotion, 160
Duhamel, Georges, 111
Durkheim, 37, 38, 41
Duty, ethics of, 67, 83-5, 104-9, 152, 195, 196, 202, 228, 238
of altruism, 191-217

Egyptian ethics, 155, 156
Eleazer, 238
Elect, the, 140
Eleusis, 175
Elysium, 279
England, 9, 244
Epictetus, 7, 51, 52, 58, 111, 116, 117, 186, 188, 214, 249
Epicureanism, 10, 138, 184-5
Epicurus, 52, 70, 116, 138, 184, 186-7, 222, 277
Essenians, 63
Ethical thinkers, 4, (*see* Wise man)

Ethics,
distinction between speculative and practical, 6-9, 20, 85, 110
in C20, 11-24, 39, 150-1
and religion, 49
the object of, 89-104
and philosophy, 91-4
metaphysics of, 98
how to achieve object of, 110-49
circumstantial, 121-3
applied, 123
and society, 150-217
elite-e. and majority-e., 195-8
Christian e., *see* Christianity
*see* Morality
Eudaimonism, 69-71, 116, 151, 152, 230, 235
Europe, 115, 137
Evil, 269-71
Existentialism, 13-16, 38, 42, 87, 101, 181, 183, 190, 234, 235, 236, 237
Existential shock, 14
Experiential knowledge, 119, 121, 123

False gods, 127-8
Fathers, of the Church, 24, 138
of the desert, 138, 180
Fatima, 177
Ford, 205
Fourier, 192, 273
France, 9, 14, 120, 244
Francis of Assissi (Saint), 51, 143
Francis Xavier (Saint), 100
Fiction, role in philosophy, 20-1, 111, 155, 254
Fortitude, 254
Friendship, 156, 186

Gide, André, 5, 86
Gilson, Etienne, 75-6
God, 23, 41, 87, 91, 102, 103
authority of, 33-4
as pure Act, 76-89
of love, 223, 237
personal and active character, 55, 72
creator, 72, 130-1, 142, 148, 190
and Christianity, 101-3, 130, 132-3, 145, 223, 236-7
idea of, 57
proof of existence, 25-6, 28-9, 36
divine transcendence of, 55, 56, 72, 89, 125-6
and value, 191-2
perfection of, 126-7
man's obligation to, 104-9
and the hero, 182
and mystic state, 241-2
and suffering, 265-8
*see* the One
Good, ordinary man's concept of, 3, 116, 175
contemporary rejection of concept of, 40-1, 87
in Aristotelian-Thomist synthesis, 79
the basis of ethics, 89, 152
the ways to, 110-49
absolute, 238-45
individual and social, 255-7
Good man, the, 1, 154-63, 199, 200, 239
Good life, the, 52-4
Gnosis, 176
Grace, 65-7
Greece, 50, 71, 88
Greek philosophy, 111, 145-8, 155, 176, 181, 189
Greene, Graham, 43
Grousset, 176
Guyau, 40, 41

Happiness, 139, 152, 174, 184, 186, 261
*see* Eudaimonism
Hegel, 12, 40, 91, 100, 103-4, 133
Heidegger, 23, 42, 277
Hemingway, 234

Marcus Aurelius, 51, 277
Marcel, Gabriel, 19, 35
Maritain, Jacques, 29, 101
Marx, Karl, 38
Marxism, 243-4, 253, 272
Mauriac, François, 43
Mazdaism, 138, 140
Metaphysics, 23-4, 78, 82, 110
Millenarianism, 272-5
Mithra, 175
Momentary, the, 233-9
Monism, 39-41, 145
Moral act, 116
Moral character of the act, 71-2
Moral choice, 45-6
Moral consciousness, 42
Moral error, 79
Moral fact, 51, 153, 157
Moral good, 79-80, 81
Moral obligation, 104-9
Moral problem, 218, 219
Moral rule, 51, 119, 120, 157,
    158, 171-3, 182
Moral sense, 43-4, 46, 55, 110-
    18, 120
Moral shock, 46-8, 157, 182,
    212
Moral teacher, *see* Wise man
Moral tradition, 118, 187
Moral truth, 153
Moral value, 118, 187
Moral virtue, 164
Moralism, 78-83, 239
    reaction against, 85-9
Morality, fact of, 1, 39, 150-1
    why study, 1-3
    reaction against, 4, 6
    rules of, 5
    wisdom m., 39, 48-54, 75,
        197, 198, 200-2, 203, 230
    code m., 39, 43, 54-68, 75,
        197, 199-200, 201, 230, 238
    proversive m., 120
    ordained by God, 126-7
    threshold of, 225-31
Moral philosophy, systems of,
    3, 5, 6, 10, 149
    professional teaching of, 6, 7,

9, 26-7, 121
    and other branches of know-
        ledge, 42-5
Morals, 61, 82, 84, 120, 154
    confusion with ethics, 171-4,
        202
More, Thomas, 281
Moslems, 160, 180
Multiplicity, 218-20
Mutual aid, 206ff
Mystics, 26, 93, 99, 110, 128,
    129-30, 148, 241, 245, 246,
    247, 248, 249

Natural ethics, 154-65
Nazism, 232, 258
Newman, J. H., 91
*Nichomachean Ethics*, 186
Neo-platonism, 10, 23, 32, 56,
    88, 101, 102, 130, 160
Nietzsche, 16, 19, 40, 75, 86,
    99, 107, 109, 122, 125, 133,
    181, 183, 187, 192, 195,
    202, 205, 224, 228, 254,
    264, 266, 267

Objectivity, of the act, 225-31
Obstacle, the, 42, 43
Obstacles to reduction to the
    One, 133-49
Oedipus, 125, 225
Old Testament, moral sense of,
    55-9
    idea of God, 124
    *see* Jews
Omar ben al-Farid, 129-30
One, the, 89, 93, 103, 117, 198
    man's effort to know, 94-6,
        98-9, 180
    existence of, 101-2
    is the Christian's god, 106
    reduction to, 110, 117-8, 128-
        33, 145-9, 157, 198, 201,
        218-9, 245-9, 252, 261, 263,
        266
    sense of, 123-8
    not inaccessible, 222
    dominates all, 281
Ontological order, 101

287